Luminos is the Open Access monograph publishing program from UC Press. Luminos provides a framework for preserving and reinvigorating monograph publishing for the future and increases the reach and visibility of important scholarly work. Titles published in the UC Press Luminos model are published with the same high standards for selection, peer review, production, and marketing as those in our traditional program. www.luminosoa.org

Amphibious Subjects

NEW SEXUAL WORLDS

Marlon M. Bailey and Jeffrey Q. McCune, Series Editors

Featuring the most cutting-edge scholarship focused on racialized gender and sexuality studies, this series offers a platform for work that highlights new sexual practices and formations within diverse, understudied geographies. The dialectic of race, gender, and sexuality is central to the spine of all books in this series—rethinking the core questions of queer theory, gender and sexuality studies, and critical interrogations of race. With an interdisciplinary scope, authors draw on innovative methodologies, produce novel theories, and accelerate the study of gender and sexuality into new worlds of thought.

1. *Panics without Borders: How Global Sporting Events Drive Myths about Sex Trafficking*, by Gregory Mitchell
2. *Amphibious Subjects: Sasso and the Contested Politics of Queer Self-Making in Neoliberal Ghana*, by Kwame Edwin Otu

Amphibious Subjects

Sasso and the Contested Politics of Queer Self-Making in Neoliberal Ghana

Kwame Edwin Otu

UNIVERSITY OF CALIFORNIA PRESS

University of California Press
Oakland, California

Suggested citation: Otu, K. E. *Amphibious Subjects: Sasso and the Contested Politics of Queer Self-Making in Neoliberal Ghana.* Oakland: University of California Press, 2022. DOI: https://doi.org/10.1525/luminos.131

Library of Congress Cataloging-in-Publication Data

Names: Otu, Kwame Edwin, 1983– author.
Title: Amphibious subjects : sasso and the contested politics of queer self-making in neoliberal Ghana / Kwame Edwin Otu. Other titles: New sexual worlds ; 2.
Description: Oakland, California : University of California Press, [2022] | Series: New sexual worlds ; 2 | Includes bibliographical references and index.
Identifiers: LCCN 2022000340 (print) | LCCN 2022000341 (ebook) | ISBN 9780520381858 (paperback) | ISBN 9780520381865 (ebook)
Subjects: LCSH: Sexual minority community—Ghana—Accra. | Effeminacy—Ghana—Accra. | Human rights—Anthropological aspects—Ghana—Accra. | Sexual minorities—Ghana—Accra. | Gender identity—Ghana—Accra. | Homosexuality—Ghana—Accra. | BISAC: SOCIAL SCIENCE / Anthropology / Cultural & Social | SOCIAL SCIENCE / LGBTQ Studies / Bisexual Studies
Classification: LCC HQ73.3.G42 A23 2022 (print) | LCC HQ73.3.G42 (ebook) | DDC 306.7609667—dc23/eng/20220207
LC record available at https://lccn.loc.gov/2022000340
LC ebook record available at https://lccn.loc.gov/2022000341

Manufactured in the United States of America

31 30 29 28 27 26 25 24 23 22
10 9 8 7 6 5 4 3 2 1

For Hillary and Siki, and to all the sasso and members of the LGBT+ community and allies who have fought and continue to fight homophobia and all other forms of injustice and oppression in Ghana

To my parents, who, despite our many disagreements, brought me into the world and tilled the soils from which I bloomed

And

To Deborah McDowell and Patricia McFadden for being there through rain or shine

CONTENTS

ACKNOWLEDGMENTS

What a joy to finally arrive at the horizon that is this book. Of course, horizons are usually animated by mirages. A material product of my mind and the other penetrating minds that embarked on this journey with me, this book may be a mirage. But I know, too, that mirages can be miracles, that they can be real. This book is, therefore, one such miracle that materialized with the support of magnificent people who are, indubitably, lampposts of brilliance. Here are people who illuminated the jagged and dark terrains I strut as a fledgling and struggling ethnographer, intellectual, and activist, Black and queer.

My sincerest appreciation goes to the community of sasso I encountered in Jamestown. You embraced me into your beautiful worlds, which both transformed and made me rethink what it means to have a self, inhabit a body, that is condemned by society, yet hopes for a future amidst precarity. You constitute my newfound family, without whom this project would have been impossible. And to the late Hillary Afful I extend my sincerest gratitude. Hillary, wherever you are, I wish you "sound sleep." You held my hand from the start of this research. You opened that vista into a new universe for me. You were an unflinching knowledge bearer whose intellectual habits and contributions are dearly missed. Your fun-loving stature, jocular habits, "divaness," and love for all that is good, continue to emblazon my mind. I also want to thank Nelson Samuel Azumah for your reliable assistance to me in the field. Fieldwork is sometimes about building, but sometimes about rupturing, relationships. I'm quite sorry to have lost you as a friend. But, I am aware that the universe, in its own way, may once again bring us together. Time, as they say, heals, and hopefully, this fracture experiences that healing power. I am also thankful to the organization where I conducted ethnographic research, Bring

Us Rights and Justice (BURJ). Many thanks to the director of the organization for bringing me in, and making me one of your own. You created an enabling environment for me to thrive as an activist-scholar.

To my adviser Susan Wadley, whose intellectual rigor and fortitude, and love and affection for this work, I couldn't have done without. Sue, I offer you a big *medaase*—thank you—for being you, and for being there for me, just when I was near giving up. You pulled me out of despair. You told me I could do it, and that nothing, whatsoever, should stop me from accomplishing what I have tasked myself to do. I listened and delightedly digested your advisement. While the work was painstaking, your presence was exactly the antidote and cushion I needed when I was wedged between a rock and a hard place. Besides being my adviser, you also blessed me with the warmth of your home. Your husband, Rick Olanoff, offered me his listening ears and provocative advice when I felt I was going nowhere, and I extend my gratitude to him for undertaking the journey beyond this book with me. I am also thankful to my committee members for believing in me: Ann Gold, Christopher DeCorse, and Vincent Lloyd. Their love for this work, and their ability to foresee that I could do this ethnography in a perilous landscape of homonegativity were instrumental. I am thankful to Ann for allowing me to nourish my writerly self in the seminar Writing Religions and Cultures: Ethnographic Practice.

How to say thank you to Vincent Lloyd? Vincent, you have nourished my curiosity from the moment you stepped foot in Syracuse. The aura of your intellect is infectious. I honestly don't know how much I'd have conceptually framed this work without your erudite and expansive understanding of the very frameworks that inform it. You, indeed, encouraged me to love Africa and its place in the African diaspora and vice versa, and exposed me to works that were trending in the field that you thought were germane for this project. I very much look forward to fortifying our relationship, especially as I pass this milestone, and to seeking your advice when necessary. I also extend my appreciation to Rudi Gaudio for being there just when I needed him. I appreciate your friendship both as an intellectual and as a mentor. I look forward to being more responsive and communicative with you. Please, kindly pardon my unwarranted absences. I am also grateful for the numerous fellowships without which the groundwork for this book would not have been possible. A Wenner Gren Dissertation Fieldwork grant, a Claudia DeLys Fieldwork Grant, and multiple grants from the Maxwell School at Syracuse University allowed me to lay the foundations for what this project has become.

I also extend my gratitude to the Carter G. Woodson Institute for African American and African Studies at the University of Virginia. The Woodson has played an unquantifiable role in the making of this book—especially Deborah McDowell, who not only believed in me but has been generously present from the moment this book was conceived to when it was completed. As a Woodson Fellow,

I had the opportunity to workshop chapters from the book in the company of LaTasha Levy, Nicole Burrowes, Ava Purkiss, Taneisha Means, and Tammy Owens, who, as co-fellows, helped to make this project bloom. What a space to discover hope and community, given how lonesome book writing can be. My sincerest appreciation to Jim Igoe and his family. Jim was not only a mentor but also a friend and advocate. To my colleagues and co-conspirators, Njelle Hamilton, Robert Vinson, and our office administrator Debbie Best, I extend my heartfelt gratitude.

Joining the faculty at the Woodson after my fellowship couldn't be more divine.

I also want to thank Jeffrey McCune and Marlon Bailey for recognizing the significance of this work by affording this book a home in the series New Sexual Worlds at the University of California Press. As series editors, they provided the assurance needed to get this book in shape. I am thankful to them and the various reviewers, anonymous and known, who read the manuscript and offered such vibrant feedback and suggestions. Xavier Livermon, Lyndon Gill, T. J. Tallie, Jesse Weaver Shipley, Patricia McFadden, Shanti Parikh, and China Scherz, as well as the many beautiful and gorgeous people who shared the wisdom that lit up the desire paths that led to the completion of the book by being unquantifiably generous. Thanks to Naomi Schneider and Summer Farah at the University of California Press for your presence and attention to detail, and making this process in the era of COVID-19 less daunting. I would be remiss if I forgot my copyeditor, Sue Carter, for her unrivaled editing prowess.

Now, I want to extend my profound appreciation to my parents, Faustina and Nicholas Otu. You have been patiently waiting for me to finish my book. You have invested in my intellectual becoming. And here's hoping that those years of emotive, parental, cultural, and social investments have not gone to waste. I love you forever. Mum and Dad, your daily calls brought me loads of joy. I also want to thank my co-conspirators, the dear friends who have been there for me just when I needed them. Thank you Delali Kumavie, James Perla, Kofi Takyi Asante, Akosua Adoma Owusu, Andrew Small, James Parker, Evan Todtz, and Tristan Stapleton for being such graceful cheerleaders. You're the eyes and minds I needed. You all fed me when I was intellectually, psychologically, and emotionally malnourished. I look forward to a deepened relationship in the future. And, my unquantifiable appreciation goes out to Ryan White and Katie Kelly, for being there for me always.

As the adage goes, it takes a village. You are my village, my community. It would be rather arrogant on my part to disagree with such a witty and deep logic. The conception of this book, its maturation in the womb of my mind, and the labor that accompanied delivering it, the birth pangs, if you will, were softened by the hues afforded by this community. Thus, from the moment I conceived this idea to the point of its delivery, I have been surrounded by countless wonderful souls, a rich community of intellectuals, activists, friends, and individuals from varied backgrounds, and of multiplex orientations, whose urgings and support have allowed this work to acquire a modicum of life. This book, like its content, is quite amphibious. While it is the effort of a community, it has been allowed to have latitude for self-assertion. Thank you all very much.

Introducing Amphibious Subjects

> We have always been here, Auntie Kwame. Which is why these days when they say we are gay or homo-what-sexual, I am like whatever happened to what we were, to being Kwadwo Besia, Ntowbea? What matters for us is that we have always been here. It is funny because immediately [after?] we became "gay" and "homosexual," the homophobia began. These labels, which were supposed to describe us as a whole were understood here in Ghana as having to do with sex, sex, sex. That is my opinion!
>
> —KK (JULY 2014)

> The place of theory in gender work refers first to theory as it is currently produced and/or used and second to the place theory ought to occupy in work on gender. In relation to the first, the notion that theory is "abstract" or "uninteresting" appears to be shared not only by participants at training sessions but also by many NGO activists in the survey who do not see its significance in their everyday lives or work. As "practical" persons seeking to deal with life-threatening problems of gender-based violence or other deprivations of rights, many activists find theory "remote" or not readily usable in their situations.
>
> —TAKYIWAA MANUH, "DOING GENDER WORK IN GHANA" (2007, 139)

Following a four-year spell in the United States pursuing a graduate degree in Upstate New York, I returned to Ghana in June 2011 to conduct an anthropological project on the tabooed subject of homosexuality. After disembarking from the plane at Ghana's Kotoka International Airport, the international gateway for air travel, I strutted quickly across the tarmac to escape the beastly heat rising from the asphalt. Like other travelers, I was greeted in the arrival hall by a poster hanging in a silver frame on the wall behind the immigration booths where arriving passengers underwent entry formalities. The sign reads:

> Welcome!! Akwaaba!! Ghana warmly welcomes all visitors of goodwill. Ghana does not welcome paedophiles and other sexual deviants [in red font]. Indeed Ghana imposes extremely harsh penalties on such sexually aberrant behavior. If you are in

FIGURE 1. I first encountered this image at the Kotoka International Airport in Ghana in 2012, which was when I took this photograph. The image hung on a wall at the section of the airport where arrivals underwent immigration formalities.

Ghana for such activity, then for everybody's good, including your own, we suggest you go elsewhere.

This poster, produced by the Ghana Tourism Authority and presented as an innocuous introduction to the country, not only provides an example of the kinds of language, signs, and gateways that gender nonconforming men, who are the subjects of this ethnographic study, must navigate in Ghana, but also exposes how gender expression is increasingly becoming the "sign" used to prop up presumptions about sexuality. Here, male effeminacy is presumed to correlate with homosexuality, a common observation shared by my interlocutors during fieldwork.[1] Known in local parlance as "sasso" (singular and plural), this community of self-identified effeminate men is part of a constellation of mostly gender nonconforming subjects whose existence in Ghana challenges the signage, which belies their complex lives and experiences. To be clear, in this ethnography, I shine light on how their self-fashioning strategies are not reducible to their effeminacy or the presumption that they engage in homosexuality. Sasso, as a label, then, transcends conventional definitions of gender (and, I would add, sexuality), which, according to the Ghanaian feminist and scholar Takyiwaa Manuh (2007), has a different purchase in Ghana.[2]

Mostly residing in the historic coastal suburb of Jamestown, in the capital city of Accra, they engage in the very "sexually aberrant behavior" the poster condemns.[3] At the same time that they are compelled to navigate within a nation-state that polices their practices, these sasso must also navigate their way through the nettlesome agendas of human rights organizations. These agendas often elide the fact that domains like Jamestown have always been vibrant sites for sasso connections. This historic suburb, while a multiethnic enclave, is mostly Ga.[4] Hence, the majority of the sasso with whom I interacted spoke the Ga language fluently or partially. Animated by edifices of slavery and colonialism like the James and Usher Forts, which dot the shoreline of Accra, Jamestown is where the Chale Wote Street Festival,[5] a carnival that celebrates Ghanaian and diasporic cultures, is held. Occurring in the middle of August every year, the celebration is a site of unconventional and nonnormative gendered plays and performances, reminiscent of the anthropologist Lyndon Gill's (2018) characterization of the carnival in Trinidad and Tobago as a fertile site of queer possibilities.

The poster is instructive for this project. It impresses upon visitors to Ghana, as well as to Ghanaians reentering the country, that Ghana screens for "sexual deviants," into which category it slots "homosexuals." In a postcolonial nation that retained a colonial-era law criminalizing homosexuality, the sign does not directly announce the criminalization of homosexuality, but nevertheless encodes its illegality.[6] In other words, the welcoming signage conveys the idea that Ghana is a heterosexual nation. Attempting to distinguish between prescribed and proscribed sexual behaviors, the language on the poster conflates unspecified "deviant" sexual practices with pedophilia and other acts of sexual deviancy, but the lack of specificity is telling.

On the one hand, the poster's inscription does not explicitly categorize homosexuality as a deviant sexual practice. On the other hand, its "welcoming" sentiment issues an implicit warning to nonheterosexual individuals whose sexual proclivities do not fall within the boundaries and expectations of the state and the image it seeks to project to the world. While it is noticeable that the poster is silent on gender, the inscription "sexual deviance" arguably indexes "gender deviance." Inevitably, sex and gender are conflated in the warning, implying conformity with the heteronormative gender regime enforced by the heteronational state.[7]

The intentions and effects of the poster are unmistakable, perhaps most especially for a self-identified queer man such as myself. When I first encountered the poster on the morning of my arrival in June 2011, my response was visceral and its effects would be long-lasting. As I continued the course of my fieldwork in the months ahead, I became guarded about my nonheteronormative sexual leanings. Further, I came to understand how this poster echoed the regulating functions of the state. Ghana takes pride in being "the gateway to Africa," a marketing slogan touted by the Ministry of Tourism, Culture, and Creative Arts and the Ghana Tourism Authority, but this poster contradicts the widely held view that Ghanaians are a very hospitable people. Arguably, such hospitality stops at the boundaries enforced by heterosexuality, implicitly underwriting the familiar representation of Africa as "the closeted continent."[8]

Between 2011 and 2012, I conducted intermittent ethnographic visits to Ghana, usually during summer break. These short-term visits were followed by long-term fieldwork in 2013 and 2014. Most of the sasso I interacted with resided in, or congregated with other sasso in, Jamestown. Their presence in a country that claims to be primarily heterosexual reveals just how fraught the boundaries and inconsistent the country's definitions of sexual citizenship are. The complex lives of sasso expose how the coordinates of queer self-making remain contested, questioning the homogenization of sexual identity and the heterosexualization of sexual citizenship. In this respect, my ethnographic exercise is freeing, not just for the bodies and voices that animate this book, but also for me as a queer Ghanaian man. These bodies challenge those fictions and fantasies of heterosexual Ghana while magnifying the contradictions integral to LGBT+ human rights interventions in Africa.

I employed participant observation and life histories, and conducted archival research at the Missionary Collections at the School of Oriental and African Studies in London. There, I undertook literary and documentary analyses while pursuing fieldwork at a local NGO, which for the purposes of this ethnography I will call Bring Us Rights and Justice (BURJ).[9] The methodologies employed in pursuit of this research allowed me to unpack just how LGBT+ human rights organizations and the nation-state were, paradoxically, mirror images of each other. Each produced inflexible identitarian ontologies for sexual minorities such as sasso. Indeed, the imposition of the seemingly liberating gay identity on sasso, I argue, actually saddled them with an obligatory "gayness" that was, in effect, not too different from the Ghanaian government's enforcement of obligatory heterosexuality. In spite of the imperial/neocolonial homonormativity undergirding LGBT+ human rights interventions, sasso *strategically* draw on the LGBT+ lexicon and its attendant iconography to embed themselves in the transnational universe of LGBT+ human rights activism in a paradoxical manner.[10]

Thus, while it is readily understood that the "criminalization" of homosexuality by the state makes sexual minorities vulnerable, it is perhaps less understood how LGBT+ human rights organizations, in attempting to address such vulnerability, ultimately exacerbate it.[11] They do so by imposing their own equally inflexible language, signage, and sexual ontologies onto sasso. I focus, in particular, on how neoliberal LGBT+ human rights organizations such as Aidspan, the Global Fund, and BURJ ignore the sociohistorical and political economic complexities that continue to appear, disappear, and reappear in sasso lives. In sum, I discuss how the Ghanaian nation-state and its civil society as well as LGBT+ human rights organizations are complicit in the production and enforcement of labels that neglect the self-making practices of sasso. What I describe in this book as *amphibious* is intended to capture how sasso navigate the "obligatory gayness" established by LGBT+ human rights organizations and the "obligatory heterosexuality" enforced by the heterosexual nation-state.

ENCOUNTERING AMPHIBIOUS PERSONHOOD

The concept of "amphibious personhood," first used by the Ghanaian philosopher Kwame Gyekye, is relevant to sasso self-fashioning. A Harvard-trained philosopher who also studied at the University of Ghana, Kwame Gyekye is one of the formative figures in African philosophy as well as a specialist in Greco-Arabic philosophy, bringing his complex philosophical backgrounds to bear on his elucidation of personhood among the Akan, the largest ethnic group in Ghana.

My turn to Gyekye's amphibious personhood does not merely represent my attempt to extend into queer space a discussion of indigenous modes of personhood-making that have queer vitality, but takes up Audre Lorde's call: "As we come more into touch with our own ancient, non-european consciousness of living as a situation to be experienced and interacted with, we learn more and more to cherish our feelings, and to respect those hidden sources of our power from where true knowledge and, therefore, lasting action comes" (1984, 37).

Invested in a process of self-discovery that disavows the structures of feeling Europeans hold most dear, Lorde invites us to break away from those configurations when she evocatively speaks of the liberatory nature of poetry for Black women. Thus: "The white fathers told us: I think, therefore I am. The Black mother within each of us—the poet—whispers in our dreams: I feel, therefore I can be free" (1984, 38). African philosophical concepts like amphibious personhood as applied to sasso lives affirm such freedom.

Etymologically, *amphibian* derives from the Greek words *amphi* and *bios*, the former meaning "both" and the latter meaning "life." In the late seventeenth century, the Latin word *amphibium* described a creature "having two modes of existence" or "possessing a doubtful nature."[12] *The Oxford English Dictionary* defines the amphibian as a "cold-blooded vertebrate animal of a class that comprises the frogs, toads, newts, and salamanders. They are distinguished by having an aquatic gill-breathing larval stage followed (typically) by a terrestrial lung-breathing adult stage." A further definition defines amphibians as "technological machines [such] as a seaplane, tank, or other vehicle that can operate on land and on water." These technologies are also labeled amphibian especially as they move between multiple spaces, conditions, and temperatures.

Gyekye does not directly reprise these definitions in his discussion on the constitution of a person. Instead, his elucidation of amphibious identification shares some similarity with the general definitions of the amphibian, most of which describe an entity, be it human or animal, animate or inanimate, that moves between two terrains. Embracing the amphibian as a useful heuristic, one which aligns with the processes of self-making expressed in the lives of sasso, I interrogate the homogenization of gender and sexuality by institutions that continue to assume that Western experiential frames are universal. To be clear, I emphasize that sasso life stories jettison the homogenization of Ghanaian citizens as heterogendered and heterosexual as well as the absorption of sasso into what Joseph Massad describes as the "gay international" (2007).

In understanding sasso as subjects who live "amphibiously," I capture how their complex lives undermine the homogenizing tendencies integral to the heterosexual investments pursued by the nation-state and the anti-homophobic projects undertaken by LGBT+ human rights organizations. As the sasso and LGBT+ human rights advocate KK hints in their remark in the first epigraph, sasso existed in Ghana before the arrival of LGBT+ human rights political interventions. Implied in that observation is how LGBT+ human rights organizations' attempts to make visible the victimized "queer" subject violently hypervisibilizes them,[13] as the recent rise in organizations that spew homophobic vitriol in Ghana indicates.[14] Furthermore, KK's endearing reference to me as "auntie" provides a glimpse into the glossary of kinship terms utilized by sasso in their daily conversations in the realm of the mundane.

This book is a queer ethnography not least because it weaves interventions from fields in conversation with each other, that is, African philosophy, anthropological studies on sex and gender, and African and Afro-diasporic/Black feminist and queer ruminations on gender, sexuality, and race. That it attends to the tensions and overlaps yielding from these conversations provides me with the framework to argue that sasso inhabit a distinct queer subjectivity. I describe this subjectivity as at once African and non-African, colonial and anticolonial, nameable and unnamable, heterosexual and nonheterosexual, visible and invisible, known and unknown, Western and non-Western, among other crucial distinctions.

Against this backdrop, I dwell within the geography of this book on the theoretical challenges that sasso lives present to hegemonic queer theory in the West, normative African philosophy, and Eurocentric anthropological approaches to gender and sexuality. Embracing the call by the Ghanaian feminist Takyiwaa Manuh, outlined in the second epigraph, that we engage with the challenges of the place of theory in gender work in Ghana, I ask: how can we make theory useful in understanding the lifeworlds of sasso without diminishing the painful, contradictory realities they navigate daily? Having engaged with sasso, some of whom are activists, and NGO workers, some of whom engage in LGBT+ human rights activism, in this book, I straddle that thin line between theory and practice by interrogating the nation-state and LGBT+ human rights NGOs' investment in the dichotomy between heterosexual and homosexual as well as gender and sexuality.

I diagram how sasso engage in gender and sexual practices that render messy existing conventions of gender and sexuality. In other words, I examine how sasso embody a gender and sexual subjectivity that circumvents homophobia while navigating the meanings of gender and sexuality circulating under LGBT+ humanitarianism. Thus, this ethnography is comparable to the Dutch-Surinamese anthropologist Gloria Wekker's ethnography on women's sexual practices and relationships in postcolonial Suriname, described as "mati work." Like Wekker, I "insist upon alternatively using 'indigenous' terminology" (2006, 68), embracing sasso as a vernacular category that troubles the reduction of sexuality and desire to identity and activity.

Moreover, I demonstrate that sasso is not merely an indigenous label since it hosts a constellation of practices, relationships, and ideas that are at once local, global, and transnational. In fact, it is a site of competing meanings. And, by relying on accounts shared by sasso themselves, I challenge how Western sexual and gender conventions get reproduced as universal even in radical liberatory sexual and gender politics. In doing so, I elaborate on how the entangling nature of sasso lives and experiences confound the homogenizing impulses of both the Ghanaian state and the LGBT+ human rights organizations who would put the country on a corrective course.

DISROBING FICTIONS OF HETEROSEXUAL GHANA

Let us for a moment return to KK, who resists such impulses by refuting the homogenized representation of Ghana as a heterosexual nation, as well as the claim that nonheterosexual subjects are "foreign" to Ghana. Instead, he foregrounds how effeminate men, who are known among the Akan of Ghana as "Kwadwo Besia" or "Ntowbea," both "man-woman" in English, have been integral to Ghana's sexual and gender landscapes.[15] Claiming that "they have always been there," KK poses the question: in what ways do LGBT+ human rights activities in Ghana displace and replace that "they" with LGBT+ nomenclature? His frustration also suggests how the increased visibility of LGBT+ human rights politics has led to the pathologization of Kwadwo Besia and Ntowbea, terms that are now associated with "homosexuality."

I echo, in part, the work of the Swiss-Ghanaian anthropologist Serena Dankwa to answer that question. In *Knowing Women* (2021), her ethnography on female same-sex intimacies, Dankwa dispels the fiction that Ghana is a primarily heterosexual nation. Exploring same-sex intimacies among women, indigenously known as "supi" relationships, Dankwa outlines a constellation of intimate practices to demonstrate the complexity of Ghana's erotic cultures. "Friendship marriages" observed among the Nzema people of southwestern Ghana by the Italian ethnologist Italo Signorini, for example, form an intricate part of this complex constellation. Known as "agɔnwole agyalɛ,"[16] which translates into English as "friendship marriage," this marriage "is considered on the conscious level as the noblest expression of friendship: the sublimation of a deep feeling which is of considerable value as a factor of social cohesion in Nzema culture and which is recognized by that society and expressed through institutions of growing complexity according to the intensity of the sentiments involved" (1973, 222). Thus, the presence of Kwadwo Besia and Ntowbea, supi relationships, and agɔnwole agyalɛ among the Nzema exemplifies the wide range of intimacies, identities, and practices in Ghana.

Even as the government considers same-sex intimacies as "foreign" to Ghana, a position underscored by the closure of an LGBT+ office run by the organization LGBT+ Rights Ghana on February 23, 2021, LGBT+ human rights groups have become increasingly visible in the country.[17] On the one hand, their presence serves to establish that LGBT+ citizens of Ghana have "rights" that need defending; on the other hand, these human rights groups come with their own homogenizing tendencies and agendas that seek to assimilate sasso in Ghana to the labels—lesbian, gay, bisexual, and transgender, and queer+—that reduce sasso subjectivity to their sexual orientation. In this book, I refer to these incidents as "heterocolonial" tropes wrapped in "homocolonial" tones precisely because they rehearse colonial and Christian projects that displaced arguably fluid precolonial gender formations. Assimilationist labels such as LGBT+ work to suck sasso into the vortex Dennis Altman (1997) frames as "global gay." The men in my study prefer the term *sasso* largely because, in their view, it does not carry the weight and currency that LGBT+ terms are presumed to carry. Furthermore, *sasso* not only avoids the negative baggage associated with LGBT+ in Ghana, but also makes navigating the homophobia spewed by Christian organizations less challenging.

Christianity and Constitutionality: Handmaidens of Heteronationalism

Ghana is undoubtedly a nation where Christian precepts are fundamental to the policing of both gender and sexuality. The pronouncement made by former president John Evans Atta Mills in 2011 at the National Convention of the Church of Pentecost is unambiguous: "Christ is the President of Ghana."[18] This statement, which epitomizes Christianity's synecdochic and irreducible prominence, boldly reinforces the perception that Ghana is a heterosexual Christian nation. The National Coalition for Proper Human Sexual Rights and Family Values (NCPHSRFV), an anti-LGBT+ NGO that wages campaigns against the "growing menace of Lesbian, Gay, Bisexual, and Transgender (LGBT+) Rights activities in the world,"[19] also perpetuates the idea of a heterosexual Ghana.

Established in 2013, the coalition's membership, which includes religious and civil society organizations such as the Christian Council of Ghana (CCG), Ghana's oldest and leading Christian organization, has taken the stance that homosexuality is the result of Westernization. Thus, the organization has been unrelenting in its opposition not only to the liberalization of LGBT+ human rights but also to efforts to incorporate comprehensive sexuality education interventions into Ghana's educational policy. Receiving funding from Western evangelical organizations like Family Watch International, the coalition is intent on preserving heterosexual family values that it believes are being "eroded" by LGBT+ human rights organizations.

Christianity's overwhelming presence is just one part of the story. Ghana's Fourth Republican Constitution reinforces Christian teachings by criminalizing what it describes as "unnatural carnal knowledge."[20] The logical corollary of British colonial legal schemes, the constitution's proscriptions and prescriptions on unnatural carnal knowledge remain vague (Atuguba 2019). In an interview conducted by the Human Rights Watch, an assistant commissioner of police in Ghana revealed that "the term unnatural carnal knowledge is vague, does not have any clear meaning in law, creates difficulties in consistent interpretation and its application is used to target LGBT+ people" (Human Rights Watch 2017). The

Ghanaian legal scholar Raymond Atuguba underscores this ambiguity when he suggests that

> Ghana's criminal statute does not outlaw "homosexuality" or "homosexual expression" in general. Homosexuality could mean the mere sexual attraction to a person of the same gender, and not necessarily unnatural carnal knowledge or sodomy. This implies that a person who identifies as "gay," but does not engage in unnatural carnal knowledge would not be caught by Ghana's criminal laws. Nevertheless, a heterosexual person who engages in "unnatural carnal knowledge" commits an offence, although (s)he is not homosexual. It may, therefore, be reasonably proposed that, a person belonging to the LGBT+ community is permitted by the confines of Ghanaian law, to live openly as a homosexual—with the opportunity at will to publicly show affection to another person of the same-sex, and engage in all acts attendant to such affection, and which fall short of the requisite degree of penetration. (2019, 114)

Despite this lucid observation by Atuguba, which disrobes the fiction that homosexuality is a criminal act, Ghanaians assumed to embody nonheterosexual tendencies are explicitly commanded to tow the lines of heterosexuality. The presence of sasso within Ghana's borders reveals the porosity of the country's supposed *cordon sanitaire*. KK's statement above, Serena Dankwa's study of female same-sex intimacy, and Italo Signorini's exploration of friendship marriages among the Nzema of Ghana bring the permeability of these boundaries to life. How, then, do sasso navigate the shifts induced by formations that have opposing interpretations of sexual citizenship? And does amphibious subjectivity, the analytic I use to make sense of sasso in this ethnography, adequately capture how they embody a distinct queer subjectivity?

FROM RELUCTANTLY QUEER TO AMPHIBIOUS SUBJECTS

When I first envisioned this project, I framed sasso responses to homophobia and LGBT+ human rights interventions as a sign of their "reluctance" or hesitation at attempts that reduced their subjectivities to their sexual leanings. Thus, at the time, I concluded that sasso were *reluctantly queer* (Otu 2014). After conducting long-term fieldwork and archival research, and engaging with African philosophy, specifically Akan philosophy and its culturally derived articulations of personhood, I moved away from reluctance as an analytic. My turn to Akan philosophy not only illuminated my understanding of how sasso navigated sexual citizenship but also underscored how they engaged in queer self-making practices contingent on time, space, and relationships. In observing sasso, it became clear to me over time that my reluctance to come out as gay in Ghana informed my own limited analyses of sasso subjectivity. Eventually, I reconciled with the fact that my interlocutors' accounts about their experiences as queer subjects in Ghana did not necessarily have to be mine. Moreover, as an ethnographer, it was important that I allow ethnography be a site of contestations, even if those tensions erupted between sasso and myself.

The sasso I encountered during my fieldwork ultimately engaged in self-making practices that challenged my global, North-based understandings of sexuality, gender, intimacy, and desire. They led me to ponder not only what gender and sexuality entailed for them but also how they understood desire and intimacy. Did these vocabularies matter at all? Or did they become significant only when they encountered and participated in LGBT+ human rights interventions? These considerations led me to contemplate whether what Judith Butler (1990) famously described as "gender trouble" had meaning in the Ghanaian context, yielding the questions: How do African bodies already trouble gender and sexuality when they exist beyond white-centered characterizations of terms that are not theirs?[21] What do we do with terms, categories, and labels that are not ours? In what ways do we reproduce oppressive apparatuses and practices by entering the labels and terms that are not of our making but the reverberations of a violent past? Although these and other questions and concerns compelled me to leave "reluctance" behind as an analytic in favor of "amphibious subjectivity," a concept derived from Akan philosophy, they also amplified the cardinal postcolonial paradox that confronts postcolonial citizens: What do we lose when we are forced to neglect what we were supposed to be for what we were forced to become? Have we become the calcified remains of a violent colonial, racist, and heteropatriarchal projects?

WHY AMPHIBIOUS SUBJECTIVITY? AFRICAN PHILOSOPHICAL ARTICULATIONS OF PERSONHOOD IN BRIEF

The place of the person and community among African societies and cultures has long been central to discussions and debates within and beyond African philosophy. African thinkers like Leopold Senghor (1995), John Mbiti (1995), Victor Uchendu (1965), Ifi Amadiume (1987b), Kwame Gyekye (1987), Ifeanyi Menkiti (1984), Julius Nyerere (1968), Okot p'Bitek (1998), Kwasi Wiredu (1992), Kwame Anthony Appiah (1992), Nkiru Nzegwu (2006), Oyèrónkẹ́ Oyěwùmí (1997), and Emmanuel Chukwudi Eze (1998), among others, have variously dissected Africans' engagement with the metaphysics of personhood and community. Notable among the aforementioned philosophers are Senghor (1995) and Menkiti (1984), who held the unwavering position that Africans are inherently communitarian.[22] Invoking the maxim "Not one tree does a forest make" as evidence to support their claim, these thinkers emphasized the centrality of the community to self-making in Africa. This proposition did not go uncontested.

Philosophers like Kwame Gyekye and Kwasi Wiredu, informed by their distinct philosophical persuasions on the making of personhood in Africa, responded to Senghor and Menkiti, arguing that self-making processes in Africa are the by-product of both individualistic and communitarian dispositions. Both Gyekye (1997, 1987, 1992) and Wiredu and Gyekye (1992) focus on the self-making traditions of the Akan people to arrive at the conclusion that the individual self and the social/collective body play significant roles in the production of personhood. While the various philosophical treatises on personhood and community invoked by these philosophers are significant, for the purposes of the book, I engage, in particular, with Gyekye's notion of "amphibious personhood."

In explaining amphibious personhood, Gyekye turns to the Adinkra symbol known among the Akan as *funtumfunefu denkyemfunefu*, which translates into English as the "Siamese crocodiles." A crocodile with two heads and a conjoined stomach, the symbol epitomizes the uneven and often complex fusion and fission that animate interactions between the individual and the community. Adinkra symbolic representations amplify how pictoral symbols and images are central to the Akan conceptual scheme. They convey values, norms, idioms, and the complexity of the ideas and practices of the Akan people in West Africa. As the Ghanaian philosopher N. K. Dzobo maintains, the term *adinkra* is rooted in "the Twi words *di nkra* meaning 'to say goodbye.' The adinkra cloth is traditionally a mourning cloth and is normally worn 'to say goodbye' to the dead and to express sympathy for the bereaved family, and so is commonly seen at funerals and memorial services. It is usually adorned with symbols that express various views of life and death" (1992, 89).

Adinkra symbology, omnipresent not only in Akan culture but also in Ghanaian and other West African and Afro-diasporic cultures, reinforces Kwasi Wiredu's supposition that "given that Ghanaian life is suffused with speculative thought, it is not surprising that many of our eminent contemporary public leaders have attached the greatest importance to philosophy by both word and work" (1992, 1).

Kwame Gyekye "endogenizes" the word *amphibian* by turning to the symbol funtumfunefu denkyemfunefu. In doing so, he reaffirms Dzobo's suggestion that "all over Africa, visual images and ordinary objects are used symbolically to communicate knowledge, feelings and values. As symbols play such an important role in the African conception of reality, a sound understanding of African patterns of thought and feeling requires an appreciation of the nature and function of symbolism as a medium of communication in African culture" (1992, 85).

Evidently, Gyekye's reliance on the Siamese crocodile in his attempts to understand personhood-making among the Akan is exemplary of how Adinkra symbology remains fundamental to the Akan weltanschauung. Articulating that the frictions between the two heads illuminate "an enduring *tension* [my emphasis] in the Akan philosophy of the individual," Gyekye underscores how this schism "offers a clear, unambiguous statement on the value of individuality" (1987, 157). The two single heads represent the two separate individuals, and the joint stomach symbolizes community, suggesting that "the uniqueness of the individual and his or her relationship to society" (1987, 159) is never diminished. This implies that the constitution of the individual is coterminously the constitution of the society precisely because "the will, interests, tastes, and passions of individuals" (1987, 159) occur in the contested space of the community—this is the very domain in which the will, interests, passions, and tastes take shape and get absorbed and redefined by the individual amidst the collective when and how they find suitable. Against this backdrop, Gyekye notes "the value of communality" (1987, 161) to the individual and the individual's centrality to communality. Through the latter, the individual is furnished with the tools to form associations between emotion and thought in order to identify their place within the collective and the latitude for their own self-formation. The Siamese crocodile embodies how the self emerges out of the entanglement between the individual and the community; conversely, the community's being is indebted to that entanglement.

Herpetologically, the crocodile is a reptile, not an amphibian. Gyekye, in his examination of amphibious personhood, does not explain why he reclassifies a seemingly reptilian creature as an amphibian. Aware of that slippage, I give two possible reasons for this lack of explication. First, I suggest that, in the Gyekyean sense, the amphibian is probably not in reference to the crocodile as a biological creature, but to the Siamese crocodile as a mythical creature. And second, since there are no records to the effect that biologically Siamese crocodiles exist, in symbolic and poetic realms, they can potentially exist.[23] Arguably, the two-headed crocodile with a conjoined belly can be seen as amphibious not just because the crocodile moves between land and water but because the two heads struggle over food absorbed by a single belly. In philosophizing the amphibian, Gyekye does not disavow the biological fact that the crocodile is a reptile; instead, he offers proof of how in the context of African philosophy, biology and philosophy can productively complement each other in ways that undermine the binary construal of biology as opposed to philosophy.

Hence, funtumfunefu denkyemfunefu, the symbolic bedrock of this theoretical exposé on sasso subjectivity in neoliberal Ghana, is arguably an example of the widespread circulation and usefulness of Adinkra symbols among the Akan people in particular and Ghanaians in general. It has both philosophic and poetic significations that are meaningful for the people who create them and use them as the guiding principles of their lives.

Consuming food absorbed by a single stomach, the two-headed crocodile is primarily invoked to signify the complex, uneven, and sometimes competing interactions between the individual and the community. Funtumfunefu denkyemfunefu, therefore, signifies how Akan people scrutinize the ways in which human social relationships are marked by a constant vacillation between the individual self and the social self. If the crocodile moves between land and water, then humans move between the selves they inhabit and the social contexts in which those selves are nested. Similarly, the environments in which they are nested are amphibious, since the boundaries between the land and water are not sharply delineated. The

FIGURE 2. The Siamese crocodile. Source: http://www.adinkra.org/htmls/adinkra/funt.htm.

amphibian thus moves between worlds by engaging in world-making practices that refuse the boundaries established to limit such movement and the potential they stand to yield. There is a queerness to this boundary-breaking trait of the amphibian that makes it appealing both as a creature and an analytic for me in this book.

Gyekye's observation that the "African social order is amphibious" is also telling not merely because it "manifests features of both communality and individuality" (1987, 154) but also because in this order, life is "lived in harmony and cooperation with others, a life of mutual consideration and aid and of interdependence" (1995, 37). For Gyekye, this life "provides a viable framework for the fulfillment of the individual's nature and potentials" (1995, 38), implying that the individual needs the community if they are to wholly develop themselves, and the community needs the individual's contributions to be adequately sustained. For this reason, then, "the African social order is neither purely communalistic nor purely individualistic" (1987, 154). And because the individual is not entirely crushed by the community, they have latitude for the self-assertion required to define their humanity and place in the collective. Despite these insightful readings, we are left with little room within Gyekye's framework to highlight the potentially boundary-breaking characteristic of the amphibian, especially as regards gender and sexuality in personhood-making.

In his essay "Person and Community in African Thought," Gyekye draws closer to an explication of self-making and personhood, especially among the Akan and the coastal ethnic Ga-Dangme, that takes on a "queer" dimension. Accordingly, he foregrounds how these ethnic groups engage in practices of the self that take on gender-neutral dispositions. For example, they use neutral pronouns to apply to both animate and inanimate objects. Gyekye observes: "In Ga-Dangme languages, also in Ghana, the pronoun *e* is used to refer to everything—stones, trees, dogs, and human beings (of both the masculine and feminine genders). The pronoun "*e*" (=it/he/she) is thus gender-neutral, encompassing all the genders: masculine, feminine, and neuter" (1992, 107).

Gyekye's observation echoes arguments on gender formations among the Igbos of Nigeria by the Nigerian anthropologist Ifi Amadiume. In her eloquent expatiation of the flexibility of gender representations and practices among the Igbo, Amadiume underscores that "another example of the looseness of gender association is the fact that in Igbo grammatical construction of gender, a neuter particle is used in Igbo subject or object pronouns, so that no gender distinction is made in reference to males and females in writing or in speech. There is, therefore, no language or mental adjustment or confusion in references to a woman performing a typical male role" (1987b, 17).

From both Gyekye and Amadiume, we glean the extent to which gender-neutral language complicates the reducibility of being and becoming a person to being male or female. In what ways, then, does Gyekye's emphasis on the neuter pronouns in Akan and Ga-Dangme conceptual schemes, like Amadiume's example of gender neutrality among the Igbos, *queer* African philosophical contributions on personhood?

What does queering Gyekye's evocative intervention on personhood do for me in this book? To queer here indexes my awareness of the limitation in Gyekye's intervention. While his framework is applicable to sasso subjectivities, it retains a heteronormative leaning that, in my opinion, presumes gender neutrality in name only rather than in action or deed. And here, I mean his invocation that a gender-neutral vocabulary exists does not correlate to the lived experience the terms are supposed to capture. In that respect, my use of *queer* here elicits the Black queer theorist Xavier Livermon's theorization of "queer(y)ing" freedom among Black queers in South Africa. For Livermon, "Black queers create freedom through forms of what I term cultural labor. The cultural labor of visibility occurs when black queers bring dissident sexualities and gender nonconformity into the public arena. Visibility refers not only to the act of seeing and being seen but also to the process through which individuals make themselves known in the communities as queer subjects" (2012, 300).

In queering freedom, then, Livermon's exposition divests from freedom the parochial understanding that it is merely a political performance by illuminating how "black queers demonstrate that far from being a Western contaminant, queerness is embedded in black communities" (2012, 300). Through queering freedom, it becomes apparent that the practice and idea of freedom need always be reworked, reframed, and revitalized if freedom's inherent vitality is to be sustained.

Similarly, the Africanist historian T. J. Tallie, in his historiography on indigeneity in colonial Natal, South Africa, conducts a "*queer* reading" (2019, 7) of indigeneity. Tallie incisively suggests that "a queer theoretical approach has allowed scholars to analyze not only instances in which subjects evince a sexual identification that is not explicitly heterosexual, but also the ways in which actions or positions can challenge larger normative systems" (2019, 7). Rendering a capacious exposition on what it means to engage in a nonnormative examination of normative systems, especially in the context of settler colonialism, Tallie writes: "A queer reading, then, can offer an exploration of how lines of assumed order are skewed by ideas, actions, or formations. If settler colonialism itself is presented as a form of orientation, of making recognizable and inhabitable home space for European arrivals on indigenous land, then native peoples and their continued resistance can serve to 'queer' these attempted forms of order" (2019, 7).

By queering indigeneity, Tallie unsettles the Eurocentric, racist anthropological roots that continue to inform understandings of indigeneity. In light of the above provocations by both Livermon and Tallie, which widen the meaning of what queering does or signifies, I not only queer Gyekyean amphibious personhood, but also demonstrate that sasso subjectivities are queer. Their engagements with LGBT+ human rights organizations, their families, ritual celebrations like christenings, weddings, funerals, and birthdays, among other things, underscore their centrality to a heteronormative culture that now publicly objects to their being.

WHEN QUEER AFRICAN ETHNOGRAPHY MEETS AFRICAN PHILOSOPHY

The queer Kenyan literary theorist Keguro Macharia, in contending with what it means to write about African and Afro-diasporic experiences, suggests we refuse the seduction to make whiteness the point of departure in our analysis of Black experiences. Highlighting the critical interventions made by African and Afro-diasporic scholars, Macharia proposes that we center their contributions while being aware of their essentialist and nationalist limitations. In a vein similar to African philosophers like Kwame Gyekye, Macharia invokes "frottage" as a metaphor to refuse the lingering specter and seduction to summon and analyze Black life through white/Western frames.

As an analytic, frottage conveys how "the black diaspora poses a historical and conceptual challenge to dominant histories and theories in queer studies, which have tended to privilege white Euro-American experience" (2019, 4). Thinking through frottage, Macharia circumvents Eurocentric theoretical models by "moving the centre," to use Ngugi Wa Thiong'o's (1992) useful terminology. Wa' Thiong'o gestures at the need to shift the center from its supposed location in the West into multiple orbits and arenas in non-Western cultures. It is important, nevertheless, to consider the intimate presence of Africa in the West, an intimacy that Lisa Lowe has described as undermining "the modern division of knowledge into academic disciplines, focused on discrete areas and objects of interest" (2015, 1). On this premise, if the constitution of Africa relies on the vacillation between the so-called West and itself, then, arguably, Africa is amphibious as it reproduces aspects of the West in its self-formation.

I find the boundary-breaking character of the amphibian to be queer. Similarly, if the crocodile, because it lives in land and water, develops abilities that sustain it in both spaces, then Africa, both as a geography and an idea is amphibious because it shares a complex and nervous intimacy with the West, and vice versa. And in view of Kwame Gyekye's formulation of the African subject's self-constitution as the outcome of their vacillation between the community and the individual, I argue throughout this book that sasso lives, experiences, and existence breathe life into the arguably abstract analytic of amphibious subjectivity.

The poster at the airport, which sets the terrain not only for this ethnography but also for the gender and sexual landscapes of Ghana, then, raises the personal, anthropological, and philosophical questions that structure the contours of this book, namely: How does the presence of sasso in Ghana unsettle the information on the poster? Does the poster demand that one's self-identity be reconstituted because they are gender nonconforming or nonheterosexual? How do sasso navigate the landscape that forms the background of the poster? Ultimately, these questions must transcend the individual, circling back to the nation-state. What does this greeting at the portal of arrival signify about Ghana? How does the country attempt to naturalize heterosexuality as the dominant sexual order for defining citizenship? Do the strong attachments to heterosexualization in the postcolonial context reinforce the colonial project as coterminously a "heterocolonial" process, a point further detailed in chapter 5? If so, in what ways do LGBT+ human rights organizations wittingly and unwittingly engage in "homocolonial" projects that reproduce the very heterocolonial practices they seek to upset?

A NOTE ON RACIALIZED NEOLIBERALISM AND DEVELOPMENTAL HUMANITARIANISM

The postcolonial African feminist Patricia McFadden (2011), extending Uma Narayan's (1997) notion of "the politics of rescue," describes how neoliberal regimes and their concomitant logics have the tendency to extinguish particular populations while coterminously producing "new privileged subjects" under the guise of saving them (see also Melamed 2011). In this book I detail how neoliberal queer politics and logics connect former colonial metropoles to postcolonial nations following a developmentalist paradigm that relies on the framework established by Global North/Global South distinctions.

The late seventies and early eighties represented a neoliberal watershed moment in Africa. During this period, Africa was sucked into a Western capitalist project that claimed to resolve the developmental woes of and dire conditions in which Africans lived their lives. The idea and science of neoliberalism ignored how forces like colonialism and slavery had wrecked Africa, which the historian Walter Rodney (1972) captured as the European and neo-European underdevelopment of Africa. The appearance of institutions like the World Bank and the International Monetary Fund (IMF) on the African political economic scene deregulated state sovereignty with the introduction of practices that upheld the principle of a free market economy.

Projects designed under the auspices of monumental interventions like the Structural Adjustment Program (SAP) and the Economic Recovery Program (ERP) forced African governments into the vortex of neoliberalism. Hence, as the

Black queer feminist M. Jacqui Alexander avers, these neoliberal projects, instead of eliminating the structures of violence for which they were implemented, merely readjusted them (2006). Saving women under the banner of neoliberal political projects calcified the tenacity of heteropatriarchy. It might be added that the intensified homophobia in postcolonial Africa is a function of gender mainstreaming projects implemented under neoliberal projects.

In an era dominated by Reaganomics and Thatcherite doctrines of the free market, countries in Africa became the recipients of funds distributed through SAP and ERP that came with strings and conditions. This era also witnessed the proliferation of NGOs that worked in concert with governmental organizations to deliver on the promise of development (Manuh 2007; Ferguson 2006; Igoe and Kelsall 2005; Pierre 2013). The proliferation of NGOs in Africa, characteristic of the neoliberal wave, disenfranchised state agencies in Africa the same way that it increasingly disenfranchised Black people, people of color, and poor working-class communities in the so-called Global North. In effect, it was a racialized project that robbed African and Afro-diasporic subjects of their access to citizenship and self-determination (Rodney 1972; Pierre 2013; McFadden 2011; Manuh 2007). These various forces animate the settings in which projects to liberate women, and, eventually, LGBT+ human rights interventions, occurred. The widespread circulation and adoption of these neoliberal projects shifted extant notions of citizenship.

Neoliberal ideologies made way for trafficking in ideas that not only enforced state deregulation but also, to a large degree, the privatization of citizenship. Not surprisingly, these shifts occurred in tandem with attempts to lift African nations from the doldrums of underdevelopment. Inevitably, developmentalism was the new civilization and new colonialism. What the first president of Ghana and ardent pan-Africanist Kwame Nkrumah persuasively captured as "neocolonialism" tilled the political economic soils in which the neoliberal turn was sowed. For Nkrumah, "the result of neo-colonialism is that foreign capital is used for the exploitation rather than for the development of the less developed parts of the world. Investment under neo-colonialism increases rather than decreases the gap between the rich and the poor countries of the world" (1965, 2).

Any analysis of the manifestation of neoliberalism in Africa requires a critical examination of how it is entwined with neocolonialism, which, to cite Nkrumah again, represented "an attempt to export the social conflicts of the capitalist countries" (1965, 3). Neoliberal political economic regimes and their concomitant ideologies and practices did not occur in a vacuum. In fact, while Africa became a large-scale laboratory for testing and affirming the veracity of neoliberal projects, such experiments had their roots in Black communities, communities of color, and working-class communities in the Global North. Nkrumah's suggestion that neocolonialism involves the exportation of social conflicts and problems from the developed world to ex-colonies anticipates the emergence and globalization of neoliberalism (1965). Neoliberalism was therefore a racial project that fundamentally restructured racist formations formerly adjudicated under colonial and imperial apparatuses that orchestrated the colonization of Africa and the enslavement of Africans.

What Patricia McFadden (2011) identifies as the "neoliberal and neocolonial collusion" at the core of the developmentalist paradigm on the continent foregrounds the consequences of structural adjustment on African nations. This collusion reinstated those old violent regimes within new apparatuses of domination. Actors in these collusion schemes include mostly Western NGOs and their non-Western representatives, as well as state and governmental agencies. Where there were Christian missionaries, colonial administrators, and merchants/traders in the era of colonization and slavery, now there are human rights missionaries, neocolonial administrators, and neoliberal corporations that participate in so-called development projects to enhance Africa. Hence, to understand neoliberalism's manifestation in Africa is to contend with its seamless attachment to neocolonialism and the fact that the neocolonial and neoliberal collusion in the Global South is distinguishable from Global North neoliberalism in a fundamental way.

The Africanist anthropologist James Ferguson, in *Global Shadows: Africa in the Neoliberal World Order* (2006), reexamines the thesis of development in Africa by interrogating conventional discourses on development that neglect the specter of colonization, which inhibits African development. Ferguson magnifies how developmental schemes in Africa execute "re-colonization" projects that racialize Africa by forcibly pigeonholing the continent into a universalist framework. Neoliberalism in Africa, Ferguson asserts, can be described by how nations in Africa are by all accounts intentionally controlled "by transnational organizations that are not in themselves governments but work together with powerful First World states within a global system of nation-states" (2006, 100).

Similarly, the anthropologist Jemima Pierre incisively outlines how neoliberal projects are coterminously scenes of racialization, even if such projects uphold radical Pan-African intentions. Pierre's reading cogently evinces the ways in which neoliberalism insidiously gets normalized in domains that are critical of the philosophy and praxis of neoliberal projects (2013). In *The Predicament of Blackness: Postcolonial Ghana and the Politics of Race*, Pierre dwells on the multiple ways in which neoliberal projects perpetuate white supremacy in their efforts to restore the histories of slavery in Ghana. She argues: "Indeed, the development of heritage tourism within the context of a neoliberal economic order that presents a narrative of slavery decoupled from racial colonization and that is without European perpetrators in fact works to neutralize the impact of the country's colonial history, silencing the effects of exploitation. At the same time, it decouples White Western power and African subordination, shifting responsibility to Africans, thereby reifying the racial and cultural differences that undergird traditional understandings of Africa's economic and political predicaments" (2013, 151).

I suggest in this book that the evolution of LGBT+ human rights in Africa, too, is "decoupled" from "racial colonization." This uncoupling enables the racialization of Africans as homophobic, and thus as solely responsible for the perpetration of the injustices against nonheteronormative subjects. Extending Pierre's point, I illuminate the coordinates and boundaries of the anti-Blackness inherent within liberalism in general, and queer liberalism in particular. Queer liberal projects, then, like the gender mainstreaming projects undertaken in the eighties and nineties to rescue African women, are sites of racialization. On the one hand, queer Ghanaians qua Africans deserve *rescuing* yet are still embedded in neocolonial networks and structures and, on the other hand, these apparatuses reinforce either covertly or overtly processes of racialization regarded as "progress-making projects."[24] The recent invasion of the office of LGBT+ Human Rights Ghana exemplifies this paradox.[25] Here, the establishment of an LGBT+ office, considered as a progressive move in Ghana, yielded what some queer Ghanaians and advocates of LGBT+ rights who supported engaging in LGBT+ advocacy expected—heightened homophobia from the nation-state and civil society—by steamrolling years of pathbreaking advocacy work.

TRAVERSING THE TERRAINS OF AMPHIBIOUS SUBJECTS: THE GEOGRAPHY OF THE BOOK

This book is divided into three parts. The first part consists of two chapters, the first of which is "Situating Sasso: Mapping Effeminate Subjectivities and Homoerotic Desire in Postcolonial Ghana." There, I elaborate on how the complex embodiments and practices of sasso can be best understood if situated in their historical and contemporary contexts. Thus, I argue, we approach sasso as a constituency inhabiting a nation that bears the marks of colonial and Christian modernity. Approaching sasso as a convoluted community, I trace the complex genealogy of sasso as a category, its various iterations and constellations.

The second chapter, titled "Contesting Homogeneity: Sasso Complexity in the Face of Neoliberal LGBT+ Politics," foregrounds the lives of four sasso; two were residents of Jamestown and two lived in other suburbs of the city. Jamestown was their congregation point. The four interludes are windows into sasso lifeworlds, and they highlight sasso heterogeneity and their navigation of homoerotic desire amid the tensions incited by LGBT+ human rights organizations and the nation-state.

The book's second part, called "Amphibious Subjects in Rival Geographies," is comprised of two chapters that ethnographically and theoretically demonstrate why sasso embody queer self-making practices that are amphibious. The third chapter, "Amphibious Subjectivity: Queer Self-Making at the Intersection of Colliding Modernities in Neoliberal Ghana," investigates several questions: How do sasso, as amorphous subjectivities, take advantage of opportunities provided them by transnational LGBT+ human rights organizations without becoming subject to and subjects of these neoliberal agendas? What are the stakes of publicly asserting LGBT+ identification? In this chapter, I focus on sasso responses to a 2014 video clip produced by Aidspan, an NGO based in Kenya, to foreground the ways in which they navigate landscapes characterized by both the collision and collusion between Christian and queer liberal modernities. In this chapter, I return to Kwame Gyekye's concept of "amphibious personhood" to illuminate how sasso navigate attempts by the nation-state to police their subjectivities and responses to such attempts by LGBT+ human rights organizations.

In chapter 4, "The Paradox of Rituals: Queer Possibilities in Heteronormative Scenes," I provide an ethnographic collage of how sasso lives imbricate with rituals of transition like naming ceremonies (popularly known in Ghana as "outdooring"), weddings, birthdays, and funerals. While rituals may not be sufficient to make sense of sasso existence in uncertain sociocultural, political, and economic terrains, their contributions to the sustenance of particular rites of passage highlight the entanglement of heteroerotic and homoerotic intimacies and desires. From ceremonies ranging from naming the newly born to weddings and birthdays, I explore how ritual, as an interstitial aesthetic, brings amphibious subjectivity-making into full relief. Focusing on an outdooring ceremony and birthday, I suggest that these events created transgressive geographies that ultimately engendered queer selfhoods.

The third and last part of the book is called "Becoming and Unbecoming Amphibious Subjects in Hetero/Homo Colonial Vortices." In the fifth chapter, "Palimpsestic Projects: Heterocolonial Missions in Post-Independent Ghana (1965–1975)," I reread the historiography and excerpts from the archive that contains evidence of projects to normalize monogamy at the dawn of Ghana's formation. I argue that to understand the fiction that Ghana is a heterosexual nation, the official vocabulary employed to dislodge and "un-citizen" LGBT+ presence by organizations like the National Coalition for Proper Human Sexual Rights and Family Values (NCPHSRFV), we need to return to these projects. I specifically reread correspondence, brochures, and conference proceedings exchanged between Christian Aid, a humanitarian organization based in Britain, and the Christian Council of Ghana (CCG) to discuss how the campaign for monogamy occurred at the expense of the racialization of polygamy, anticipating the waves of homophobia in Ghana today.

In chapter 6, "Queer Liberal Expeditions: The BBC's *The World's Worst Place to Be Gay?* and the Paradoxes of Homocolonialism," I illuminate the complex entanglements between local NGOs and queer liberalism by suggesting that the screening of the controversial BBC documentary on International Day Against Homophobia (IDAHO) reinforced "homocolonial" tropes in the same way Christian NGOs in the sixties reinforced "heterocolonial" tropes. I focus on disagreements among BURJ employees preceding the celebration of IDAHO, contentions that amplified the complexities and anxieties around NGO work that addresses LGBT+ human rights issues in nations that neglect the existence of queer subjects.

In the conclusion to the book, entitled "Queering Queer Africa?," riffing off of W. E. B. Du Bois's (1903) widely cited statement that "the problem of the twentieth century is the problem of the color line," I ponder whether the problem in Africa in the twenty-first century is the problem of the queer line. Queering queer Africa, a phrase used by Ugandan feminist Stella Nyanzi (2014), underscores the need to avoid rehearsing the mistakes that hindered a radical feminist movement in postcolonial Africa. Thus, I ask what the stakes are for pursuing LGBT+ human rights in a heteronationalist state intent on clamping down on LGBT+ human rights pursuits. Queering queer Africa embodies recognizing that the radical project to dismantle oppression in its various manifestations is unending. It is a process that must be constantly attuned to the machinations of neoliberal and neocolonial regimes.

PART ONE

Setting the Scenes

1

Situating Sasso

Mapping Effeminate Subjectivities and Homoerotic Desire in Postcolonial Ghana

> I have always, I think, opposed the stereotypic definitions of "masculine" and "feminine," not only because I thought it was a lot of merchandising nonsense, but rather because I always found the either/or implicit in those definitions antithetical to what I was all about—and what revolution for self is all about—the whole person. And I am beginning to see, especially lately, that the usual notions of sexual differentiation in roles is an obstacle to political consciousness, that the way those terms are generally defined and acted upon in this part of the world is a hindrance to full development.
>
> —TONI CADE BAMBARA, *ON THE ISSUE OF ROLES* (1970, 123–124)

When I first arrived in Accra to do my fieldwork in 2011, little did I know that there were clusters of self-identified effeminate men, collectively known as sasso, in the city and surrounding suburbs. I had heard rumors that there were bars and hangouts that catered to gays, like Chester's in Osu and Terry's in Adabraka.[1] Although it was widely known that these spots existed, that they were associated with homosexuals kept many from visiting these bars lest they be identified as homosexual. Those who patronized these spaces did so at night.

I first encountered the term *sasso* during the early stages of my ethnographic fieldwork in 2011, when I was invited by Gina, a public health official working at the National AIDS Control Program (NACP), to meet with a group of six men in their mid-twenties to early thirties. The men initially introduced themselves to me as men who have sex with men (MSM) because of their active participation in HIV/AIDs outreach in Ghana. Admittedly, MSM was a public health label popularized by NGOs that undertook projects to minimize the transmission of HIV/AIDS and sexually transmitted infections (STIs) in Ghana. At the time, I was unfamiliar with the term *sasso*. It was during my ethnography that I discovered that the term described self-identified effeminate men and persons, who, irrespective of their gender, engaged in homosexual sex.

Following this discovery, I pondered whether LGBT+ human rights organizations working in Ghana knew of the existence of sasso and if the term featured in their public health programs for sexual minorities alongside MSM. I came to understand that the existence of sasso was paradoxically a peculiarly Ghanaian articulation of sexual subjectivity laced with neoliberal, neocolonial, and postcolonial influences. The complex interweave of the local, the transnational, and the global was made palpable during my encounter with Iddrissu. In his late twenties at the time of our conversation, here is how Iddrissu described his initial encounter with the sasso community:

> I was invited to this party at Terry's by a friend. At the party there were many people, men, old and young, and women, also old and young, in attendance. Most of the people in the party acted in a certain way, you know? The men I saw there, some of them were very effeminate. They were cross-dressed, while others danced very suggestively with each other without restraint. These are things that people of the same sex no longer do in public. Before, it was OK for men to dance with men and women to dance with women with nobody saying that they are gay. These days if you go to a wedding, funeral, or outdooring [christening ceremony], you can't even do that because you will be accused of being gay. But when I went to that party at Terry's and I saw the way people were acting, it was interesting to me. I suddenly felt comfortable and proceeded to ask my friend why he invited me. And he promptly said he did because he knew I was sasso; that I liked men like him. In response, I asked what "sasso" meant. To which he said it refers to a man who likes to have sex with men, a man who acts effeminately, and women who like to have sex with women or also act masculinely. I said to him but I don't act effeminately and he said but I know you like men by the way you eye men like me who act effeminately and pay attention to us. I didn't know how to respond to his observation, Kwame; because I know that it was true, that I was sexually attracted to men and that maybe I was gay. Never did I know what sasso entailed until I went to the party, which was attended by people some of whom identified as gay, lesbian, while many others quite comfortably self-identified as sasso. It was a surprising event, to say the least. I say that I am "sasso" to those who are aware of the term. Sometimes, too, I use "gay" only when I believe the person with whom I am interacting will not be familiar with the term [*sasso.*]. However, I am very, very cautious who I tell I am gay. One never knows in this country.

Iddrissu's initiation into the sasso community threw him into overlapping and multiple worlds that decentered rigid Eurocentric framings of gender and sexuality in non–Euro-American contexts while paradoxically reinforcing these categories. Furthermore, his account magnified how the increased visibility of LGBT+ human rights, concomitant with a hyperattentiveness to gay subjects, eroded those homosocial practices so prevalent in the public sphere. Iddrissu's narrative reminded me of an experience I had during college. A group of students hurled homophobic epithets at my cousin and me simply because we had our arms around each other's shoulders. At the time, I did not fathom why that measure of affection between men had to be reduced to sexual attraction, nor did I comprehend how two men publicly displaying emotional intimacy constituted an act of sexual indiscretion.

The narrative shared by Iddrissu and my encounter in college capture the contests between local terms (sasso) and global categories (LGBT+). In general, sex and gender, as African feminists have observed, shift in meaning when they appear in African contexts. The Nigerian sociologist Oyèrónkẹ́ Oyěwùmí, in her critical assessment of the category "woman" among the Yorùbá people of Nigeria, notes that "the woman question is a Western-derived issue—a legacy of the age-old somatocentricity in Western thought. It is an imported problem, and it is not indigenous to the Yorùbá. If it has become relevant in Yorùbá studies, the history of that process needs to be told" (1997, ix). Oyěwùmí's position on the controversy surrounding the place of women among the Yoruba is illuminating not only because it invites a deeper engagement with the category of woman in this West African culture but also because it pays attention to the historical processes that introduced the "the woman question."

Like Oyěwùmí, I approach LGBT+ categories in the Ghanaian context by asking how sasso, in their engagements and practices, might complicate what it means to be LGBT+ in neoliberal Ghana. In this chapter I diagram how "sasso" (Ga) (or "saso" [Akan]), a category encapsulating self-identified effeminate men, men and women who engage in homoerotic sex, and men who act effeminately (but are not self-identified effeminate men) and women who act masculinely, challenges received ideas and notions that capture Ghana as a heterosexual nation.[2] I elaborate on how the term confronts and confounds normative and hegemonic Western framings of gender and sexuality by illuminating how these categories get challenged when trafficked from one cultural context to another (Amadiume 1987a; Oyěwùmí 1997; Wekker 2006; Gaudio 2009; Banks 2011).

As the Black feminist Toni Cade Bambara (1970), in her essay "On the Issue of Roles," suggests, the implicit assumption that gender categories are reducible to the male/female binary is not merely inadequate but "antithetical" to the construction of persons. In other words, the masculine/feminine dichotomy, central to Western ideologies, stultifies other ways of embodying gender and sexual difference by generating false equivalences that leave in their wake "the madness of "masculinity" and "femininity" (1970, 125). Elsewhere in the essay, Bambara questions the need to use the West as a point from which to evaluate our identities by elaborating on how "we make many false starts because we have been programmed to depend on white models or white interpretations of non-white models, so we don't even ask the correct questions, much less begin to move in a correct direction. Perhaps we need to face the terrifying and overwhelming possibility that there are no models, that we shall have to create from scratch" (1970, 133).

What will it mean to turn away from "white models or white interpretations of non-white models"? Embedded in a milieu where vernacular articulations of sexual and gendered subjectivities like sasso intertwine with nonvernacular articulations like LGBT+, I argue that collectively, sasso embody a constellation of identities and practices that reveal the scrambled nature of postcolonial subject formation.

SASSO AND SASOFO: CONSTELLATIONS OF EFFEMINATE MASCULINITIES IN GHANA

To be specific, I use *sasso* to describe the assemblage of men bonded by effeminate identification, and homoerotic intimacy and desire. Since the majority of my interlocutors resided in or converged in Jamestown, which is predominantly Ga-speaking, *sasso* is ethnolinguistically of Ga extraction. In that regard, these effeminate men are not very different from *sasofo*, the community of effeminate men studied by the anthropologist William Banks (2013). Perhaps a minor difference is that the sasso I interacted with during my fieldwork mostly interfaced or were familiar with LGBT+ human rights NGOs like BURJ, among other organizations that engaged in public health programs addressing the health needs of sexual minorities. In his anthropological study of this community, Banks observes that "saso is an in-group term used to refer to members of this community and their subculture. Members are referred to as Sasofo (in Twi, lit. 'Saso people'). Many of my interlocutors trace the origin of the term 'Saso,' to the expression 'Mi Saso,' which they translate as 'my mate' or 'my colleague'" (2013, 265).

Building on Banks, I insist that sasofo and sasso share overlapping lifeways, the only distinguishing marker being that the former is found in an area dominated by the Akan whereas the latter is found in a predominantly Ga area like Jamestown, my ethnographic site. Hence, geographic location and ethnicity are key but not mutually exclusive sites for the construction of difference among sasso. For example, the sasofo studied by Banks mostly reside in the Central Region of Ghana, and sasso can be mostly found in Accra and other parts of Ghana. Though not entirely exclusive, sasofo operate in worlds in which traditional African spirituality remains a defining marker of their identity.

In sum, sasso describes a sexual subjectivity that both interweaves and interplays with being Ghanaian and global, vernacular and transnational, Christian and un-Christian, and rural and urban. The men whose stories and excerpts inform this book also bear some resemblance to the *'yan daudu* among the Hausa of Northern Nigeria, whose lives have been richly documented by the anthropologist Rudolph Gaudio; yet sasso are also quite distinct from them (2009). Gaudio notes that he "found tantalizing references to 'yan daudu in relation to 'prostitution' [*karuwanci*] and *Bori*, the Hausa cult of spirit-possession whose practitioners are widely condemned by orthodox Muslims as 'pagan' [*arna*] or 'heathen' [*kafir*]. In most of these texts the term 'yan daudu was translated as 'homosexuals,' 'transvestites,' 'pimps,' none of which turned out to be truly accurate, though they all convey a partial sense of 'yan daudu's activities and social identities" (2009, 17).

If the sasofo studied by Banks are enmeshed in spiritual practices, the lives of 'yan daudu are similarly entangled with the Islamic religious virtues of being, becoming, and belonging, while being influenced and shaped by shifts wrought by colonial domination and trans-Saharan connections. Sasso subjectivities overlap with but are also distinct from 'yan daudu. For instance, sasso and 'yan daudu are perceived as men who act like women. Unlike the 'yan daudu, however, most of the sasso I interacted with had their experiences shaped by Christianity. Yet it can be adduced that sasso and 'yan daudu are both shaped by the ongoing histories of colonialism, neoliberalism, global human rights interventions, and more. In effect, sasso, like most postcolonial subjects, are scrambled by a violent past, the effects of which continue to be visible in their relations to institutions such as the church, marriage, family, political economy and the law, and human rights NGOs. Sasso are constituted and distinguished by class, grades of effeminacy, ethnicity, educational level, and their degree of involvement with transnational NGOs and related Eurocentric identities. To be clear, their self-making strategies also challenge our understanding of "normal," drawing from—and complicating—established values and practices of their communities.

TRACING TOPOGRAPHIES OF QUEER INTIMACIES AND DESIRES: JAMESTOWN AND THE COMPLEX OF SASSO SUBJECTIVITIES

Jamestown is one of the oldest suburbs in Accra, Ghana's capital city. Located on the coast near the central business district, it is predominated by the Ga-Adangbe ethnolinguistic group, or in simpler terms, the Ga ethnic group (Kropp-Dakubu 1997; Odotei 1996; Fayorsey 1992).[3] Economically, fishing, the dominant profession in Jamestown, has been generally male dominated. The suburb also hosts the large open market, Salaga Market. Jamestown's close proximity to Accra's central business district means that most of its residents are either fully or partially involved in the informal or formal economic sectors of the region.

Ongoing diversification of Ghana's urban economy, evidenced by changes in the service, information technology, and financial sectors, to give but a partial list, is shaping fishing as the lynchpin of Jamestown's economy. That Ghana is embedded in a global economy also implies that residents in this community participate in and contribute to global economic circuits in various degrees. Despite the reverberations of a neoliberal economy that restructured Ghana's largely informal economy through projects orchestrated by the World Bank and IMF, and later, the European Union and China, fishing continues to be a key part of Jamestown's economy. The fisheries industry animating the suburb connects it to other coastal towns in the Greater Accra Region, the Central Region to the west, and the Volta Region to the east. The sasso who participated in this ethnography had a variety of connections to fishermen, ranging from intimate, to familial, to commercial.

Besides fishing, the community has a rich culture of pugilism. World-class boxers and title holders like Azumah Nelson, Ike "Bazooka" Quartey, and "Bukom Banku," among others, all have connections to Jamestown. Markers of slavery and colonialism such as the Usher and James Forts, historically slaveholding posts, are scattered through the suburb. Insignia of a past whose effects continue into the present, Jamestown remains a transhistorical and transnational space animated by people whose identities are nervously linked to and constitutive of the making of the Black Atlantic world. Not too long ago, these slaveholding forts functioned as medium security prisons. The historical and enduring presence of these carceral complexes reminds us of Jamestown's deep connections to the present prison industrial complex, and the extent to which the transatlantic slave trade incised the veins of Africa through invidious and violent systems of human capture, displacement, and dislocation (Smallwood 2007; Mustakeem 2016; Pierre 2013; Rodney 1972).

The commencement of this ethnography in 2011 was sparked by an observation made in passing by the Ghanaian sociologist Akosua Darkwah to me that "when two Ga women say they are going to a funeral or a wedding on a weekend, it is an alibi or a coverup for an opportunity to engage in homoerotic intimacy." It did not come as a surprise to me when the sasso I encountered at the National AIDS Control Program (NACP) office shared that they were from Jamestown. These sasso have been involved in projects that centered on access to health care for key populations, which included men who had sex with men (MSM) in Jamestown in different capacities. Most served as peer educators for local and international health and human rights organizations.

Local NGOs like the Centre for Popular Education and Human Rights, Ghana (CEPHERG), founded in in 1998, and the Ghana-West Africa Program to Combat AIDS and STI (WAPCAS), established in 1996, are examples of early organizations that had LGBT+ issues on their radar. These organizations worked in concert with international NGOs like Family Health International, now known as FHI 360, to support outreach projects on access to health care among key populations, specifically men who have sex with men (MSM), female sex workers (FSWs), persons living with HIV/AIDS (PLWHAs), and the survivors of gender-based violence. These various projects mainstreamed terms such as MSM and FSW in public health discourses, and the sasso I encountered at the National HIV/AIDS Secretariat in Accra in 2011 participated in some capacity on the various projects undertaken by these organizations.

Between 2011 and 2014, I undertook several visits to the community—the longest visit occurring between May 2013 and August 2014—hoping to understand the complex of homoerotic desire and intimacy in Jamestown as well as the roles NGOs played in sasso life. My ethnographic research entailed engaging in participant observation, collecting life stories, and serving as the resident consultant of the NGO Bring Us Rights and Justice (BURJ), which offered free human rights services to sasso and other sexual, gender, ethnic, disabled, and class minorities. Incidentally, this was also a period during which news about homosexuality in Ghana dominated the news media. Clergy and members of the civil society alike were vocal about what they perceived to be Ghana's diminishing moral standards.[4]

It can be assumed that this moral and political coverage partly explains the antihomosexual violence that rocked Jamestown following rumors that sasso had organized a homosexual wedding in the community for a lesbian couple. Before this incident, Jamestown, for most sasso, was a space where they could express their femininity and engage in clandestine sexual encounters with men without fearing sanctions from the community. The wide acceptance of effeminate masculinity together with the invisible presence of homoerotic practices is arguably linked to the nature of social organization among the Ga people on the coast.

Understanding Jamestown's Profuse Homoerotic Networks

Anthropological studies of the Ga, the indigenous ethnic group in Jamestown, shed some light on the vibrant homoerotic economy in the suburb. The copresence of homoeroticism and heteroeroticism among the Ga people can be linked to the duolocal pattern of postmarital residence characteristic of the Ga. Here, the bride and groom reside in separate residences (Field 1940; Fayorsey 1992; Odotei 1996). Margaret Field, in her ethnography entitled *Social Organization of the Ga People*, asserts that "Ga men do not live with their wives. They live with their 'brothers' in groups of from three to ten, and their sons join them as soon as they are too big for the women's compounds" (1940, 3). The Ghanaian social anthropologist Clare Korkor Fayorsey, like Fields, observes that "due to the separation of spouses in Central Accra female matrikin reside together, whilst their husbands live elsewhere. The co-residence of urban Ga women enables them to engage in joint economic ventures" (1992, 20). I draw on Fields and Fayorsey to argue that this pattern of after-marriage interactions not only influenced economic connections but also shaped political and gender relations, thus creating an environment for the copresence of heteroerotic and homoerotic intimacies. Economically, if husbands embarked on fishing expeditions, wives remained in their natal homes awaiting their husband's catch. The fish caught during these expeditions were either smoked and sold in the market or sold fresh on the market by the women. These economic contexts served as social and political domains for women to define and assert their agency.

The absence of husbands enabled married women to bond with other married and single women in the community in spaces like the market and at ritual gatherings like weddings, naming ceremonies (outdoorings) and funerals. Despite their heteronormative qualities, these rituals, some of which are elaborated in chapter 4, were paradoxically sites at which homoerotic connections were established between men and men and women and women. These complex homosocial bonds notwithstanding, there was also the ritual involving cross-dressed boys who accompanied fishermen on their fishing expeditions.[5]

Although the act of cross-dressing has received scant historical and ethnographic study, it draws attention to the fluidity of gender categories in Jamestown, justifying the profuse network of sasso, some of whom cross-dress on occasion. The coincidence of a culture of male cross-dressers in a town animated by male-dominated professions like fishing and pugilism paradoxically both troubles and reinforces heteronormativity.

The current vernaculars and worldviews that shape the sasso with whom I interacted—both in Jamestown and other parts of Accra—are therefore the byproducts of a complex environment, the history of which is irreducible to traditional vocabularies of human sexuality and the transnational lexicon on gender and queer identities which mostly use the Western world as a starting point. If, as Toni Cade Bambara (1970) suggests, to begin with the West as point of departure is to assume a "false start," then what would it mean to make a nonwhite location as the point of departure?

SASSO VERNACULARS AND WORLDVIEWS

Who are sasso? What are their locations in the community of Jamestown, Accra, and Ghana? How should they be positioned in ongoing debates between the nation-state and LGBT+ human rights formations? While these questions do not have simple answers, the rather obscure etymology of sasso bespeaks this difficulty.[6] In the Ga language, *sasso* means "coequal" or "to occupy the same status." A similar term, "sɛso," which translates into English as "coequal," exists among the Akan, Ghana's largest ethnolinguistic group. Among the Akan, *sɛso* is expressed to distinguish the status of a person within a hierarchy defined by age, gender, class, ethnicity, and urban or rural location.[7] When used to denote gender difference, the term is used to emphasize masculinity as the domain of men, deemphasizing femininity as a result. The following anecdote, shared by my mother, is a good example:

> Growing up in the mid-sixties to the mid-seventies, it was often presumed that education was not for girls. But for some girls, especially those born into Christian and educated families, the opportunity to access primary and secondary education was quite easy. Those who made it into the university were very few nevertheless. As for me, I was asked by my elder brother to go and learn to sew. He thought that, as a girl, my destiny was to become a seamstress or a stay-at-home wife, who helped with the upkeep of the household and the family. School was no place for a girl, he often said. I was, however, obstinate. You know that I don't leave anything to chance. I chose instead to go to school. With the support of my mother, that is your grandmother, I went to school, and I excelled very well. Because I refused to pursue what your uncle had suggested he called me "obaa akokonini" (female rooster). He thought that my refusal implied that I had challenged him. By calling me a female rooster, he was intent on putting me in my place. He wanted to prove to me that I was not his coequal [sɛso].

Thus, some men primarily deploy *sɛso* to fortify their masculinity, as my uncle does. Referring to my mother as a female rooster, he reminds her that she is acting unconventionally by refusing to comply with his commands. The configuration of coequality also actively operates in the domain of class-making. In the latter dimension, the affluent use it to brace their class location to prevent its potential breach by those at the lower rungs of the class ladder. For example, people in positions of power are, without hesitation, served by their guards, drivers, and laborers, sometimes called houseboys, who are not their coequals.

Below, I turn to the use of *sasso* among the Ga, arguing that while it is similar to *sɛso*, it has a polymorphous meaning. Therefore, the following question is key: why do self-identified effeminate men utilize *sasso* as their terminology for their community and various groups? I provide no definite answer in this book, especially when we consider that sasso imbue several meanings to the term. However, I share the following speculations. First, *sasso* is a term distinguishable from *Kwadwo Besia*, a term used derogatorily to describe effeminate men. Second, *sasso* could possibly describe same-sex relationships as sex among "equals"—whereby such equality is presumed to be based on the same gender of those engaging in a sexual act.[8]

INTRODUCING KWADWO BESIA

To understand Kwadwo Besia, I briefly chart the naming system among the Akan, who, according to the Ghanaian linguist Kofi Agyekum, have names that "are very unique because each person has an automatic birthday first name that points to the day of the week that s/he was born" (2006, 212). For example, my first name, Kwame, references the fact that I was born on Saturday. In a similar fashion, Kwadwo, sometimes spelled Kojo, the first name in Kwadwo Besia, is the name among the Akan that refers to males born on Monday. Among the Ewe, an ethnic group in the southeastern part of Ghana, the variant of Kwadwo/Kojo is Kodzo. In general, the naming system among the Akan and other ethnolinguistic groups in Ghana tends to incline toward dual gender configurations. Thus, if Kwadwo is the name assigned to the male born on Monday, then "Adwoa" is his female counterpart.

Etymologically, Kwadwo can be interpreted as "calm" or "peaceful" (Agyekum 2006, 215). The prefix (Kwa) is a hanging syllable, and the suffix (dwo) means "cool," "calm," "passive," and "patient." *Besia* is the Akan—specifically Fante, a dialect—term for "female." I speculate that Kwadwo is assigned the suffix *besia* because it means "calmness," "patience," "tenderness," and "passivity," as opposed to "haughtiness," "impatience," and "aggression," which are considered masculine traits in this milieu (Agyekum 2006, 214).

Growing up in Ghana in the late eighties and early nineties, I was socialized to interpret Kwadwo Besia as a derogatory category and was often referred to by that label because of my effeminate mannerisms. I was taunted for being girlish because I did not exude aggressively male traits. Name-called incessantly by friends, family members, and strangers, I was always reminded to act according to existing gender ideologies. Just as my mother was called a female rooster by my uncle, Kwadwo Besia was hurled at me to compel me to conform to customary gender expectations set for boys. It shoehorned my gender identity into the pigeonhole of masculinity despite the contentious conditions that animated becoming a man in Ghana, a convoluted process documented by the historian Stephan Miescher (2005). In *Making Men in Ghana*, Miescher provides rich historical details on how missionary Christian and colonial educational ideologies on gender and sexuality conflicted with indigenous notions of masculinity. The irreconcilable nature of these tensions scrambled the masculinities and femininities of colonized subjects in the colonial situation.

Kwadwo Besia has increasingly surfaced as a deprecating term. In Ghana's intensifying homophobic landscape, the term has become synonymous with homosexual. Despite the invidious transposition of homosexuality onto Kwadwo Besia, sasso occasionally deploy the label among themselves, oftentimes offensively and jocularly on certain occasions. If *sasso* is now a popular term, it is not because it avoids the freights Kwadwo Besia carries but because it allows effeminacy some room for flexibility in a context that disciplines nonheteronormative bodies. Little surprise, therefore, that the term *sasso* interweaves alternating parts of speech; in particular, noun, verb, and adjective. In this book, however, I focus mainly on self-identified effeminate men.

BLURRING PARTS OF SPEECH: SASSO SUBJECTIVITIES AS MULTIPLICITOUS INSTANTIATIONS OF DESIRING SELVES

The historically evolving distinctions and definitions in terms used to refer to homosexual men highlight the fact that *sasso* is not simply a neat placeholder. In other words, its etymology is a matter of debate. The search for etymology sometimes leads to the essentialization of origins in the same way that the quest for sources serves to fictitiously portray the "original" as authentic, untouched, and unproblematic. Retreating from reducing *sasso* to its etymology, I unpack how *sasso* blurs the multiple parts of speech that define it, alternating as it moves through time and space. The assemblage of meanings that converge in *sasso* constitutes the amphibious ground for the performance and embodiment of the "multiplicitous self."

In her highly influential anthropological study of female same-sex intimacy among Afro-Surinamese women, the anthropologist Gloria Wekker captures the multiplicitous self as "a self that is multilayered, complex, integrating various instantiations of 'I'" (2006, 12). The phenomenon of "mati work," which describes "an old institution . . . in which women have sexual relations with men and with women, either simultaneously or consecutively" (2006, 2), is central to the ethnography. For Wekker, the relationships that formed within this institution did not easily align with Eurocentric conceptions of homoeroticism and homosexuality; rather, they undermined hegemonic conceptions of gender and sexuality. Indeed, they were reminiscent of "the West African-based cultural archive of sexual subjectivity as slaves belabored it under specific demographic and colonial political circumstances in the former Dutch colony, Suriname" (2006, 2). I find Wekker's meditation insightful for two reasons. First, it presents an entirely different sexual and gender framework for dissecting intimacy and desire. Second, her reading refuses to capitulate to Western models of gender and sexuality. The institution of mati work is an example that shines light on the limitations of Euro-American-centric labels that circulate hegemonically in both scholarly and nonscholarly worlds.

Aware of the many meanings of *sasso* in this project, I focus, in particular, on effeminacy as one of sasso's key distinguishing markers. It is not my intention to reduce *sasso* to effeminacy, rather I am interested in highlighting the contestations and complexities encoded by the term. Just as Wekker observes that mati work among Afro-Surinamese women is not limited to the sexual acts between women, so I argue that *sasso* is reducible to neither effeminacy nor engagement in homosexual acts. The elasticity of *sasso* signals its "amphibiousness," defying any attempts at homogenization. From its etymological meaning as "coequal" to its various iterations as a noun, verb, and adjective, *sasso* constitutes a constellation of sexual and gendered practices and relationships. And as an assemblage, it does not easily map onto Western articulations of gender and sexuality that circulate in heteronationalist state and homonationalist LGBT+ human rights discourses. The irreducibility of *sasso* is evidenced by how its usage is contingent on whether it is employed as a noun or a verb or an adjective by members within or outside the sasso community.

BEING AND DOING SASSO AND WHAT MAKES ONE SASSO: NOUN, VERBAL, AND ADJECTIVAL DIMENSIONS OF SASSO SELF-MAKING

It became apparent during my fieldwork that effeminacy does not necessarily make one sasso and that *sasso* was a capacious term. Terry, forty-five at the time of our interview and one of the oldest sasso to participate in this ethnography, aptly captures the byzantine nature of effeminacy and sasso identification:

> There are some men who display effeminate mannerisms and have no idea what *sasso* means. We, in the sasso community, that is, those self-identified effeminate men who call ourselves "sasso," will call those effeminate men "sasso," but they may never have heard of the term and, even if they have, will choose not to use it. This is an important distinction to remember, Kwame. Not all effeminate men are sasso, especially if they choose not to identify themselves in that manner. Sasso (self-identified effeminate men) may call those men "sasso," but that by no means implies that they want to be called "sasso" until they comfortably choose to identify with the community and become part of us. Effeminacy is still an important marker for us though. It allows us to know our "sisters," even if they are not yet in the collective. If these

> men are associated with professions like food vending, interior design, tailoring and dressmaking, the list is long, we also know they are sasso because in Ghana most of these professions are mostly female oriented.

Sasso does not merely reference effeminacy, as Terry's insightful description evokes. In this narrative, he evinces how the assertion of agency is paramount to how one embraces or rejects sasso identity. Against this backdrop, while sasso are likely to address an effeminate man as "sasso" because he supposedly exhibits feminine tendencies, the person in question may not willingly self-identify as such.

What does it mean to "do" sasso in a world in which the possibilities of queer intimacy and kinship are imagined as impossible? What communities and connections are born out of this "doing"? These questions have been tackled by several performance studies theorists, especially those invested in Black queer performance and the performance of queer people and women of color in marginalized settings (Butler 1990; Muñoz 1999; Bailey 2013). As I asked in the introduction, in what ways do sasso embody a gender and sexual subjectivity that troubles Western conceptions of gender and sexuality? How do they already trouble gender and sexuality in a manner that already troubles the gender trouble about which Judith Butler (1990) writes?

Scholars of Black queer performance have long plotted how nonheteronormative Black subjects, precisely because of their racial, gender, and heterosexual nonnormativities, make worlds within frames that attempt to circumscribe their being (Johnson 2005; Bailey 2013; McCune 2014; Madison 2005). Touching on what performance engenders, especially in ballroom culture, Marlon Bailey suggests that "performance makes it possible to revise, negotiate, and reconstitute gender and sexual categories and norms" (2013, 18). Bailey's intimation demonstrates that nonheteronormative subjects straddle structures that shape them and, in the process, shape those structures in contentious and sometimes incoherent ways. Hence, if sociocultural and political-racial structures are positioned to socialize subjects into preexisting categories of identity, then, by that very logic, subjects uneasily shape the institutions that make subjects out of them.

In other words, to do sasso, to be sasso, and to become sasso are part of a constellation of strategies, both implicit and explicit, intentional and unintentional, employed by sasso to traverse a terrain assailed and made precarious by the tensions between the heteronormative nation-state and homonormative LGBT+ human rights organizations. Thus, to "do" sasso is irreducible to the performance of effeminacy and intertwines uneasily with the act of engaging in homosexual sex.[9] For example, Ayikwei, a sasso who works as a hairdresser in Jamestown, when asked what sasso meant quickly retorted: "To put it simply, all sasso are not the same. We have different styles and we express them differently. Sometimes these styles result from who we associate with, whether or not we go to church, if one attended a private or public school, and many more." Ayikwei's definition of what sasso entails casts light on how problematic the homogenization of sasso by the nation-state and LGBT+ human rights organizations can be. He notes, too, that sasso are not a uniform constituency.

This lack of uniformity is evidenced by how sasso create and navigate worlds differently by drawing on the distinct yet overlapping resources at their disposal. These world-making processes are contingent on factors including but not limited to class, ethnicity, and proximity to whiteness. "All sasso are not the same" can also reference how the sexual position one takes in the moment of the homosexual sex—whether the sasso is a top or bottom or either—shapes their construction of sasso identity. It also captures the degree to which religious affiliation impacts how one embodies and performs effeminacy. This means that identifying as Muslim, Christian, atheist, or traditional African can influence how a sasso molds or distinguishes themselves from other sasso. I have shown above how the community of sasofo studied by William Banks in Ghana's Central Region are distinguishable from the sasso in this book because spiritual practices are significant to the constitution of their subjectivity.

Another interpretation of sasso is offered by Desmond, a food vendor in Jamestown, who agrees with Ayikwei's interpretation that sasso are not all the same and that factors and forces abound to explain why sasso are a variegated constituency. Desmond goes a step further to describe sasso as a man who "sashays around, swinging [his] waist in a twirling fashion, throwing [his] wrists about effortlessly without fear of sanctions, and possessing the gait of a model. I will call such a person a sister, or, better still, auntie. Sasso are like that. Sometimes, too, when we exaggerate, it is like you see in RuPaul. Some of us like that show."

This encapsulation not only rehearses assumptions about gay men in Western mainstream popular culture and sexological discourses, but also condenses the markers of a sasso, limiting it to one's bodily techniques and performance in everyday life. Indeed, this description evokes what I describe as the "auntie trope," which appeared to be widespread among the sasso I interacted with during my ethnographic study. The reference "auntie," which is another characterization of sasso, is a placeholder that, to a certain degree, mixes gay identity in the West with vernacular articulations of effeminacy. Hence, it is possible that "auntie," too, is a category that not only captures "effeminate man" but also draws on the widely used familial "auntie" to describe elderly women in many Ghanaian contexts. These contextual meanings are neglected by both LGBT+ NGOs and the nation-state in their various projects on sexual citizenship. Desmond's insightful attribution also undercuts hegemonic understandings of queerness such as those espoused by the NGOs and the heteronational state by weaving practices of gender enacted in RuPaul's *Drag Race*, an American reality show that has an internet presence, with vernacular understandings of gender nonnormative men.

It may appear that effeminacy is a significant reference point among sasso; however, on occasion, an overly effeminate presentation of the self by a sasso will invite rebuke from sasso who prefer to cloak their effeminacy. Consider, for instance, the following anecdote by Richard, a sasso who was regarded by other sasso as too effeminate and derided as gay, a label with which he did not openly identify.

> As for me, I cannot control my effeminate mannerisms. Whenever I am walking in town, clearly the way I walk betrays my effeminacy. I did not used to be called names before. Now people jeer at me, calling me "gay, bati man, homosexual." Some call me "Kwadwo Besia," and some sasso do it too, although to laugh at me. Despite the name-calling I know that I am not in control of how God created me. I always tell them that I was born that way so they have to deal with me being in their midst or walking on their street. Sometimes too I remark that their jeers and mockery will not change my looks. I have had friends over the years too, some of whom have praised me for how bold I am. For instance, the women at the market where I go to do grocery always shower me with gifts. Some say that I am beautiful, and that they wished that I were their daughter.

Richard illuminates the adjectival distinction of sasso, while also revealing the degree to which effeminacy is now rendered as analogous to homosexuality or gay identity. This iteration of sasso can potentially also describe a kind of gender nonconformity, of being "wrongly gendered," which presumes engaging in homosexual practice, a correlation that has recently entered the public sphere with the increased visibility of LGBT+ politics in Ghana. That he's referred to as "bati man" instantiates the trafficking of the derogatory Jamaican term for a homosexual, *battyman*, into the Ghanaian context through dance hall music, which is very popular in Ghana. Moreover, it is difficult to determine whether the gendered nature of this acceptance is a kind of polite derision or mere mockery. What I know, however, is that the appreciation shown Richard by the market women is sometimes protective, one that is intended to guard him from unwanted stares and attacks. Drawing on biblical Christianity, he validates his nonnormative gendered self in a context in which being effeminate is viewed as antithetical to masculinity, and, in particular, Christian masculinity. Adriaan Van Klinken's (2019) *Kenyan, Christian, Queer* captures how Christianity, read as inimical to queer subject formation in postcolonial Kenya, was recycled as a site of radical queer possibility and freedom. Richard's anecdote reinforces Van Klinken's observation by showing how Christianity is central to their subject formation and queer self-fashioning.

Richard provoked unpredictable responses, even in sasso circles. He says: "I don't know what is going to happen to me anytime I go out there. I leave my life in the hands of God. At least, I know that my family loves me and that they will come to my aid should anything devastating happen to me." For example, Kobby, a human rights officer at BURJ, once reproached Richard for being "too auntie" in a public space. He instructed him to learn to manage his effeminacy, which he perceived as hypervisible. To be clear, Kobby is known among sasso to suppress his effeminacy to avoid homonegative responses from his family, strangers, and sasso themselves. Kobby's discomfort with overly feminine sasso is apparent:

> I am OK if they do it in spaces that will not incite trouble. Things are changing in Ghana. As you know, sasso are viewed as gays these days. As for me, I always say that people like Richard have to be careful because if anything happens, they are those most likely to be attacked. He can display his effeminacy when he is with us, or at Terry's, which, as you know, is a safe spot for all of us. But when you walk on the streets of Accra, and in a place like Nima, you have to be watchful and careful about how you present yourself.

It can be inferred from Kobby's account that being overly effeminate was acceptable, though in remarkably complex ways, until the transposition of gay identity onto sasso. It appears that Kobby's unabashed objection is employed to caution sasso like Richard to be watchful of the heightened homonegativity, yet it also reinforces homophobia. In other words, there is an exercise of "social discipline," to use Goffman's (1959, 57) terminology, among sasso circles, in the same way sasso face disciplinary forces outside their circles. "Through social discipline," Goffman asserts, "a mask of manner can be held in place from within" (1959, 57). Hence, Kobby's assertion, by being disciplinary, preserves particular ideas about proper masculine behavior that sasso are required to adopt when moving between and within most public spheres. Besides spaces such as Terry's, a joint owned by an older sasso called Terry, and Clubhouse, a bar frequented by sasso, many places in and around Accra were not too safe for sasso like Richard. Richard and Kobby thus had varying degrees of amphibious self-styling.

Sasso as Homoerotic Act

If doing (verb) and being (noun) sasso are uneasily entwined, then what does it mean to engage in homosexual sex if the person involved does not share effeminate characteristics? Doing sasso exceeds effeminacy to include the act of engaging in homosexual sex itself. Thus, noneffeminate men per their engagement in homosexual sex are likely to be described as sasso if they have a sexual preference for men (effeminate or noneffeminate). This also applies to women, as the anthropologist Serena Dankwa (2009, 2021) observes in her ethnography on female same-sex intimacies in Ghana. Here, whether the men or women who engage in homoerotic sex displayed characteristics that were considered to belong to the opposite gender has no bearing on their place in the universe of sasso. What is stressed is the expression of same-sex desire. In other words, the act of same sex can mark one as sasso regardless of gender presentation, making the amphibious dimensions of sasso more palpable especially as it crosses sexuality and gender in rather convoluted ways.

To be clear, emphasis is placed on the act of sexual engagement and with whom. Thus, there are self-identified effeminate men who have clandestine sexual engagements with noneffeminate men, who, in Western sexual nomenclature, may be heterosexual, bisexual, or homosexual. This mode of classification also makes it plausible for women to be sasso. In that respect, a woman or man does not have to act masculinely or femininely to engage in homoeroticism.

For those men who appeared masculine, sharing homoerotic experiences did not require embracing gay identity. A litany of studies in sub-Saharan Africa have shown how sexual bonding between masculine and effeminate men, while transgressive, paradoxically reiterates heterosexual modalities (Lorway 2015; Epprecht 2008; 2004; Reid 2013; Gaudio 2009). Such accounts also reveal how masculine-looking men form an integral part of the homoerotic worlds. Indeed, sasso (self-identified effeminate men) have a predilection for "straight-acting men."[10] The more manly a noneffeminate man, the more likely they will be approached by a self-identified effeminate man. The following story disclosed by Hillary, a sasso who was actively involved in the LGBT+ human rights movement, reinforces this position.

> I have always liked this guy who lives in my compound, he is a gentleman with a good job. His body looks good, he takes good care of himself, and most importantly, he is younger than me. We have been eyeing each other, but I don't know if he is aware I do sasso or that I am sasso. I know he reads my effeminacy, and that, one day, it will draw his attention. He is on my radar. I know I will have him one day although I think he is shy because he fears that we may be caught when we have sex. I don't think about the consequences that will result when we are caught. He is a real man, and that's all I want now. Don't think I am selfish, I just have needs, and I believe he does too.

Hillary's expressions "I do sasso" and "I am sasso" collapse sasso as a noun and a verb. While the young man described above is not sasso—a self-identified effeminate man—Hillary wonders whether he might be interested in a homoerotic encounter with him. Moreover, his noneffeminate disposition, epitomized by "gentleman," made him a person of sexual interest for Hillary.

OUR MANLY MEN: *GENTORS* AND *LOGS* IN THE SASSO UNIVERSE

I distinguished between two kinds of noneffeminate men within the sasso universe: "gentor" (pronounced *jentor*) and "log." Deriving from *gentleman, gentor* presupposes a particular view of masculinity that is refined, educated, and preened. Log, unlike gentor, belongs in the lower stratum of the working class, doing menial jobs or being partially employed. Very often, they have no access to a fixed income. Yet, they, too, like the gentors, are quite prominent in sasso worlds. In sasso vernacular, log is euphemistically the placeholder for the "working-class phallus." Together, these men do not self-identify as effeminate, yet their desire for homoerotic intimacy with sasso situates them in sasso worlds. Considered "straight-acting," they exhibit virile traits that distinguish them from the traits of effeminacy that denominate sasso subjectivity. Evidently, sasso-embodied plays of "ladylikeness"—which occur through a complicated effeminate matrix, sometimes subject to social discipline—present them as the counterparts of gentor and logs in this nonheteronormative situation. That gentors and logs form an integral part of the sasso universe reinforces William Banks's assertion that "Ghanaian men who only have sex with women do not locate their sexual identity in some sort of in-born psychological disposition. Instead, by emphasizing that they follow the culturally constructed tradition of Ghanaian heteronormativity, and by avoiding self-referential terms such as 'straight' or 'heterosexual,' these men frame their sexual preference as a 'natural' outcome of proper social ideals and cultural fulfillment" (2011, 277).

Western sexological discourse on homosexuality and heterosexuality is frayed by gentors and logs, who, like sasso (self-identified effeminate men), reconstitute gender and sexuality in a manner they deem fit. In a context currently contending with the "global cultural wars" resulting from the clash between LGBT+ human rights organizations and African governments (Kaoma 2009), these gender and sexual reconfigurations are significant. Logs and gentors, like the sasso animating this study, need to be situated in this nettlesome context. Despite their engagement in homoerotic intimacy and being part of the sasso universe, these men refuse LGBT+ identification. Although they *do* sasso, such engagement does not, per their worldview, make them homosexual or gay.[11] In other words, the blurring of the lines between gender and sexuality, of the barriers between homoeroticism and heteroeroticism, conducted by gentors and logs offers a different origin from which to begin to decenter analyses of gender and sexuality.

Gentors: Gentlemen and Homoeroticism

Gentor is derived from the word *gentle* and designates men of a certain caliber and social status. Gentors are likely to be in heteromonogamous relationships, residing in upscale, middle-class, and low-middle-brow residential neighborhoods in the capital and surrounding suburbs. Some gentors, most of whom are bachelors with university degrees, are young and likely to court women their age or younger. Gentors enter the worlds of sasso (self-identified effeminate men) through furtive channels, which implies that they are rarely seen with sasso in public spaces. Gentors and sasso occasionally have long-term relationships. Emmanuel, a tailor in Accra, recounts his relationship with a gentor:

> These men [by which he means gentors] do not come into Jamestown, you know? We meet them at weddings or funerals. There we give each other looks, and when I like them I just go to them and make a move. However, I am not always very direct like I do with the logs, who I have to pay to have sex with anyway. For the gentor, because they are wealthy, they want to be treated with respect. So, when we meet for the first time and they like me, we exchange numbers and then the relationship begins. Sometimes we do it in the car, and then a hotel, and may be eventually in their house.

> My boyfriend was a very rich man who had traveled to Europe and America. He was married, but his wife continued to be based in Europe, while he often traveled to Ghana to do his usual business. He was introduced to me by a friend at a wedding, and, in fact, revealed his feelings about me to my friend. Although my friend liked him, it appeared that he liked me more. I moved in with him after a few dates, and we really had such a great time together. He called me his "wife." And I called him my "husband." It was a great relationship.

As Emmanuel's story suggests, the relationships that occur between sasso and gentors parallel relationships between heteronormative couples, as some sasso use heteronormative terms such as *husband* and *wife* to refer to the relationships that obtain between them and their lovers. Sasso relationships with gentors highlight the power differential determined by the gentor's class and their sexual position as the dominant partner.

On Logs: The Hustlers/"Kubolor Boys"

Logs are men who belong in the working poor or are unemployed.[12] The Jamestown community, like several Ghanaian low-income suburbs, has been hard hit by unemployment and economic debacles. The emergence of logs on the scene of sasso thus provokes the question whether they indulge sasso for sex because of the uncertain and precarious states in which they live or because they genuinely have feelings for sasso. Moreover, it is unclear whether sasso, most of whom are self-employed, take advantage of the desperate situations that logs face to have sexual and sometimes long-term intimate connections with them. While these questions arose in my conversations with some sasso, there seemed to be an agreement among both logs and sasso that they truly enjoyed each other beyond the realm of sexual intimacy. Logs are likely to be hustlers, who in local parlance are also known as "kubolor boys," and who engage in a range of activities including pugilism and fishing, among other menial and semi-skilled jobs. Evidently, sasso engagement with men with a preference for homoerotic intimacy generates a peculiar "political economy of homoeroticism" (Lorway 2015; Livermon 2012; Gaudio 2009; Epprecht 2004). This economy circulates in a radius defined by the class orientation of sasso and the class status of their homoerotic partners. As Kissi, an exuberant sasso and shop owner, once reminded me:

> Kwame, we make the gentors have sex with us just for their money. I am not saying we are sex workers, but it is something like give and take, or I give you my tit and you give me your tat [laughs]. It is not like you have to ask for the money. They know that they have to give you something for the road, for the day, to survive, you know? And, we, too, when we do it with the logs, we have to give them something. They, too, have to live. Because in a way when we are with the gentors we are like them [logs], because we need the money and when they [logs] are with us [sasso] we become like the gentors. The only difference is that the logs like the gentors penetrate us, although occasionally some will demand that we penetrate them. There was this

time when this well-built young man I had a sexual encounter with demanded that I too penetrate him. It was not something I was expecting since I thought that he was only into penetrating. These guys are interesting, you know? So, when I sleep with a log, for example, I have to give him something [money] for the road, for the day, in order for them to survive. It is hand go, hand come, you know.

The transactional dimension of homoeroticism that Kissi speaks of here might be interpreted to mean that sasso engage in sex work.[13] We should not reduce this transaction aspect to sex work, though, since in this erotic world, sasso, gentors, and logs acknowledge that homoerotic sex is only available under conditions governed by codes of secrecy and security. And with the growing tide of economic insecurity, pseudohomophobia, and the transformation of the public secrecy of homoeroticism into public knowledge, some tactics and strategies have to be enacted to deal with both homoerotic and economic scarcities. Logs are also likely to have girlfriends, while retaining clandestine or sometimes open relationships with sasso in Jamestown.

POLITICAL AND AFFECTIVE ECONOMIES OF HOMOEROTICISM AND PHALLIC CAPITAL

As a suburb where homoerotic desire is both overtly and covertly expressed, Jamestown is a site that enables creative ways of acquiring homoerotic sex; the exchange of gifts is but one example. Gentors, for instance, provide gifts and money to sasso in order to get sex from them. Sasso, too, offer gifts to logs in hopes of receiving sexual satisfaction from them. Shadrach recounts his back-to-back sexual experience with a log and gentor to illustrate his statement that sasso "get paid to get fucked and we pay others to fuck us":

I remember having sex with both my gentor and log consecutively on one occasion. I enjoyed such serial encounters. It made me feel good. You know? My log needed money, and had come to me for financial supplication. But, I did not have any money at all. He demanded sex in exchange for something small, you know [he pauses and looks me in the face]. I so badly wanted to have sex with him because he has a big "something" between his legs, and could also gyrate his waist very well whenever we had intercourse. In fact, he knew how to make love to me more than many of the other men I had encountered. Because I cared for him, you know like I loved him, I called my rich boyfriend [gentor] and asked if I could have a brief meeting with him. He knew that whenever I called him, I was interested in having sex with him, and I often gave him my best skills [laughs loudly]. He, too, loved me very much, especially as I gave him the much-needed satisfaction. He didn't hesitate to have me over.

He drove over to Jamestown to pick me up [and bring me] to his house. I had already notified my log before my departure that I was going out and that I would be back home later that evening to make him some sumptuous dinner and also have some money ready for him. You see, you don't only give money to these people for

> sex; sometimes you have to go an extra mile to cook for them too. As they say, a way to a man's heart is through his stomach. Because my food is delicious, whenever these men come they get stuck to me. So, I knew that if I invited him over for dinner, he would have no reason to reject my invitation. Sometimes, all one required was to make food for the logs in exchange for sex. Because when you give them money, either they will give it to their girlfriends or buy drugs.
>
> My log had a girlfriend in the community, who somewhat knew about our relationship. But she didn't care because I was giving her boyfriend money that he invariably used to sustain her upkeep, and several people knew that. Here, it was like everybody did what I was doing, so nobody had to say anything, and if they did, it had to be done secretly. Now let me return to the food issue for these guys. In my opinion, a sasso is always better off cooking for them. So, to be able to meet my log's needs that particular evening, I went off with my gentor, spent the afternoon with him, and gave him what he wanted. He, in turn, gave me some money for groceries. And, when I got home early that evening, I made a tantalizing meal for my log, after which we bathed together and did our little something, something.

Shadrach's anecdote evokes a complex of homoeroticism that both coexists and conflicts with heteroerotic expressions. For instance, it is apparent that his log has a girlfriend. His allusion that it doesn't bother the heterosexual couple complicates the presumed watertight compartments separating heteroerotic and homoerotic bonds. The dynamism of this pattern is indeed crucial for understanding how nonheteronormative sexual subjectivities are expressed here, and their links to particular political economies of intimacy and desire in neoliberal and neocolonial times (Valentine 2007; Decena 2011; Gill 2018; Allen 2011).

Carefully skirting heteronormativity either intentionally or unintentionally, I argue that sasso transform restrictions into potential sites for subversive erotic self-making and play. As a result of their connections to gentors and their entrepreneurial prowess, sasso experience class mobility in low-income Jamestown. This affords them the resources to have intimate homoerotic experiences with logs. The following anecdote by KK explores this further:

> As for me, I like logs more than the gentors. Logs are simply my preference. Because I have a stable job and money, I would rather go and get them and just do whatever I want with them. Remember, they want the money because they are frustrated. There are the coconut sellers, shoeshine boys, truck pushers, driver's mates, and car mechanics. I honestly like them rough like that because they know how to do it very rough. All I have to do is to just ensure that they clean themselves very well before any sexual action takes place. To do this, I provide them with a place to bathe, give them clean towels to clean their bodies, and then the action begins. They always appreciate when you value them as human beings too, you know?
>
> When you see them on the street for the first time, you may think that they are very dirty and untouchable. But, give them an opportunity by making them bathe with hot water and, in addition, get them clean and you will see a crystal difference in their appearance. Some of these men are princes underneath the terrible conditions

> that Ghana creates for them. I know that it is fate that has made them what they are. As for me, I see it as my God-given duty to make them bathe thoroughly and then proceed to have intercourse. I have actually had some of the best sex with these guys. After the sex, I give them money and I ask them to leave. Whenever I want to see them again, a phone call is just a stretch of an arm away. Having sex with these guys comes easy for me, and because of their "wretchedness" [he shrieks], people hardly look at them. As for me, I think that being with them sexually is like eating a juicy chicken and then wiping your lips with a tissue afterward [he smirks at me]. Nobody will ever notice that you have eaten a juicy chicken, if and only if you wipe your lips well. Never leave a trace behind else they will find out.

KK's penetrative allusion reveals the complicated nature of both normative and effeminate masculinities. KK assumes the role of gentor in his relationship with the log, as a result of his middle-class location. The log takes on a passive class role because he is a hustler. If, socioeconomically, the log remains economically subservient, that position does not necessarily imply that they are coterminously sexually passive. As KK takes on the sexually passive role during his intimate homoerotic encounters with logs, his statement further reveals the degree to which sasso themselves play a role in the making and shaping of dominant or hegemonic masculinity. Logs may be heterosexual men, yet their low-income class status combined with the likelihood of unemployment diminishes their masculinity.

Additionally, KK suggests that cleaning the low-income logs makes them look like gentors. He asserts: "I make them into princes." Occupying a class position higher than the class status of the logs he engages with, KK draws on his resources to become "friends" with logs. This role switch in class puts the log, who is a non-effeminate man, in a submissive position. KK, who is a self-identified effeminate man, takes on the dominant role. An amphibious process that troubles gender and sexual binaries and expectations ensues from KK's interaction with logs. The "straight-acting" log not only transgresses the boundaries of heterosexuality by having homoerotic sex with KK, but also embarks on crossing the boundaries between two different classes, from their lower class to middle class—KK's class, albeit temporarily. These behind-the-scenes microsociological connections are barely acknowledged by LGBT+ human rights NGOs.

NEOLIBERAL VORTICES: SASSO IN QUEER, HUMAN RIGHTS, AND PUBLIC HEALTH NGOS

The complex distinctions characteristic of the sasso universe have significant implications for the categorical imperatives of transnational LGBT+ rights NGOs. Sasso subjectivities, particularly in the site of my fieldwork, are necessarily influenced by the presence of international LGBT+ human rights NGOs whose interventions, which include LGBT+ empowerment programs and projects on access to health, overlook the fluid character of sasso self-making. Indeed, whether or not sasso identify as gay is situational, depending on time, place, and with whom they are interacting. Sasso in Jamestown and surrounding suburbs embody selves that unsettle the presumed distinction between being heterosexual and homosexual, as well as the presumed distinction between Ghanaian and un-Ghanaian. Sometimes, too, in their practices, they appear to reinforce these distinctions. On some occasions, sasso participate in the tendency of NGO interventions to homogenize them as gay men in some contexts, while actively rejecting it in others. In other words, sasso "interface with different subcultural fields" (Muñoz 1999, 5) to navigate the precarious environments in which they live. The paradoxical relationships sasso have with NGOs ultimately illuminate how they deploy tactical strategies in a landscape defined by the collusions between neocolonial and neoliberal apparatuses.

Evidently, sasso complex historical and contemporary situations appear to summon transnational LGBT+ rights advocates to cultivate more careful attention to the unexpected ways in which their interventions interact with queer politics in the contexts in which they intervene. It must be noted, then, that sasso lives permit us to witness the ways in which neoliberal human rights projects paradoxically create value out of and for particular subjects under the guise of creating diversity and embracing multicultural worlds. As the literary scholar Jodi Melamed has argued, "Neoliberal multiculturalism has created new privileged subjects, racializing the beneficiaries of neoliberalism as worthy multicultural citizens and racializing the losers as unworthy and excludable on the basis of monoculturalism, deviance, inflexibility, criminality, and other historico-cultural deficiencies" (2011, xxi).

Like Melamed, I suggest that on the stage of neoliberal human rights politics, sasso are represented as bodies worth saving precisely because they are homosexual subjects existing in environments disemboweled by homophobia. Yet, at the same time, other postcolonial subjects like the working poor, of which sasso are a part, are deemed unworthy because of their homophobic tendencies, impoverishment, and supposed religious conservativism. LGBT+ human rights NGOs represent sasso as vulnerable, yet they simultaneously displace them by heightening homophobia. To be clear, sasso are likely to be members of the working poor, engaging in jobs that are erratic, much of the proceeds from which they use to supplement or fully support their families. These precarious positions are intensified by neoliberal and neocolonial regimes of exploitation.

Sasso networks in Jamestown include homoerotic encounters that operate through nuanced connections of secrecy and disavowal. Thus, in this context, the transnational imperative of being "out," which mostly animates Euro-American LGBT+ politics, aggravates established strategies of queer self-making in ways that provoke the very homophobic violence the LGBT+ human rights NGOs are seeking to combat. It is not my intention to dismiss the leaps that have been made by LGBT+ NGOs like BURJ, one of the key NGOs addressing LGBT+ rights and improved health access for sexual minorities such as sasso. These leaps include, most importantly, the increasing politicization of LGBT+ issues in Ghana and the emergence of organizations that distinctly address LGBT+ human rights as a human rights concern. The proliferation of these organizations exposes Ghana's supposedly unblemished heterosexuality as a heteronationalist fiction which circulates as a fact in anti-LGBT+ rhetoric. As the anthropologist Michael Taussig argues: "When the body, a nation's flag, money, or a public statue is defaced, a strange surplus of negative energy is likely to be aroused from within the defaced thing itself" (1999, 1). In this case, heterosexuality is the "nation's flag," celebrated as a sacred dimension of the Ghanaian nation-state. Amid the increased visibility of LGBT+ politics, effeminate men are increasingly being rebranded as gay because their presence "taints" the supposed purity of the Christian heteronationalist state. Not only are they the focus of LGBT+ organizations but also targets in campaigns to end HIV, which elide the constituency of men—gentors and logs—who engage in sexual activities with sasso. These men distinguish themselves from sasso by rejecting effeminacy and publicly dismissing homosexuality, a technique of separation reminiscent of their rejection of gay identity. In fact, the secrecy that shrouds their homoerotic engagement echoes accounts discussed by C. Riley Snorton (2014) and Jeffrey McCune (2014), respectively, on the phenomenon of "down-low" in the United States. These scholars suggest how down-low remains a key site of racialization and a practice used to code Black men who discreetly engage in homoerotic encounters as vehicles for the transmission of HIV/AIDS.

Thus, for sasso and the men who clandestinely engage them for sex, contemporary public health engagements and LGBT+ human rights interventions must acknowledge these subjectivities as tethered to particular histories of racialization in both Africa and its myriad diasporas. Moreover, these marginal sexualized and racialized groups are convoluted by histories of displacement and dislocation (Pierre 2013; McFadden 2011; Kanneh 1998). Throughout this book, I insist that the relegation of these histories to the background does violence to these subjects, who undoubtedly continue to both confront and resist anxieties wrought by a violent past (Pierre 2013; Gill 2018).

Sasso subjectivities are reminiscent of the colonized subject described by the cultural studies theorist Stuart Hall, whose "identity is formed at the unstable point where the unspeakable stories of subjectivity meet the narratives of a history, a culture. And since he/she is positioned in relation to cultured narratives which have been profoundly expropriated the colonized subject is always somewhere else, doubly marginalized, displaced always other than where he or she is, or is able to speak from" (1987, 6).

The conditions in Jamestown, a low-income suburb that sits on periphery of the city, together with sasso, most of whom live in the margins, reflect the displacements triggered by such unspeakable stories of history and culture in contemporary neoliberal rescue interventions. Within this framework, the nation-state, invested as it is in heterosexual citizenship, and LGBT+ human rights organizations, invested as they are in homosexual citizenship, both paradoxically displace sasso identities.

2

Contesting Homogeneity

Sasso Complexity in the Face of Neoliberal LGBT+ Politics

> The fiction of identity is one that is accessed with relative ease by most majoritarian subjects. Minoritarian subjects need to interface with different subcultural fields to activate their own senses of self. This is not to say that majoritarian subjects have no recourse to disidentification or that their own formation as subjects is not structured through multiple and sometimes conflicting sites of identification.
>
> —JOSÉ ESTEBAN MUÑOZ, *DISIDENTIFICATIONS* (1999, 5)

> Queer visibility, then, is not only about finding acceptance for difference within black communities but also about a defiance and a subversion of blackness in ways that are potentially transformative, thus creating the very liberation promised by the constitution and giving freedom its substantive meaning.
>
> —XAVIER LIVERMON, "QUEER(Y)ING FREEDOM" (2012, 301)

In this chapter, I discuss how queer self-making among sasso remains unstable, manifold, and complex thus complicating binary articulations of gender and sexuality. The sasso whose accounts are discussed here are Hillary, Terry, Shelley, and Alajo. I call them by their first names because that is what they preferred. Their narratives reveal how sasso selfhood intersects with other articulations of identity, thereby confounding LGBT+ nomenclature in particular and hegemonic/dominant meanings of gender and sexuality in nation-state discourses. These interludes illuminate how LGBT+ human rights politics in Ghana and state-sanctioned homonegativity, both of which homogenize heterosexual and homosexual identification, undermine the capacious character of sasso.

Inhabiting different and contested worlds, the lives of the men featured here capture how marginalized subjects deploy complex self-fashioning techniques to, as José Esteban Muñoz suggests, "activate their own senses of self" (1999, 5). Among the questions posed in this chapter are these: How do the stories shared by these sasso foreground their negotiation of the tensions between the nation-state and LGBT+ human rights organizations on the question of sexual citizenship? What kinds of worlds are created amid these seemingly stifling environments animated by the collision between homonationalism and heteronationalism? I argue that these sasso engage in self-fashioning processes that amplify the merits and demerits of what Muñoz famously described as "disidentifications" (1999). If disidentification "is meant to be descriptive of the survival strategies the minority subject practices in order to negotiate a phobic majoritarian public sphere that continuously elides or punishes the existence of subjects who do not conform to the phantasm of normative citizenship" (1999, 4), then to a degree, the men whose stories animate this chapter engage in disidentification.

It is apparent that disidentificatory self-making practices are evoked by sasso. Nevertheless, I am also quite aware that Muñoz's theory of disidentification has a different import in a sociocultural context congealed by the collusion between neoliberalism and neocolonialism. For example, can sasso lives be understood through the theory of disidentification? Do their lives broaden the breadth of this theory or reveal its limits in the context of Ghana? Clearly, Muñoz, aware of the limits of disidentification, avers that "it is *not always* [his emphasis] an adequate strategy of resistance or survival for all minority subjects" (1999, 5). In that light, I outline how Hillary, Terry, Shelley, and Alajo live complex lives that evoke disidentification while simultaneously spelling out the possible deficits of that theorization in the age and context of neoliberal LGBT+ human rights politics in Ghana. These men not only vie for visibility, but also, to reiterate Livermon's point in the second epigraph, "queer" visibility in ways that contest liberal ideas of queer visibility circulating in Western LGBT+ human rights discourses. The stories shared here also foreground the richness of ethnographic writing, which the anthropologist Michael Herzfeld describes as "both a social and poetic act" (2004, 24).

The sasso discussed here corporeally embody feminine qualities, yet such identification is refracted through class, religious identity, educational level, geographic location, involvement in NGOs, and degree of effeminacy. Let us take Shelley, for example, whose striking effeminacy makes him both vulnerable and appreciated depending on the time and space and with whom they are interacting. He confronts public shaming and mockery, but also celebration, adulation, and love. Despite this uncertainty, Shelley always celebrates his feminine attributes, saying, "I am proud of myself. All the features I have are natural. Whether I am man or a woman I am simply who I am." To reduce the state of being and becoming sasso only to sexual identification, as is the tendency both by transnational LGBT+ activist NGOs such as Aidspan, and by the nation-state, effectively depoliticizes queer identification as a variegated constituency, as Cathy Cohen (1997) and Lisa Duggan (2003) remind us.

Sasso have variable interactions with LGBT+ human rights organizations that address health rights for men who have sex with men (MSM). For instance, Hillary comfortably and confidently identified as gay in the space of NGOs like Family Health International (FHI), Bring Us Rights and Justice (BURJ), and the Centre for Popular Education and Human Rights, Ghana (CEPHERG). In Jamestown, where he resided with his mother and sister, he identified with the term less frequently, embracing *sasso* instead. In the same vein as Hillary, Alajo both straddled and struggled with uneven geographies that LGBT+ activist NGOs and the contested category of sasso produced. It is worth noting, however, that Hillary, when among Terry and his peers of diasporic Ghanaian returnees, was more likely to identify as gay than sasso, a move reflecting how sasso and gay were considerably influenced by one's class position.

Comparable to women in non-Western contexts who, according to the Turkish feminist Deniz Kandiyoti (1988, 275), engage in "patriarchal bargaining," these sasso *bargained with heteronormativity* in an amphibious manner. Patriarchal bargains, Kandiyoti argues, "exert a powerful influence on the shaping of women's gendered subjectivity and determine the nature of gender ideology in different contexts. They also influence both the potential for specific forms of women's active or passive resistance in the face of their oppression" (1988, 275). Kandiyoti's insightful analysis raises questions about the reducibility of patriarchy to "male dominance, which is treated at a level of abstraction that obfuscates rather than reveals the intimate inner workings of culturally and historically distinct arrangements between the genders" (1988, 275).

This interpretation of patriarchy suggests that women, often viewed as the victims of patriarchal structures and ideologies, can internalize patriarchy to oppress other women. In that regard, white women's proximity to white patriarchy, for instance, grants them access to patriarchal privileges shored up by whiteness which nonwhite women have no access to. As a result, racial and gender privileges blend to advantage white women while undermining nonwhite women. In a similar vein, women in Ghana who are ethnolinguistically Akan, the largest and most privileged ethnolinguistic group, are more likely to wield and enjoy patriarchal privileges not available to non-Akan women. Within this calculus, Akan dominance conditions Akan patriarchal dominance and vice versa.

In this chapter, however, I elaborate on how sasso navigate homonegativity and heteronormativity through a complicated, sometimes incomprehensible prism of bargaining. To be clear, bargaining is arguably a jujitsu tactic, which when exercised passively, actively enabled their navigation of a system that chronically disenfranchised them. The sasso discussed here consistently yet unpredictably treaded multiple minefields of contentment and despondence. In the process, they revealed the scrambled nature of sexual and gender identity in the postcolonial context, as well as the inconsistent composition of the postcolonial subject in a context conditioned by the uneasy alliances between neoliberal formations and the neocolonial nation-state. Multiple contradictions are at play in their narratives, contradictions that foreground the significance of amphibious subjectivity.

INTERLUDE 1: ENTERING HILLARY'S LIFE

In summer 2011 I arrived in Ghana for the first time in four long years as a lone ethnographer. I first encountered Hillary, one of seven self-identified effeminate men to interact with me during my first short-term fieldwork, a few days after my arrival. Returning to the country of my birth, I encountered a culture at once familiar and strange. I was no longer the Kwame who had departed the shores of Ghana in 2007. The "I" of 2007 was supposedly a self-identified heterosexual with repressed homoerotic tendencies, who was initially preoccupied with doctrinal Christianity and raised by staunchly Presbyterian parents. The "I" that returned to Ghana in 2011 was a self-identified gay man unsure of what to expect after trudging through the arrival gates at the Kotoka International Airport, the main portal of arrival for travelers entering the country by air.

The shift from before to after, marked as it was by a stint of five years away from Ghana, implied that there was no guarantee that fieldwork at "home" and on a prickly subject like homosexuality was going to be an easy task. I was introduced to the sasso by Gina, a public health nurse, shortly after my arrival. Gina was a mature student at the University of Ghana's Department of Sociology and a senior nursing officer (SNO) at the National AIDS Control Program (NACP) Office, located on the premises of the Korle Bu Teaching Hospital, Ghana's largest and most advanced teaching hospital at the time. She facilitated my meeting with Hillary and six other self-identified effeminate men: Kissi, Crystal, Ben, Mawuli, Foster, and later Kobby. Apparently, Hillary and the other sasso present had participated in an HIV/AIDS outreach project as peer educators and were also recognized as ambassadors between the public health NGOs and members of the sasso community.

Admittedly fond of Hillary, Gina noted that he "possessed leadership qualities and was also very familiar with the sasso community." She added further that "Hillary's ability to mobilize other sasso on demand for local human rights organizations and HIV/AIDS outreach agencies both in Accra and other cities in Ghana is profound." For this reason, she added, "he might be a very good person to interact with. He is also very formidable, and I am sure he will be able to offer some security and cover should you need it." As this was my initial ethnographic foray into Ghana, Gina assumed the position of gatekeeper for the purposes of the meeting with Hillary and his crew of sasso. I made no effort to question her nomination of Hillary, as I was confident that her decision to have him be a part of my research was sound. Sadly, toward the end of my long-term fieldwork, Hillary, after a long battle with HIV/AIDS, succumbed to the disease in June 2014, some few weeks following his thirtieth birthday. This account about him is my homage to him.

At the meeting held at the NACP office organized by Gina, Hillary projected a strong and a vociferous attitude toward all issues homophobic, sexually circumscribing, and stifling. Although it was our first encounter, Hillary vented—unreservedly—his opinions regarding Ghanaians' hypocrisy on the subject of same-sex sexuality. He unequivocally declared that "even pastors, teachers, and leading government officials secretly have homosexual lives. I know so many of these hypocrites. On Sundays, they mount the pulpit and give the impression that they are holier than thou. In fact, they are worse." Hillary's jousting made him an interesting candidate for an informal interview, and his actions at the meeting confirmed everything Gina had said about him. His socially attuned and clever political and rhetorical analyses of life amid the heightening homonegativity in his community made him an especially provocative interlocutor to consider.

> These politicians say homosexuals are morally bankrupt. Yet Ghana is one of the most corrupt countries in the world. They say we, gay people, are morally corrupt, culturally corrupt, we are this, and we are that. However, they are the very people who are sending our nation down the toilet. As for me, I will never trust a politician in this government. Neither will I trust a lot of these pastors. While we need them to use money judiciously, for instance, to help provide antiretroviral drugs, nearly all the time, they spend the money on themselves. They inflate their stomachs. They are the fat cats who embezzle funds from the poor. And in doing so, they steal our lives too. How can people living with HIV continue to fight if the government embezzles the funds required to provision them with antiretroviral therapy? Kwame, I mean that these people embezzle our lives too, and because we have no money we have no power at all.

Hillary's astute sociopolitical analysis foregrounds his disdain toward the widespread public corruption in Ghana. He directed his statement unabashedly at a public health official who unwittingly uttered homophobic remarks at sasso attending the meeting. Appearing offended by the presence of sasso, the official who attended the event was shocked by how sasso confidently talked about their sexual encounters with men without fear of sanctions, while demanding that the government expand public health services to key populations. Observing this man's negative disposition, Hillary took it upon himself to take a jab at him, saying, "Even health officials who are aware that everyone in this country has a right to health also abuse and infringe on some people's rights. I wouldn't be surprised if there are some in our midst right now. In fact, I am looking at some now. What are they here for, if not to speak with us on how to secure rights for sexual minorities and other marginalized folks?"

Notably, Hillary had a profound knowledge of current affairs and public health issues and thus did not hesitate to challenge anybody whom he found suspicious or regarded as homophobic. Hillary had been to one of Ghana's constitutional review sessions in Akosombo, in the Eastern Region of Ghana, and described to me his experience at the meeting in a manner that reinforced both his knowledge of Ghana's sexual politics and his refusal to be constrained by them.[1]

> Kwame, I was the only sasso who decided to go. I wanted to speak for us and relate to the review committee that being gay was not wrong. It was part of being human. Not even that Marcus, who had perched himself as a leading advocate for gay rights, came. I singlehandedly went there to challenge these constitutional lawyers. I had only one lawyer, called Barrister Atuguba, there to back me up. I stood in front of the commission, can you imagine, me, with no university degree, standing before these men who at times made me feel like a nobody, because my English wasn't as good as theirs. Me, who was not able to finish university, standing before these people dropping big words, big legal language. But, I did it, because I care about myself. I want freedom. I want to be free to be me, here, in Jamestown, in Accra, and in Ghana. I went there to speak for freedom, but the so-called learned people refused to listen. I wonder why they went to school, to open their mind or to be close-minded. I am surprised, the leaders of this country. Maybe they should let the illiterates run it, I believe they might do a better job governing the country. This whole thing is a struggle. Hopefully, in the future, things will get better. But, that is something I hardly envision. We must pray for this country, Ghana.

Hillary was an advocate for sasso and gay rights in general, and this description establishes that he had been involved in a litany of human rights activities for sexual minorities in Ghana. Following my brief meeting with seven sasso, Gina asked Hillary to stay behind, proposing that he go out to lunch with me. With a smirk on his face, Hillary consented, suggesting that we have lunch at one of the posh restaurants on Oxford Street, Frankie's Restaurant in Osu, Ghana's popular expatriate center.[2] Our lunch date afforded me with the opportunity to request an informal interview with him. At the restaurant, Hillary provided me a basic account of his life, from his boyhood to his current position as a peer educator in HIV/AIDS and human rights organizations, charged with addressing the concerns of MSMs and sex workers in Accra. The following is an entry in my fieldwork notebook describing my initial impression of him in the restaurant:

> It feels great to now be quenched by the coolness that the air-conditioned space that the restaurant affords. I am at Frankie's with Hillary. It is his choice, and I decided to follow him there. Somehow, I am wondering why he would bring me to Oxford Street, which is that part of town with a lot of obronis—white people—around. In the restaurant, Hillary clearly feels excited. He talks about the coolness of the restaurant following our rather long stride from the HIV/AIDS control program office. He begins his conversation about how he became sasso, but he stops just when the waiter comes to us with a menu. He looks at the waiter in a manner that makes me wonder whether he is merely suspicious of him or simply being flirtatious. Now, I am thinking, what should I say to him about our meeting? From where do I launch the conversation?

How to begin a conversation about homoeroticism and homosexuality in a context that completely disavows the presence and even the possibility of these erotic engagements and arrangements?[3] Initiating a conversation about homosexuality, a tabooed subject in this milieu, was a conundrum I had to overcome at the beginning of my fieldwork. Evidently, it was for Hillary, too. Despite his commitment to LGBT+ human rights activism, Hillary appeared guarded in the moment, and the fact that we were in public—a restaurant—further restrained the ease of our conversation. We conversed in hushed tones. While I struggled to disclose that I was gay, he equally contemplated whether or not to come out to me.[4] Eventually, I revealed to Hillary that I was interested in men, and that there was a man in the restaurant I found very attractive. He laughed, saying he already knew I liked men and that my gestures and gait betrayed me from the moment he saw me. "You are sasso," he declared laughingly. Hillary's allusion reinforced the adjectival dimensions of sasso that I have already described. My effeminate mannerisms, according to him, were what made me his coequal. "We are all the same, Kwame. One big family," he remarked.

As lunch unfolded, Hillary began to share the following story with me.

> I am not going to declare my age to you because it is a deeply held secret. I don't like sharing my age with strangers anyways. Maybe when we become friends, if I get to know you more, I will give you the chance to know me more. I hope you are not mad [I nodded to affirm that I wasn't offended at all]. I have always lived with my mother and my older sister. I really care about them. I was born not in Greater Accra, but in Western Region, which is where I believe my parents met. They lived for a while until my mother moved to Jamestown. As for my father, he has never been a part of my life. In fact, I have very little relationship with him. Unlike my mother, he is not Ga; instead, he is Fante, which is why my last name is Afful. My parents divorced long ago, and then my mom left her marital home back into Jamestown, her hometown. I followed suit. But eventually, I had to move to Teshie-Nungua to live in my grandmother's house.
>
> Since it was my grandmother's house, I had a lot of extended family members residing there as well. My uncles, my aunties, cousins, the list continues. I enjoyed being with my grandmother, although I dearly missed my mother too. It was she [grandmother] who took care of the financial burden that came with my education. So, I had no option but to stay with her as long as I was going to school. However, living with uncles and so many boys in the same house proved to be such a challenge for me. Unlike the males in the house, I behaved like a girl, at least, so I was told, and was very often jeered at for being Kwadwo Besia. Anyone who set their eyes on me in the neighborhood either assumed I was a girl or Kwadwo Besia, because I acted effeminately. It was tough for me wherever I went. In school, at church, with friends, people will mock me. It was so miserable and nobody came to my rescue.
>
> Kwame, life growing up in my grandmother's house was truly depressing. But I managed to get by eventually, following an incident that will leave a bitter mark on my memory and in my life. One of my uncles began molesting me sexually when I moved into my grandmother's house. At night, he would sneak onto my mat and then have sex with me. This went on for a long time to a point where I wanted to run away, to go someplace very far away. I was afraid to tell anybody because he

> threatened that if I did I would die. And, in addition, I was afraid to disclose the act to anybody given how shameful it was. Imagine your own uncle having you from behind, Kwame? How can you tell someone of something as embarrassing and shameful as that? That was the difficulty I encountered. Upon completing junior secondary school, I decided to move out of my grandmother's house to live with my mother in Jamestown. Because, not only did my uncle have sex with me, some older boys in my school, who were bullies, began having sex with me too. It was frustrating, but these incidents describe my initial experience as sasso. They threw me into a world where I knew it was impossible to act on my feelings for men. Of course, I didn't like what my uncle and the boys did, but in a way, they also showed me that there was nothing wrong with me, because it was they who fucked me, and enjoyed the process in no small way.

The way Hillary authors his life story allows us to see how his being in the world is irreducible to his sasso identification, but also extends to include other forms of identities, spaces, and formations traversed by him. Negotiating multiple scenes of self-making as a queer subject, Hillary ultimately strategically disidentified with those familial and educational structures that were all too frequently violent spaces that reminded him of his difficult upbringing. These structures were created to instill in heteronormative subjects an unquestioned acceptance of heterosexuality; however, for Hillary, they were ultimately founts of violence. His story indexes how queer subjects experience a heteronormative socialization process that leaves behind traumatic scars.

Schooling Passions? Family, School, and Church

It is evident that the family, school, and church are contested sites of effeminacy and the virtues of proper masculinity, as Hillary's narrative reveals. In effect, he was a living palimpsest, not one "self," but rather a multilayered subject, with a scrambled self. Relocating from his mother's house to reside with his paternal grandmother in another suburb of Accra following the dissolution of his parents' marriage, Hillary suffered repeated sexual abuse and violence at the hands of his uncle and other family members, and then, much later, from schoolmates in high school. The narrative, then, combines experiences about the personal and the collective, as he traverses both familial and educational milieus. To understand Hillary's subjectivity as sasso is to fathom his history as shaped by physical, emotional, and psychical violence and the dissolution of familial relations.

Lamenting his parents' divorce, he declared that "they never considered the effects of the dissolution of their marriage both on me and my sister." Moreover, he speculated all too frequently that had they remained together, his lifelong passion for education would not have been ruptured. And in addition to that, he occasionally regretted being effeminate. It was the very reason why he had to face expulsion from school. Reflecting on the rupture of his education he says:

> I have always pondered the fact that had my parents stayed together in their marriage, I would probably have ended up just like you. I am sure your parents are still

> married. I could not even finish senior secondary school because of a relationship I had with a senior. I was caught once with him in his dormitory and was reported to the housemaster that I had been having sex with other students. Therefore, when we were caught the housemaster decided to use me as scapegoat, and the senior was seen as the victim. Can you imagine, Kwame? [He shakes his head in disbelief.] The world is such an unfair place to be. I guess he was let go because, unlike me it was quite difficult to prove that he was homosexual. He wasn't effeminate, you know? I, on the other hand, was very effeminate, exuding auntie quality in school.
>
> I would hear people muttering under their breath whenever they walked past me. Life was difficult. Following our exposure, I was expelled from the school. My hopes were dashed. I couldn't tell my mother and sister the cause of my expulsion. How to tell them that I was engaging in homosexual acts? How to convey such an act, Kwame, and in what language? Now the senior who forced me into having this relationship is somewhere married with a wife and children, and possibly cheating on his wife by sleeping with men. I have always argued that once you do a sasso, you never stop, because it is in you, it lives with you, and it will follow you into your grave.
>
> My life now relies on doing peer educator jobs and workshops for these NGOs. Although I do the groundwork with a lot of my friends, we get little to nothing. And these days life is increasingly becoming difficult. At least I can say that I have acquired some qualification following my active involvement in the workings of these NGOs. My life therefore is better, but I wish I had more job security, and had better education like you. Had I taken my education seriously, I would have ended with a university degree that would have catapulted me into success.

Expressing utter regret for his dismissal from high school, he states: "Had I carefully and secretly guarded my relationship with my boyfriend in high school, I would have graduated with a senior secondary school certificate and then continued to the university." Although Hillary submitted to the language of shame and self-blame in narrating his story, he nonetheless never claimed to be fully remorseful. Indeed, he felt that he had productively lived his life in spite of the circumstances that had derailed his ambitions. Moreover, he frequently acknowledged that his life was better than others—especially his sasso friends. Affording me an ethnographic journey into his life, his account revealed the rather complex nature of heterosexual regimes in neoliberal political economic landscapes. His story reveals how educational institutions, like the secondary school he attended, were active sites for politicizing heteronationalism and for "schooling" heterosexual passions, to use Veronique Benei's illustrative terminology.[5] In the context of the boarding school, homosexuality was sanctioned as an affront to citizen-making.

The details of Hillary's story, particularly his precarious financial situation, which meant that I occasionally remitted him some money to take him through the day or helped pay for his medications, solidified our connection. Our developing relationship provided an opportunity to interact with the other actors and institutions in his life, including close relatives, coworkers, consorts, other sasso, politicians, renowned human rights activists, clergy, choristers, and the various organizations in the orbit of his life. While offering a tragic narrative, his story exposes the alliances between family and education as institutions that attempted—albeit unsuccessfully—to mold his passions in order to consolidate heteronormativity. Additionally, they uncover how these institutions provoke queer possibilities and entanglements in ways that on the surface may appear impossible.

Don't Do unto Others What You Don't Want Others to Do unto You

In Hillary's opinion, being sasso or engaging in same-sex eroticism did not interfere with his relationship to religion. The church played an integral role in his life:

> I am an ardent chorister, which means that I love my church. I was born and raised Anglican, and I have been in that church for almost my entire life. As a chorister, I have to always make it a point to attend choir practice. My reverend knows me very well and is even aware that I am sasso. Although we have not broached the topic, we don't let it interfere with the services I give to my church, and what I derive from the church too. However, my overt effeminate mannerisms draw attention to me as sasso. For example, one member of our church, a woman, went around spreading bad stories about me. Sometimes, she would tell people that I was dangerous, and that I was a homosexual. I did not know what I had done to merit her badmouthing me all the time. But one day, the least expected happened to her, as she had to come face to face with what she feared most. Her oldest son caught her youngest son having sex with another boy in the community. And this was during Easter, can you imagine? Now, when I heard her story, I thought about how the world we live in is surely a strange place. And then I immediately thought about that verse in the Bible, which says that if you would not feed a snake or stone to your child, why would you feed it to someone else's.
>
> Payback, payback, it is sweet, but also not very sweet. We have to love each other. As for me, I learned a lot from that woman's experience. When she saw me again, she tried to be nice to me. I however knew in my head that she did not empathize with me. Do unto others what you want others to do unto you.

The interspersion of Christian allusions in Hillary's narratives with local proverbs and idioms represents an attempt to make himself legible and to be viewed as "normal" in a setting that limits his desire to be sasso. Here, he attempts to make comprehensible the consequences of a church member's castigation of him as a homosexual, applying the biblical proverb that "you reap what you sow." Rather than draw on doctrinal Christianity to discipline his homoerotic disposition, he recycled aspects of a religion that disciplines homosexuals by declaring that "I am what I am because that is how God created me." In making this inference, he was referring to the Christian God.

Hillary's resort to Christian discourse illumines the paradox undergirding his homoerotic desire. In the larger Ghanaian Christian universe, his justification might be construed as blasphemous, yet his invocation reconciles his conflicting identities as sasso, Christian, Ghanaian, and, ultimately, queer. In this rendering, too, it doesn't matter whether Christianity has left a homonegative legacy; what matters is how Hillary recycles aspects of this religion to his advantage. In that respect, although he is well aware of the limitations of Christianity on his being, he finds recourse in it nonetheless. Hillary's narrative reminds us of the complex tapestry of contradictions that work together to make his self-identification as sasso possible.

INTERLUDE 2: NAVIGATING TERRY'S WORLD

I was introduced to Terry, an affluent sasso whose life often intersected with the lives of other sasso in Jamestown and beyond, by Hillary. Known to be able to fix problems for sasso who lacked the resources to navigate the problems that beset their lives, Terry had both sasso and nonsasso friends. Terry was ethnically Ga, and his posture in the sasso community made him seem omnipresent, attracting gay men not only in Jamestown but also in the upscale suburbs of Accra. In effect, Terry's reputation afforded him access to multiple settings in ways that other sasso did not have. Unlike Hillary, Terry did not interface much with LGBT+ human rights organizational efforts. Hence, he was less likely to be present at meetings sponsored by organizations such as BURJ. In fact, he was more invested in organizing gatherings such as parties that mostly brought sasso together.

Middle-aged, Terry wore a shiny dark skin and generally exuded confidence. He always wore a smile. "My large smile is my signature," he once uttered loudly. Terry owned a provisions and accessories shop that was regularly patronized by sasso in the community, as well as people in Jamestown. Called Terry's, the shop functioned as a transit point for the different strokes of sasso from Jamestown. It also, on occasion, served as a bar for Terry's wealthy friends, most of whom were clandestinely gentor. There, sasso converged to engage in wide-ranging sociopolitical and economic conversations about matters that deeply affected their lives. It was the kind of spot where one could receive a loan, buy an item on credit, grab a drink, or find and enjoy much-desired company. A makeshift plywood structure covered in brown oil paint, Terry's obviously offered the sasso who visited some sense of community and family. Through their association with a man believed to have access to considerable wealth in the community, the sasso who gathered there felt validated and protected. It was ultimately home for many, buffering them from intermittent homophobic onslaughts. As Terry put it,

> Life is definitely not easy for these young sasso. I know some sasso who have been rejected by their families. Where do you expect them to go? In a country where effeminate men are called homosexuals, and beaten as a result, it is hard to let them go out into the world, homeless and helpless, when there is nobody out there to help them. I have come across a lot of young sasso who have attempted suicide. I actually know someone who took his life last year. He was a very brilliant young man. In fact, you remind me of him, which is why I have taken a strong interest in your work.

> It is by a Ghanaian who also identifies with the community. It will be good for the sasso community and for Ghanaians in general. Since I opened this shop, I have had young men come up to me asking for a place to stay. Now I think I am the mother and the father of all these abandoned kids, abandoned because they are gay. Some of them need good and quality education to become successful in these times. But, unfortunately, they are not being taken care of, basically because their families have accused them of engaging in homosexual sex. What kind of stupidity is this? People need to change from their ways. When these young men come to me seeking solace, I offer them whatever assistance I feel I am capable of affording, and I move on. I know that is the good thing to do. The two young men in my shop were thrown out of their homes for fear of being gay. Now they are under my care. They are brilliant and industrious. Just imagine the kind of resourceful people families in Ghana are losing because they are seen as different because they are gay. And even worse is the fact that they are sometimes told that they are possessed by demons. What nonsense! Without these men in my shop, I wonder how successful it would have been, Kwame. I simply wonder!

While providing support to his sasso patrons, Terry's shop was a low-grade structure by design. The gutter, like most open trenches in downtown Accra and other urban centers in Ghana, showed traces of silt and spirogyra. The façade of the shop had a rusty awning which provided shade on sunny days and prevented rain from entering the store on rainy days. Two wooden pillars, firmly thrust into the concrete floor, supported the porch. On this verandah, Terry and his two shopping assistants, Abdullah and Nana, always rested on a raffia mat. His shop assistants also doubled as his "children," as Terry adopted them following ostracism by their families. According to Abdullah, Terry presented them with the opportunity to refashion and build their lives. "He saved my wretched life," says Abdullah, "when I was down on my luck." Sasso often filled the shop to capacity, sometimes in the company of their consorts. Between intermittent power outages, Terry would blast loud music, heightening excitement at the shop. The space was constantly abuzz with entertainment, with sasso coming and going as they pleased. Indeed, it served as a liminal space where sasso revived their relationships with each other.

When Class, Race, and Queer Capitals Converge

Besides managing his provisions shop and bar in downscale Jamestown, Terry lived in one of Accra's upscale suburbs, called Roman Ridge. His residence, unlike his store, was a hotspot that saw a mix of sasso and wealthy gay men. They often gathered there to have semiprivate homosexual soirees and get-togethers. The sasso at these events were of a certain status. To be invited, as I was reminded once by Terry, the sasso had to be of a certain stature; respectable, with a certain level of education, and prim and proper. At such events, Terry would treat his friends to sumptuous meals and drinks. On these occasions, too, he would mock me by speaking in a diluted American accent. Not responding in an American accent, I retorted that I resisted speaking like an American. He laughed at my rejoinder.

Terry spoke fluent English. Having lived in England for a while, relocating to Ghana in the early 2000s to take care of his mother, who lived in another suburb, he was betrothed to an older Englishman called Edward. Terry visited the United Kingdom a dozen times a year to fulfill his matrimonial duties to his husband. When he finally decided to move back to Ghana, he established what was arguably one of Ghana's first gay bars—Terry's. I interpreted Terry's disclosure of some of the most intimate aspects of his life as deriving from the symbolic esteem and status derived from his association to whiteness through marriage.

Like Terry, the other men I met at his soirees highlighted their triumphs in Ghana and abroad in a fashion reminiscent of Pierre Bourdieu's description of "the forms of capital," by which he means that "capital can present itself in three fundamental guises: as *economic capital*, which is immediately and directly convertible into money and may be institutionalized in the forms of property rights; as *cultural capital*, which is convertible, on certain conditions, into economic capital and may be institutionalized in the forms of educational qualifications; and as *social capital*, made up of social obligations ('connections'), which is convertible, in certain conditions, into economic capital and may be institutionalized in the forms of a title of nobility (1986, 241).

Terry's life distinguished him from most sasso. He obtained his diploma from one of Ghana's technical universities, proceeding to the United Kingdom in search of a better life and to also escape what he once described to me as "the tragedy of being a man interested in having homoerotic encounters with men in Ghana." He provided me with a brief account of how he had always wanted to leave Ghana for a place where he could be himself without feeling alienated.

> I always knew I was sasso. My siblings always laughed at me. I only have sisters, so it was not surprising that I behaved like a girl. As I became a teenager, I was preparing to go to senior secondary school. Aware of my feminine attributes, I was quite afraid that seniors in the school would bully me. For many people in Ghana, boys who act like girls will grow out of it. I don't think I did. The only option I had was managing my girlishness. My parents wanted me to go to boarding school. I was forced to go there because they shared the view that I was going to be toughened up. When I arrived in school, I was quite afraid. So, I had to act tough to avoid getting bullied by other students. I began exercising my body by visiting the gym regularly. I still do this even today. If people see me, they think I am just like any other man because of my looks. However, while I have the musculature of a man, I believe that I have the heart and the feelings of a woman beneath the ruggedness that defines my body. It is this softness in me that Edward finds attractive. He always says that when he first saw me, he knew I was very calm and soft from within. These attributes, he claims, were what drove him to approach me. We first met in a gay bar in London. I had never been to a gay bar at the time and was quite terrified by the idea. However, I decided to go, disguising myself so as not to be seen by Ghanaians who lived nearby. Once I entered the bar and heard the music I saw many men on the dancing floor briskly dancing to music. I couldn't believe what I was seeing. I convinced myself that night

> that if men can fall in love with men, then there is nothing wrong with my feelings for men. In Ghana, we're socialized into believing that having homosexual feelings is wrong. Meeting Edward, I was convinced that was untrue. I discovered my true self.

Terry's marriage to Edward, which occurred in the late nineties, gave him access to British citizenship. In Terry's narrative, he sees England as a space of queer freedom, whereas Ghana is figured as a site of queer abjection, a position made quite clear in the 2011 BBC documentary entitled *The World's Worst Place to be Gay?* Often representing England as a liberal domain, Terry, much like LGBT+ human rights organizations that are based in the West or sponsor LGBT+ human rights organizing in Ghana, elevated England as a citadel of queer tolerance, a mecca every homosexual in Ghana should experience at least once in their lifetime. No longer solely Ghanaian, he had the opportunity to visit England with much ease. Moreover, his dual citizenship status marked him from the other sasso as the outsider within, one who had access to the privileges of a Westerner.

Terry's narrative bespeaks his multiple "transformations" in the service of heteronormativity. First, because he perceived that he possessed feminine attributes, Terry regulated his effeminacy while in Ghana. Second, his marriage to Edward encouraged him to embrace his effeminacy unapologetically in England, reinforcing my observation that he imagined England as a site of freedom. The fluidity and tensions between selves in his narrative clearly complicate his location in the community of sasso, his family, and the class of clandestine gay men. Unmistakably, his narrative expands how his desire for queer self-making remained unstrapped from the pressures of heteronormativity. Not only was he now able to easily travel between Ghana and Britain, but also between Jamestown, that low-income suburb, and his swish estate in Roman Ridge.

Sasso Contestations, Gay Confrontations

When Terry returned to Ghana from London to open his bar, he wanted it to serve as a space for gay men in and around Accra, expatriate workers, and Ghanaians returning from overseas. His experience in the UK informed his desire to create a space that served men who wanted to share their lives with other men. "For me, a bar that catered to gay men was also a place where people who were not free to come out and be themselves could get some luck. It was in a gay bar in the UK that I found myself." Although the space was intended to serve as a bar open to the public, Terry wanted to create a space where gay men in Ghana could converge without facing umbrage from the public. In his narrative, coming out and being gay was what essentially defined one's sexual identity, and having a space in which to express such identity was crucial. In Ghana, that was difficult. Terry named the bar after himself, "Terry's." When it opened, it attracted a large clientele, including sasso, gay men, and nonsasso. The majority of the bar's patrons were Ghanaian returnees and expatriate workers in Ghana. The bar was located in Adabraka, an area popularly known to be a hotspot for swanky businesses and hotels, and the opening of the bar brought together what Terry described as unlikely patrons. Terry recounts how there were occasional squabbles among his mixed clientele.

> When I opened the bar it was my hope that all the gay men I knew could finally get together. It was going to serve as a place where they could be comfortable about their identities. Of course, sasso are not necessarily gay. It appears that to be gay here implies having wealth and obtaining some level education. As you know, very few sasso know who gays are or even understand what it means to be gay. My goal was to let this space permit sasso to learn from these men. I have always had sasso as friends, and I have always regarded myself as one of them. But in the bar, I had to occasionally distance myself from that identity. This does not imply that I ignored my friends who were sasso; rather, I was more comfortable with calling myself gay, so as to make those patrons who self-identified as gay feel comfortable. Clearly, Terry's was a space for all men who had sex with men, and it was open to the general public too. But I was more comfortable with the idea that gay men and sasso alike could come there to enjoy themselves. I have always been appreciative of my sasso friends. Without them, I couldn't have opened the bar. They are truly resourceful. On occasion, they can present problems. For instance, my wealthy guests often fought with sasso, calling them out on their nuisance. They thought they were tarnishing the image of the bar, given how loud they were, and most especially, their open display of effeminacy. I was OK with that, but I could only take that so far. The bar had to close down because there was a fight among sasso. When the fight broke out, there were straight clients at the bar. Being witnesses to the fight, they reported me to the authorities without hesitation. The case they built against me revolved around the fact that Terry's catered to gay men in Ghana, and that since it was illegal to be gay in the country, the bar had to be shut down. Moreover, my neighbors always complained about the blasts from the music. They said I was disturbing what used to be a serene environment. I am certain that was not the problem. In fact, they too had been given the information that my bar had a large gay clientele. A few years after I opened Terry's I had to shut it down because of these complaints. I used some of the profits derived from that business to set up my provisions store in Jamestown. My hope is to open a bar again. I shall. I believe in myself.

The role of politics around sexual identification is prominent in Terry's telling anecdote. Here, it is clear that class differences were at the heart of the conflicts that arose at the bar. For example, middle- and upper-class gay men reminded sasso, who were viewed as belonging to the lower class, and considerably less educated, to respect the boundaries between them. Confronted by this dilemma, Terry distanced himself from sasso when surrounded by his coterie of wealthy gay friends, most of whom had lived abroad. Sasso who patronized the bar also agreed that the gay men they engaged with were no different from them because they had sex with men. Besides, they detested the idea that the former often emphasized their class status to distinguish themselves from sasso. With different selves colliding, all of whom were queer but scrambled by amphibious, class, and effeminate subjectivities, the space amplified the differences among sasso, as well as their fractious relationship with self-identified gay men. Terry's shifting allegiances between gay men and sasso mirror the tensions that emerged between these constituencies, and the fact that there were heterosexual patrons made this space convoluted.

Terry conveniently gravitated toward sasso while in Jamestown and distanced himself from them in the swanky suburb where his bar was located. Here, Terry faced a dilemma. He worked to manage his class status in a manner that did not declassify sasso, whose class status was lower than the gay men in the bar and were regarded as being too loud and lacking courtesy. It is clear that class difference emerged as a source of tensions in the community, and Terry became a source of both envy and emulation for several sasso. Evidently Terry's class, his proximity to whiteness via his marriage to Edward, and his ability to act manly when and how he pleased not only elevated him but also protected him from the encumbrances of homonegativity and economic precarity.

INTERLUDE 3: INTERACTING WITH SHELLEY, AN ETHNOGRAPHIC EXCURSUS

Shelley's story invites us to witness the multiple ways in which he navigated being an overly feminine sasso amidst increased homonegativity in Ghana and also how he bargained with heteronormativity. Shelley ethnically identified as Akan yet lived in Jamestown for much of his adult life. For him, life in Ghana was a complex experience that entailed not only having to deal with being marginalized because of one's gendered or sexual identification, but also having to deal with a sociopolitical economy that made life miserable for sasso and the poor. He was in his early forties at the time of our encounter.

> I stood on the edge of the dusty field, watching as the older boys played football. Wild imaginations about having sex with them ran amok in my head. The weather had the usual sunny and humid tinge, and the boys' bodies were drenched in sweat as they briskly played. I staged myself at my usual location, the periphery of the field, to get a better view of them. I was in the company of my girl playmates, who accompanied me to the field every other football day. They, too, enjoyed consuming their sculpted appearances, and the streams of sweat that rained down their torsos. The smell of dirt and sweat diffused ineluctably in the dusky air of the sunset-lit field. I basked in the moment. The boys' sweaty bodies enhanced their physique, exposing the veins in their arms and the contours of their abdomens. Although they never lifted weights, they did possess the bodies of "macho men" [weightlifters]. In fact, you know who they reminded me of: Captain Planet [laughs]. I loved football days.
>
> On such days, I would dash home to quickly finish my household chores in advance to ensure that I had ample time to spectate [pauses, looks at me]. You know what I mean? And it was certainly the delight I absorbed by watching their penises prance back and forth that made the experience one to crave. The end game usually climaxed with the boys mobilizing around me and fondling my body. It was truly the climax [bobs head]. Some slapped my bum, caressed my breasts, and played with

my phallus, but only when the coaches weren't looking. On several occasions, they would demand that I follow them to secret hideouts in the bushes bordering the field, and there, I fellated them. This was like a normal routine. However, they would usually divulge information about our sexual encounters to others, and in doing so, cast me as the perpetrator, because I allegedly lured them to "play" with me.

I was often teased and subjected to name-calling, and always had to deal with the uncontrollable spread of stories about my sexual acts with them. I must admit, however, that I was never ashamed. In fact, I continued to give them fellatio without remorse because I enjoyed it too. These circumstances led to my first anal sex. I was about fifteen years old and it was with a football captain. He approached me one afternoon after a game. A very handsome dark, tall, and well-built boy, every girl admired him, and I did too. I think he is a Northerner. He asked me to follow him into the bushes, and while there, he played with me again and again. It was painful, but I enjoyed it, every bit, in fact. We did it again and again thereafter. He told the other boys about our sexual encounters, and they, too, would begin to solicit sex from me time and again. Some accompanied their solicitations with money and gifts, and this is how I got into sasso.

My excessive sexual encounters began to have its payoff, however, when I developed severe anal fissures. I was quite bedridden for a while and did not want anybody to know about my condition. I bled whenever I attempted to walk and the blood soiled my pants. I considered getting pampers and sanitary pads per the suggestion of my friends to help minimize the incontinence. But that did not stop me from bleeding. Traumatized by my condition, I was afraid to go to the doctor. Furthermore, I feared disclosing my condition to my mother. You know, they tell us that getting fucked in the ass is a bad thing, so it is also difficult to complain when you find yourself wanting. I developed symptoms like anal warts and some other related sexually transmitted infections. As I remember it, those days and nights were terrible, and I could hardly sleep. I was distressed and traumatized, cursing myself for not considering the possibility of having sex infrequently.

My condition worsened over time, and I had to finally reveal to my mother this unpleasant thing in my behind. She was petrified and could not help but admonish me. She said that it was God's retribution for the evil things I had been doing, and for backsliding as a Christian. She was very upset with me; however, she saw my condition as an opportunity to preach the gospel. Imagine groaning with pain, and being bombarded with verses from the Bible, Kwame? It is nothing to savor. In her numerous teachings to me she would say that only a change in my habits would let God heal me. And for this reason, she said God had given her a remedy. The remedy was that I sit on a bucket of hot water twice every day for two weeks, once at dawn and once before going to bed for the sore behind me to heal completely. The steam from the hot water was the antidote. In two weeks, I was completely healed and then went back to the guys again for sex. Since this incident, hot water has been my friend [we both laughed at his last statement].

Shelley shares this story with me at his *kelewele* (spicy caramelized fried ripe plantain) joint one evening in the organized anarchy of Jamestown. Seated behind his food vending table, which was pitched right next to one of the thoroughfares in the neighborhood of Swalaba, *okada* riders buzzed around, injecting smoke that had both Shelley and me coughing incessantly.[6] Amid the cacophony and unperturbed by the crowds that surrounded us, I recorded his story, which he shared while his friends and the consumers of kelewele interrupted us intermittently during the course of our conversations.

Shelley waxed nostalgic about how beautiful he had been, and how the failing economic conditions in Ghana made life weary for him. "Life," he would often say, "is hard in Ghana these days. But I will overcome. I keep on praying." In spite of the dire economic circumstances in which he lived, he still managed to retain a degree of optimism. In our first encounter, I misrecognized his gender by assuming that he was a woman. On the spectrum of sasso identification, Shelley was an "auntie," given his overt effeminate presentation and his profession as a food vendor. His feminine embodiment mirrored the women in Jamestown, most of whom bleached their skin and were also industrious. I was not alone in mistaking him for a woman: on several occasions, others, inside and outside the community, did the same. Overall, Shelley's stories reflected his nostalgia for a past in which he was a desirable sasso. Compared to other sasso in the community, his appearance gave him a youthful demeanor and disposition.[7]

Shelley's light and shiny skin, doctored flawlessly with brighteners, complemented the crown of his iridescent dark, curly hair. On occasion, he would apply a large dose of curl activator to give some oomph to his already coiled hair, on which he invested large blocks of time, equal to the time he spent on grooming his body in general. Shelley often applied bleaching creams to his skin. The extensive use of these creams had left his hands, neck, and arms sinewy, exposing green varicose veins.[8] Standing at six-foot-two, his well-preened, slender figure made Shelley hypervisible in the community.

When he visited the market to purchase the food items for his business, he often towered above the market women. His skillful bargaining power—touted as genuinely exceptional and too good for a man—earned him the admiration of the market women. In fact, for his dramatic flair at bargaining, the market women often gave him their produce at a reduced price.[9] Shelley luxuriated in the fact that his bargaining skills and economic talents also earned him the envy of his fellow sasso. He would often say: "I am blessed. I possess a God-given trait, which gives me plenty in these harsh economic times." Laughing boisterously, he asked playfully, "Am I not blessed, Kwame. Am I not?"[10]

Shelley subscribed to Christian beliefs." He often used the phrases "a church benchwarmer" and only an "occasional churchgoer" to capture his affiliation with Christianity. Unlike Hillary, Shelley was not involved in HIV/AIDS organizations because he was convinced he did not possess the wherewithal to educate others, nor did he have the educational capital to venture out and be involved in such projects. He uttered this line to me: "I am not like you, the degree holders. I have very little education, which is why I sell kelewele here. If I had some education, I would have joined my brother, who currently lives in the United States. I, however, think that this will not be possible, given his awareness that I am sasso. He doesn't even talk to me now."

Shelley cared surprisingly little about his overt effeminacy, perhaps because he was relatively older. At the time of our interview, he had just turned forty-five years old and emphasized that he was not the "coequal" of sasso precisely because he was older, despite the fact that his effeminacy placed him among the other sasso. Here, Shelley participates in reinforcing his position as an older sasso by virtue of his age. Yet, his age blended with his effeminate self-identification, which like the self-presentation of Hillary and Terry, placed him squarely in the ambivalent space created by being a man without masculinity or exuding femininity without being a woman.[11]

On occasion, Shelley reflected on the fact that effeminacy deprived him of privileges of masculinity such as being a husband and a father. The market women with whom he interacted were subdued by their knowledge that he lacked "manliness," which, they believed, kept him from the rungs of potential marriage and fatherhood. In fact, these attributes made Shelley one with them and the market women one with him. In a culture where fathering children and marriage are considered as the ultimate crown of masculinity, to possess a quality that, as popular belief had it, prevented one from having an active phallus left an indelible mark on their personhood.[12] In Jamestown, it was a public secret that Shelley had sex with men, which many deduced from his feminine attributes. As can be extrapolated from the stories of the other sasso in this chapter, Shelley embodied and expressed competing masculinities and femininities. In this milieu, his "masculinity" could be described as "effeminate masculinity."[13]

Are You a Man or a Woman? Gender Misrecognition in Action

It was a rainy day and Shelley had to go to Salaga market, the open-air market in Jamestown, to buy cooking oil for his kelewele business that evening. With puddles everywhere in the unpaved market, Shelley's struts, his impeccable sashaying and negotiation of every mound of mud with utmost care, revealed how adroitly he maneuvered the muddy waters of the market. Arguably, such navigation was analogous to how sasso traversed the precarious conditions created by transnational LGBT+ activism and the heightened homonegativity faced by them.

Shelley moved to Jamestown when his mother asked him to pack his bags and vacate his natal home in Tema, the harbor city located east of Accra, following rumors that he was a homosexual. Jamestown became his home; when I met him, he had been residing there for more than a decade.[14] There he could comfortably be himself, as he once reminded me. "Here I wear my embroidered white elbow length shirt, and my skintight knee-length jeans without flinching. I also don't have to worry about indignant looks." For Shelley, to express effeminate identity was to adorn his body in beautiful clothes. That act, he emphasized, offered him the latitude to show off his curves, especially the protrusion of his buttocks.

In Jamestown, unlike other parts of Accra, Shelley had the freedom to overtly express his effeminacy. There, he could also claim and embody a sociophysical appearance that challenged hegemonic gendered categories. Beyond the confines of Jamestown, however, Shelley, like other sasso, was confronted by questions like "Are you a man or a woman?"

> Not very long ago, I was out on one of my usual errands in the city. I ran into a very attractive young man somewhere in Accra who expressed an interest in me. He was a butcher in Accra but resided in Kasoa. Following a brief conversation, he invited me out to a nearby drinking bar. I remember enjoying every second we spent together in the bar. This guy caressed my arms and then fondled my thighs with his large palms, which seemed to have been toughened up by years of wielding the butcher's knife. After a few drinks at the bar, we left to go have a meal in a chop bar. In fact, he enjoyed hanging out with me. I assumed that he knew I was a man who resembled a woman. When the night fell, he asked that I come with him to spend the night at his house. This was a proposal to which I happily consented, because I, too, liked him a lot. He quickly hailed a Kasoa-bound taxi. We arrived at his house around 1 a.m., which was nested in a wooded neighborhood that had poor dirt roads with no lights. I was terrified. I remember pondering what to do at this time of the day should something bad happen.
>
> Upon arriving, he took me to his bedroom and asked me to undress so he could admire my body. As I undressed he came to the realization that I was a man. He began to yell and call me names. Not far from where he stood on his side of the bed hung a big machete. He drew my attention to the machete, prompting me to wonder what he might do with it. Grabbing the machete, he brandished it at me. With my eyes completely welled up and bloodshot, I was overpowered by my emotions. I pleaded with him to release me, convincing him that I had thought that he knew I was a man and that I was never going to let this happen again.
>
> Following my plea, he dropped the machete and offered me money to quietly leave his house. I dressed and slowly left his room. I dashed out, running quickly to a nearby road, where I waited a while to catch a taxi back to Jamestown. While running, I looked behind me to make sure no one followed, as I feared he might have changed his mind and come after me with the machete to butcher me to death.
>
> Kwame, this experience not only terrified me, but also stayed with me. Eventually I had to regulate my movements in and outside of Jamestown in particular and Accra in general very carefully. And anytime I went outside of Jamestown, I had to manage my looks, appearance, and voice, even. I had to put on clothes that did not encourage people to ask the question: Are you a man or woman? Sometimes you've got to be careful, especially as you will not know what is coming to you.

Shelley's narrative articulates the embodied interenactment of masculinity and femininity that confused his consort. In the different domains he traversed, his presentation of self and interactions with others determined how he was interpreted.

In fact, his "I," so to speak, remained an ambiguous domain that inevitably threatened and blurred both gender and class binaries. In Shelley's case, effeminacy is not merely a performance but a way of life and of being and becoming. For instance, it is quite difficult to know whether his consorts misrecognized his gender, or if Shelley, too, misinterpreted their intentions.

How is one to read the misrecognitions and misinterpretations figured here? Must they be read as just another effect of the disenchantment with or perhaps the failure of gendered and sexed categories in this context? These microincidents represent the everyday experiences that sasso like Shelley and Hillary faced. And for the most part they are not investigated by the LGBT+ human rights organizations that purport to rescue sasso from the homophobic claws of the nation-state and civil society. I suggest that these incidents invite us to probe beyond facades of the supposedly homogenous categories established by heteronationalist and homonationalist politics in order to plumb the fissures and contradictions that they mask.

Another scene of gender misrecognition is relayed by Shelley. This time, however, the misrecognition occurs not in Jamestown but at the place of his birth. Hence, misrecognition was not unilateral but bilateral on occasion, as the following anecdote encapsulates.

> A few years ago, when I still lived in the house of my extended family in Tema, a man approached me and asked if I had a boyfriend. I told him that I did not have one. He asked to be my friend and then I decided to exchange telephone numbers. Beginning our friendship over the phone, it later became sexual, and we began to have phone sex. On one occasion he said he had fallen for me and was intoxicated by my beauty. He even called me Eve, because I was his forbidden fruit. He convinced me to have sex with him one evening. We arranged to meet at Nick Hotel in Tema Community Seven one night. The man, an exporter of local produce, was very rich and could afford to pay for us to go to this four-star hotel.
>
> Before this encounter, which he deemed special, he would always buy me gifts ranging from clothes to jewelry. I think he really loved me and had good intentions for me. And I loved him too. I did not know if he knew I was a man, although I assumed that he did. At the hotel, he reserved the king's suite for us, and was ready to christen our relationship with a sexual encounter. I, too, was looking forward to the moment. I could tell that he was very well endowed and couldn't wait to enjoy him just as much as he did me. Together in the suite with him, he treated me to drinks that he had ordered from the bar. This was accompanied with assorted foods from the restaurant, too. Kwame, I really enjoyed being with him until the unexpected happened. So, he began to kiss me and then fondle my breasts. Just when he began to unzip my tight pants, the "thing" sprang out. He jumped out of the bed in shock, grabbed his belt, and locked the door.
>
> Kwame, he lashed the hell out of me that night with his belt in a way that I have never experienced. I was jumping around the room looking for a way to escape, but the door was locked. He told me he was going to phone the police to tell them what had happened. I also quite remember him saying that he was going to call a radio station to come and capture the event. As he moved to pick the phone and call the

> police, I quickly grabbed the keys, which had been left on the bed, unlocked the door, and fled from the room. I can't believe this happened to me. And sometimes I laugh whenever I reflect on the incident.

These anecdotes detail Shelley's constant confrontation with misrecognition. For example, in retelling these stories, Shelley recalled how people read the physicality of his body, such as his curvaceous and bosomy appearance in a milieu that confines gender performances to the masculine and the feminine. Shelley's embodiment and navigation of effeminacy complicate the idioms of homosexuality and heterosexuality. Furthermore, his sasso identity, as well as that of others, tells us more about how sexual subjectivities and forms of self-making occur among sasso themselves, and in ways that are far from parallel and even. Shelley's misrecognition bespeaks the failings of dichotomized gender, showing how it confuses the very subjects who enforce the rules and grammar of gender based on the physical and performative presentation of an individual. The homophobic reaction from the man in the hotel room can be read as representing a moment in which the deregulation of gender invites quick retribution. Arguably, homophobia is an instance of heteronormative retribution at gender misrecognition; hence heteronormativity's failure to comprehend nonheteronormativity puzzlingly enables homophobia and queer possibility.

INTERLUDE 4: TRAVERSING ALAJO'S UNIVERSE

I was introduced to Alajo by Hillary. When we met, he had just turned twenty-five. Alajo was truly animated and unlike any sasso I had encountered. An only child, he lived with his mother in one of Accra's coastal suburbs, Nungua, which is east of Jamestown. Mixing ambitions with loss and disappointment, Alajo unmasked his difficulties reconciling his identity as sasso with being an only child, and his unwavering ambition to become a journalist. Like Terry, Alajo was quite well educated, possessing the ability to debate any subject with alacrity. He was biethnic, being of Akan and Ga extraction.

Alajo occasionally distanced himself from his sasso comrades, seeking their company at his convenience, especially during weddings, funerals, and other ceremonies. He often commuted to Jamestown to visit Terry at his shop. Our first meeting was in 2011, in the twin city of Sekondi-Takoradi, located on Ghana's west coast. Alajo was participating in a health-care outreach project that was under way and being monitored by the West Africa Program to Combat Aids and STI (WAPCAS). The project was part of WAPCAS's campaign to offer flexible services to MSM in the metropolitan area of Sekondi-Takoradi. In sasso circles, these acronyms are widespread, which bespeaks their interaction, encounter, and perhaps involvement with both local and transnational NGOs that address issues related to HIV transmission.

Fair in complexion, Alajo was slender, standing about five-eleven. He exuded conventionally feminine attributes while engaging in performative masculinity in spaces and on occasions where any expression of femininity could potentially raise eyebrows and frowns. He regarded himself as being less effeminate than Hillary and Shelley. Among the sasso in Jamestown, he was touted as a beautiful man. Like Shelley's, Alajo's beauty sometimes drew positive attention. On other occasions, he was jeered at for being Kwadwo Besia, a term he sought to avoid. In our conversations, Alajo would hint that his gait betrayed his effeminacy. One day, as we walked through one of Accra's suburbs, a group of men started calling him Kwadwo Besia, referring to me as his homosexual partner. Fearing for our lives, Alajo asked that we catch a taxi to escape the unknown. Alajo's gait highlighted the contours of his hips and buttocks in a manner that was beyond his control. "I can't control the way I walk, or the way my ass looks," he would often say to me in a polite and soft-spoken manner.

During our encounter, he told stories about his ambition to become one of Ghana's greatest journalists. Having attended one of the elite senior secondary schools in Ghana in the Central Region, from which he graduated with honors, Alajo secured admission at the Ghana Institute of Journalism, where he pursued a bachelor's degree. Following his graduation, however, he found the job market to be challenging. "There were virtually no jobs, and if there were, employers only sought out applicants who had obtained a university degree," he told me. He expressed frustration with the absence of jobs in his field.

> I had always seen myself going to the school of journalism. Following my graduation from Adisadel [historically an Anglican private school for boys in Cape Coast], I quickly hopped on that bandwagon that was going in the direction of Ghana Institute of Journalism. You know, growing up around my mother I loved to read. Although my mother has very some minimal education, she always encouraged me to take my studies seriously. She did this by buying me books. Dickens, Brontë, Shakespeare, Achebe, Wa Thiong'o, Soyinka. I have read them all. My mother was very supportive of my education. As someone with little to no education, I was quite amazed at her ability to invest in my education. Growing up reading the writings of these people, I managed to secure a place in Adisadel.
>
> There, I did general arts, and my electives were literature, Christian religious studies, and government. I enjoyed these courses very much, passing with flying colors. After my stint in Adisadel, I gained admission into GIJ, where I worked with some of Ghana's prominent journalists. I had a great cohort that supported each other. In fact, my time at GIJ was great. For me journalism was one of the ways by which I could tell the story about those whose lives remain under the carpet of our deteriorating economy, politics, and culture. I thought of journalism as one of the most effective and efficient ways to expose the inconsistencies in our country. Coming from a poor family, I was inspired and motivated to see Ghana become a much better place for all.

> My mother had very little education, and my father abandoned her just when I was born. These experiences really informed my decision to pursue journalism. Also, another reason for the pursuit of that discipline was my own location as someone who grew up knowing that he was interested in having sex with men. Although my homosexual feelings were never considered as I embarked on getting a degree, I had seen and heard in the news how homosexuals in this country were being treated. I often objected to how journalists represented homosexuals in the media. For me, journalism presented an opportunity for as to ask questions, dig deeper into the things we do. Ask ourselves why we do the things we do, with some level of circumspection and introspection. That is how I envisioned it. So, when I graduated and realized that I was not going to get a job, it frustrated me. Most of the jobs expressed an interest in someone with a bachelor's degree. At the time, GIJ only offered diplomas in journalism. Can you imagine, Kwame? I felt so lowballed.

Alajo often shuddered at the idea that he couldn't get a job in journalism despite his laurels from the Ghana Institute of Journalism and the secondary school he attended. Moreover, he felt that the system in Ghana did not work well for him, largely because it was against sasso like him and, for this reason, undermined their prospects for growth. As he reminded me once: "Kwame, the system here only operates on the basis of who one knows. Here nepotism and cronyism remain the rule. I am the first in my family to get this far by way of education. Most of the people I know are not that influential. I am hoping to find someone who will offer to give me a job on a merit basis rather than just because they know me or are familiar with me outside of my expertise."

Amidst uncertainty, however, Alajo landed a job with human rights and public health NGOs, one of which was WAPCAS. As part of his work in these NGOs, he traveled the length and breadth of Ghana, counseling MSM, female sex workers (FSW), and persons living with HIV/AIDS (PLHIV).

When I met Alajo, he was part of a research team that was conducting "The Men's Study." At the time, Sekondi-Takoradi was undergoing an oil boom. The economic turnaround attracted a large number of foreign workers who mostly worked on the oil rigs in the Gulf of Guinea. The discovery of oil off the western shores of the country drastically transformed the sexual demography of the city, suddenly making it one of the areas in Ghana to witness an upsurge in HIV cases. The Men's Study was being conducted to examine the sexual behaviors among men amid the transitions that were happening. Alajo collected data for WAPCAS, asking MSM about their sexual behaviors.

We arranged to meet at the Akroma Plaza Hotel. I arrived at the hotel earlier than anticipated, following a seven-hour trip from Accra. As I waited for Alajo, I became quite concerned about our safety there. The past few months had witnessed growing claims that homosexuals were invading Sekondi-Takoradi.[15] Media stories maintained that a group of gay men had begun throwing parties there, and that the government needed to intervene immediately. Responding to media reports about the increasing presence of homosexuals in the city, the then minister of the Western Region Paul Evans Aidoo issued a statement that asked law enforcers to "smoke out" homosexuals in Ghana.[16] An idiomatic expression, "to smoke" out literally translated as hunting for rodents such as rats, grasscutters, ground hogs, and reptiles using smoke to fumigate the holes they dig. These creatures were regarded as destructive and invasive to crops such as cassava, yam, cocoyam, and other root tubers. The smoke forced these animals to come out of burrows and tunnels.

The minister's statement, while legitimizing attacks against men perceived to be homosexuals, received little to no attention in the country. The minister imagined homosexuals as invasive individuals scourging Ghana's purity, for which they needed to be "smoked out" at all costs. Our meeting was, therefore, discreet, to say the least. The danger was likely somewhat less for the queer ethnographer based in the West than the sasso living in conditions governed by homonegativity; but it was not safe for either of us.

Strange Bedfellows: Heteroerotic Entanglements with Homoerotic Pleasure

Alajo arrived at the restaurant just in time for dinner. He was decked in a pink polo shirt that was tucked into well-ironed denim pants; he looked splendid for our meeting. Asked why he was so well preened, he rejoined: "Well since I am coming to a four-star hotel, the onus is on me to appear in a fashion befitting of the location, Kwame. You know in Ghana, the guards will ask you to leave if you come in rags, tattered clothes, looking all disheveled." Alajo was truly articulate, possessing the ability to be lucidly expressive.

Our conversation at dinner ranged from his sexual experiences with men to the uncertainties accompanying being sasso. A story he told me left an indelible mark. It was about how a woman in Jamestown proposed that he have sex with her husband.

> I was walking on the streets of Jamestown one hot afternoon, to this place called Clubhouse, you've been there, right? On my way, a woman, who stood at the entrance of a compound house,[17] hissed at me, gesturing me to come. She had an Adinkra cloth with a Gye Nyame symbol print wrapped around her bosom.[18] As I approached her, she asked me to follow her into her compound. I wondered what was going on, asking myself if the woman was normal. But, I just thought that she was a woman, and that should anything happen at all, I could overpower her. She offered me a bench once I entered the courtyard and a cup of water. She immediately entered her room, returning with a bottle of Coca-Cola to quench my thirst.
>
> Relaxing on the bench together with her, she told me that I was a very handsome, and, in fact, very beautiful man. I delightedly responded to her praise, saying that I knew that. As you know, I get these statements thrown at me all the time by both men and women. In this case, I did not know what the woman's intentions were. I assumed that she liked me, and that she wanted me to become her boyfriend. But I also held the belief that she was aware I was sasso, since I had a lot of friends in this

> part of Jamestown, and I hung out with them at Clubhouse almost every night and every other Saturday.
>
> As our conversation grew, the woman finally revealed the reason for her impromptu invitation. She wanted me to become her husband's boyfriend and lover. She did say that she would give me some money if I chose to sleep with him, and also if I established a relationship with him. This request came as a surprise. I knew for a fact that in Jamestown anything could happen, but something like this was all too rare. She asked me if I was interested, and said that she could give me some time to think about it. To this question, I responded in the negative.
>
> In fact, I made up the lie that I had a very jealous boyfriend who would not take kindly to her request. At the time I had been out of school for a couple of years and was ready to return to pursue journalism, too. So, I saw no reason to have any homoerotic relationship, or being embroiled in this love triangle that this woman so desperately suggested. I just couldn't believe that she tried to pay me to sleep with her husband.

Heteroeroticism uneasily intertwined with homoeroticism in this incident. In fact, homoeroticism, as I understood it, was preferred because it preserved the sanctity of heterosexual relationships. By proposing that Alajo become her husband's boyfriend, the woman hoped to sustain her heterosexual bond with her husband. In a milieu where homosexual relationships are forbidden, Alajo did not threaten her heterosexual marriage. Homoerotic dalliances were therefore preferred. If the husband had been in a heteroerotic relationship, the likelihood of him asking for a divorce would have been higher. Arguably, homoeroticism consolidated heterosexual marriage.

The entanglement of homosexuality with heterosexuality here needs magnifying, since these nuances are often obscured by the largely abstract critiques of African homophobia that lose sight of the cultural nuances of sexual and gendered relationships. These critiques are often articulated by Western-based organizations and Western-produced documentaries like *The World's Worst Place to Be Gay?* (Alcock 2011) and even more radical ones like *Call Me Kuchu* (Zouhali-Worrall and Fairfax Wright 2012), both of which imagine in distinct ways how the queer African subject is constantly assailed by homophobic regimes. Similarly, heterosexuality's furtive yet complex entwinement with homoerotic networks, as Alajo's story illuminates, clearly questions the Ghanaian government's normalization of heteromonogamy and the assertion that Ghanaians qua Africans naturally have heterosexual dispositions.

PART TWO

Amphibious Subjects in Rival Geographies

3

Amphibious Subjectivity

Queer Self-Making at the Intersection of Colliding Modernities in Neoliberal Ghana

I note, for instance, that the work now circulating as queer African Studies in the United States is indifferent to many of the conceptual frames in African Studies.

—KEGURO MACHARIA, "ON BEING AREA-STUDIED" (2016, 185)

Sometimes, one must know when, where, and how to be gay.

—HILLARY (JULY 2011)

The Aidspan film *I Didn't Want to Bring Shame on My Family: Being Gay in Ghana* features a young Ghanaian man who self-identifies as gay, living with HIV in Jamestown. The documentary begins with a close-up of the interviewee moving his lips, announcing his name and his age. He says: "My name is Hillary Afful. I am twenty-nine years. I am gay. I am HIV positive. And I live in Accra, the capital of Ghana." He gives away a smile that reveals two of his silver-plated incisors in this scene, telling a story that dismisses any assumption that men who have sex with men (MSM) in Ghana do so because of the money, since he had always enjoyed it. There is a voiceover animating the background, presenting the viewer with statistical figures of the increased rates of HIV infection among MSM.

The narrator discloses how external donors have helped to minimize transmission rates. "Ghana has made tremendous strides in tackling HIV by bringing its general prevalence rate down to 1.3 percent. A lot of this can be attributed to support from the Global Fund, which pays for around 90 percent of the antiretroviral drugs used in treatment." In the sequence that follows, a medical professional presents her opinion, expressing how nobody in Ghana really wants to acknowledge that being gay is a global thing. She further adds that the stigma and taboo nature of homosexuality means that gays are not comfortable with utilizing health facilities for their upkeep and protection against HIV and other sexually transmitted infections. In view of this, they have to rely on self-medication.

In another scene from the clip, Hillary, the young man at the heart of the documentary, remarks: "When you have HIV, for instance, it's like a shame on your family and I didn't want to bring shame to my mother." Here he sobs. The documentary concludes with the following quote from Hillary: "There's more to be done than what we've been doing previously. Lack of knowledge my people perish. We need to do something to reduce the risk of infection among the gay community in Ghana. Now I believe there's hope for me, but at first, I lost hope."

Aidspan, the organization that released the video, is a transnational health and human rights NGO funded by the Global Fund, which is an international NGO headquartered in Geneva, Switzerland. The video by Aidspan was filmed in Jamestown because Hillary lived there, and not because of the organization's awareness of the town's history of boys cross-dressing or the complex entanglements of homoeroticism and heteroeroticism. The video went viral both in Jamestown and across the country, resulting in verbal attacks on the sasso featured in the video beside Hillary. In turn, they demanded, reasonably, that the clip be removed immediately, although Aidspan did not comply. As an organization, Aidspan engages in continent-wide projects aimed at stopping the spread of HIV, opportunistic infections, and contagious diseases.[1] Moreover, the organization addresses the obstacles to its mission to eradicate these conditions. The organization thus perceives homophobia to be a bottleneck hampering access to health care for MSM. However well intentioned, the approach adopted by Aidspan to address health care for these men, who identify as sasso, was paradoxically insensitive to the nettlesome social, cultural, sexual, historical, political, and economic environments in which they are embedded.

Several questions animate this chapter, namely: How are we to critically comprehend the responses incited by Aidspan's attempt to rescue Hillary and other sasso who participated in their health projects? How are we to understand their rationale for publicizing the video? What sociocultural frameworks must be considered when elucidating how sasso responded to a video that supposedly sought to bring them assistance and redress? How do sasso subjectivities and processes of self-fashioning amplify the complexities of self-making among queer subjects in a terrain animated by uncertainties triggered by the collusion between neoliberalism and neocolonialism?

In this chapter, I respond to the queer African theorist Keguro Macharia's felicitous "litany of complaint" in his critique of the emerging subfield called queer African studies. In "On Being Area-Studied," an excerpt of which appears in the first epigraph, Macharia expresses disappointment at queer African studies' failure to engage with existing conceptual frameworks afforded by African studies, and African scholars, to be specific. For Macharia, "it is difficult to imagine that African philosophers, including John Mbiti, Kwesi Wiredu, and Nkiru Nzegwu, [and for the purposes of my argument here, I include Kwame Gyekye] have ever written anything that conceptualizes personhood, individuality, or community" (2016, 185).

In this chapter, I illuminate how Hillary's remark in the second epigraph foregrounds how sasso carefully navigate the changing scenes of Ghana. Thus, I show how sasso craft sexual subjectivities that sit at the vexed intersections of what I describe as African Christian and queer liberal modernities. These competing modernities are the outcome of complex colonial, neocolonial, and neoliberal histories of exploitation that scramble sasso subjectivities, making amphibious subjectivity an insufficient heuristic on occasion.

INFLECTED SUBJECTIVITIES: SASSO AS AMPHIBIOUS, POSTCOLONIAL, AND QUEER SUBJECTS

I contemplate how sasso like Hillary position themselves within, against, and on the frontiers of postcolonial identifications and the queer liberal categories supplied by NGOs such as Aidspan, examples of which are MSM, gay, lesbian, bisexual, and transgender. Sasso lives consistently reveal that these categories are unsteady, shifting, possessing different assigned meanings. For example, Hillary's self-identification as gay in the Aidspan documentary drew on queer liberal nomenclature, a term he rarely deployed in Jamestown. Being sasso, for Hillary, thus required a degree of tactical and strategic circumspection, and there, the ability to engage in pretentious conformity was apparent. In the following conversation, which transpired between us in the summer of 2012, Hillary reveals how he carefully navigated the muddied terrains of his subjectivities. Asked if his family knew about his sexual encounters with men, Hillary responded:

> It's really hard to tell. I don't tell them that I do sasso. They only know that I am sasso. I respect them, and so when I am around them, I am very careful about what I say or what I do. I may be comfortable joking around with friends about my sexual encounters; however, I have to be sure that jokes about my sexual encounters with men are muted when I am around members of my family. It is very difficult to even tell my mother that I am a peer counselor for men who have sex with men at the NGO. She only knows that I work on HIV-related projects. As for my sister, I believe she is aware of my homosexual encounters because she has female friends who sleep with women and are also my good friends. However, I believe she understands. On the other hand, my mother is very humble and a respectable member of my family and the community, and I don't want to break her heart. Kwame, many sasso are in the same shoes as me. Most of us don't talk about our lives with men. For those who have done it, the consequences have been grave. We'd rather live our lives under the carpet rather than live openly as gay men. You know, all of this is out of respect. Because, once you say you are gay in this community, it reflects not so well on your entire family and community. People will talk and say stuff about your family. And most of us want to avoid the consequences that our homosexuality can bring. So, one better plays in secret.

Hillary's response points us to the many selves—at once contradictory and coherent—he embodied. Neither Aidspan workers, nor the nation that criminalizes and polices homosexuality, could fathom such complexity. In this account, Hillary articulates a self that is deeply embedded in his family, and in that context, he meticulously avoids exhibiting any traits or actions that would draw his family's attention to his engagement in homoeroticism or even his health-care outreach for MSM. In these hidden textures and transcripts, he engages in a self-fashioning process analogous to Gyekye's amphibious identification.

Although his family partially relied on him for financial support, derived from his participation in NGO activities directed at sexual minorities, Hillary, as well as those aware of his employment, kept such associations shrouded in secrecy. Significantly, Hillary's family members engaged in similar forms of secrecy, hiding their perceptions about his homoeroticism. While his public secret was "known" to them, to employ Taussig's (1999, 5) assertion, it was not "publicly articulated"; rather, it formed part of a social protocol observed by both Hillary and his family to avoid potential tensions within his nuclear family.

In order to fully understand Hillary's subjectivity, his lifeworld and choices, it is important to consider not just the complicated role of human rights organizations in postcolonial Ghana, but also how these organizations scrambled his subjectivity. How, then, does Hillary as sexual dissident manage these selves, especially when the body suddenly confronts the vagaries triggered by epidemiological uncertainties wrought by HIV? In what ways does the HIV-positve self, which, like the queer self, is cloaked in silence, complicate the politics of making queer bodies visible?

THE UN/RESPECTABLE POLITICS OF SILENCE: WHEN HIV/AIDS SCRAMBLES SCRAMBLED SUBJECTIVITIES

Here, I set the stage with Hillary's scrambled past to expound on how his subjectivity/ies shine/s light on how he was grounded in and defined by his family and the community in the suburb of Jamestown and its environs and the contradictions such situations generated in his NGO work. The Aidspan video presents us with a different Hillary. This Hillary is positioned as a person living with HIV in a milieu where bodies living with HIV face severe ostracism from a world that pathologizes the disease. The slice of the subjectivity Hillary offers here altogether obscures how Jamestowners and Hillary's family and friends, sasso, and actors from local NGOs such as BURJ supported him during seroconversion. In light of this, I reckon how life for Hillary, and for sasso more generally, constitutes a composite experience that generates multiple, unpredictable responses, including vacillations between hope and despair.

Residing in a state governed by homophobic reason, to paraphrase Amar Wahab (2012), Hillary at times, and surprisingly, asserted his Christian and queer

FIGURE 3. Gracing a Muslim wedding with Hillary at the Aviation Social Center in August 2012. Photo by author.

selves in an unbothered and confident manner. At events organized by the church and in other venues such as weddings, outdoorings, and funerals, he was regarded as an important figure in the sasso community and beyond.

As an ethnographer, I acknowledge that my experience with Hillary, constitutive of my own ethnographic journey and navigation of being queer in this uncertain, often dangerous, milieu, presents but a slice of his life. Perhaps, like Aidspan, I am complicit in articulating a self that may not adequately give Hillary his due. I am of the view, nevertheless, that one of the struggles emanating from the business of ethnography might be that the stories we tell are distinctively informed by perspective and mood, and perhaps the reasoning that we contribute something "distinct" to the field.

Residing as Hillary did in a sociocultural and medical landscape where people living with HIV (PLHIV) faced considerable difficulties in accessing health care, his articulation of an amphibious self was perhaps intended to mask his ailing condition. Surrounded by family and friends, Hillary's self-fashioning enabled him to keep his head above the proverbial water. Jamestown's uneasy relationship with PLHIV, economic desperation, and the homophobia engendered by neoliberalism's unhallowed wedlock with neocolonialism occasionally interfered with his sense of being (Alexander 2005; McFadden 2011). Since survival was of the essence, at least for Hillary, he invented and imagined otherworldly narratives of his life that provided an explanation (if only to himself) of his condition, the source of which lay beyond scientific reason and medical explanations. Hillary drew, for instance, on narratives of misfortune and witchcraft. By reducing the symptoms of his condition to supernatural causes, he positioned himself as the victim of another world where unseen forces could be blamed for occurrences that were believed to have unknown causes (Farmer 2006; Epprecht 2008; Ashforth 2000).

Racialized Epidemiologies: Being Black/African and Gay in the Age of HIV/AIDS

The Aidspan video froze Hillary's amphibious, scrambled, and messy subjectivities, rendering it homogenous and simultaneously queer, yet victimized and plagued by HIV. Here, I move beyond narratives of queer victimology and gay men as vectors of HIV. These Pavlovian discourses, which often reinforce racialized tropes of African homophobia and sexual intolerance toward sexual and gendered minorities, also neglect the historical and persistent configuration of the Black body as a vehicle of HIV/AIDS. In other words, the association of HIV/AIDS primarily with gay men and the Black/African body constitutes an epidemiological project to construct the Black body as a stand-in for and vector of epidemiological failures. A discursive regime tethered to histories that produced scientific, religious, medical, cultural, and moral enquiries that vitiated Black corporeality, the epidemiological composition of the Black body in the age of AIDS indubitably suffers from these "controlling images" preceding the HIV/AIDS pandemic (Gill 2018; Collins 1991, 69; Cohen 1999).

The distinction between the Western gay AIDS narrative and the African AIDS narrative, for instance, both ruptures and blankets the connection between gay and African AIDS. Let us for a moment consider how Haiti was touted in Western media as the origin of the "brand" of AIDS that afflicted gay men in the eighties to lend evidence to how the Black/African body is consistently racially marked as the source of HIV/AIDS (Cohen 1999; Farmer 2006; Brodwin 1996). Thus, while Aidspan attempted to highlight Hillary's disenfranchisement and tragedies in a video that sought to rescue him from the claws of homophobia, the portrayal also racialized the gay Ghanaian subject by neglecting the discursive regimes in which that subject was both embedded and constituted. In light of this, if we return to the origins of HIV/AIDS as ultimately a spectral scene of racialization for both the African and gay subject, then Hillary's subjectivity is also "messily" racialized by the Aidspan video, although such language or vocabulary is foreclosed by the video. The controlling image born out of the intersection of being Black, gay, and a carrier of HIV nourishes contemporary public health attempts at eradicating HIV.[2] Precisely intended to rescue perishing subjects like Hillary, these campaigns obscure the hidden fact that these bodies already perish under legacies that continue to exact racial terror on Black bodies.

Complicit Silence: HIV Stigma and the Politics of Avoidance

In the summer of 2012, Hillary was clearly battling chronic illness. At the time, I was reluctant to conclude that he had contracted HIV. Having visited the hospital on several occasions, he consistently said that it was malaria plaguing him and so not to worry. Whenever I paid him a visit in the one-bedroom apartment he shared with his "girlfriend,"[3] I found scores of antimalarial drugs, ranging from artesunate amodiaquine to vitamins to concoctions such as blood tonics. These pills were intended to help rejuvenate him and enhance the quality of his blood. The drugs were strewn on the table next to the couch that also doubled as his bed. The state of his health was disquieting, requiring that he remain in bed for long periods of time.

In spite of his condition, Hillary offered to let me conduct an interview, expressing that he enjoyed my company and the funny anecdotes we shared. As my key respondent, Hillary undoubtedly reveled in the attention I gave him, and I was drawn to his aptitude for storytelling punctuated by moments of head-bobbing.

When I arrived in his apartment that afternoon, the humid atmosphere of Jamestown was infused with the smell of smoked fish. To overcome the heat, Hillary burrowed in a long couch with deep-blue cushion covers in the living room, basking in the breeze generated by a noisy standing fan nearby. He entertained himself with episodes of RuPaul's *Drag Race*, which he viewed on an old Samsung color television that sat on a TV stand. After a few dozen episodes, he switched to regular cable. Serendipitously, the midday news on Metro TV, one of the TV channels in Ghana, was on. Making breaking news that afternoon was the death of the president, John Evans Atta Mills. The news filled Hillary with a mixture of sadness and relief. The president had been noted for taking a stance against homosexuality, condemning Western governments for attempting to impose bad values on Ghanaian culture.[4]

An ardent member of the opposition New Patriotic Party (NPP), Hillary saw the loss of the president as an opportunity for his party to be victorious in the next election against the ruling National Democratic Congress (NDC), the deceased president's party. Despite his condition and acute pain, he was enthralled by the state of events unfolding in and around the country in the wake of the president's death, prancing about his room following a long and hearty phone conversation with a friend. While our interaction that afternoon centered on the death of the president, he went on to inform me that, had it not been for the wonderful attention from his mother and sister, he would have been completely immobilized. He was also thankful to his friends (sasso), roommate, and some young children in the compound who occasionally attended to him. Before my return to the US that summer, I paid him one last visit. I said this to him in Ga language upon arriving: "Auntie Lɛ [big woman],[5] how are you feeling today? You know I leave in a few days, right?"

> Kwame, I can't believe you are leaving so soon. Time flies! So, you are going to be leaving me alone, for a long year. Don't forget about me. Anyway, by God's grace, I am feeling much better today. I don't know why this malaria won't leave me alone, because it comes and goes. Now, I cannot even go out to work, and, as you know, I need the money I accrue from work to survive. When you are sick, too, you don't want to go to your boyfriends, because sometimes, they give you some money after giving them what they truly desire, sex!

While I was bothered by Hillary's ill health, there was very little I could do. Sometimes the thought of him having contracted HIV/AIDS crossed my mind, but I was also troubled by that conviction, given his continued resilience and zest even in his weakened state. In retrospect, I could see that Hillary's allusion to chronic malaria as the affliction that made him chronically weak masked the etiology of his condition and the associated costs of his ailment.

Since the income derived from his part-time work as a peer educator at West Africa Program to Combat AIDS and STI (WAPCAS) was inadequate, Hillary was unable to defray the costs of his medical bills and rent. Furthermore, he had been out of work for months. Support, in the form of money, came mostly from friends and family. It is worth noting that Hillary never considered himself a sex worker. For him, it was customary to receive money from boyfriends with whom he had intermittent sex. Upon my return to the States, I periodically called to inquire about the state of his health and learned that his sporadic fevers continued, although they were not as severe as before. I advised him to seek the services of health professionals as quickly as possible to avoid any further decline in his health. To ensure that he received regular medical treatment, I also provided him money on occasion when I was in the field.

I mention these encounters with Hillary because I knew from having observed his relentless fevers that he was showing signs of HIV. The sasso who were close to him also knew he had become infected. Who was I to reveal that he was seropositive? Maybe it was his profound involvement in the sasso community, especially in relation to such issues as improving access to health care for key populations, which prevented us from discussing his symptoms. My assumption is that those sasso who shared my awareness were silent out of respect. As a community, they understood that telling Hillary that he had contracted HIV could worsen his condition. Our hesitation, therefore, reflected an expression of our amphibious subjectivity, one that was driven by our empathetic considerations for him and the community of sasso that we were all a part of. At Hillary's memorial, Mawuli, a close friend of his, had this to say:

> You know, it is very hard to tell someone to go in for an HIV test, especially when you are aware that they know that they should do it. In Hillary's case, it was even more complex because none of us had the strength in us, not even Kissi, the one who always managed to stand up to him or dare him. Telling someone that you suspect they have HIV is nearly impossible, and such was the case for us. Hillary had a strong personality. In fact, he was like our mother, protecting us from the people who brutalized us. So, who were we to even gesture at any suspicion? And more so, nobody wants to be told to go for an HIV test especially when they themselves are familiar enough to know what is right from wrong, and to recognize that regular testing was necessary always. I, for one, and some of the "aunties," thought that he was probably on medication. Hillary, until he was diagnosed, never bothered to go in for a test. But, I believe that if we were silent, then we were so out of both respect and fear.

As a leading peer educator in the sasso community, Hillary had ample awareness of all matters related to sexual health and safer sexual practices. He was also the key person that public health NGOs reached out to when they needed peer educators. Assuming that Hillary's involvement in these activities perhaps provided him with the knowledge about his condition, I was reluctant to bring up the possibility of his seropositivity. Other sasso shared the same concerns, and the excerpt from Mawuli echoes this. Hillary's stature in the community inadvertently required that his seropositivity be kept in the realm of silence.[6]

Inventing Causation

In late April 2014, I arrived at the BURJ office to news that Hillary's condition was worsening. Kobby, a sasso and an employee at BURJ, related the story to me. Hillary first introduced me to Kobby in 2011, right after my first meeting with them at the National AIDS Control Program office. The two had known each other a long time and were taken for siblings on several occasions. Shortly after my arrival that morning, Kobby dragged me onto the balcony of the one-story office building to break the news that Hillary was engaging the service of a traditional herbalist who had ostensibly identified the cause of his infirmity. The herbalist's services had been sought to help cure Hillary.[7] Demanding very high fees for his service, the herbalist claimed that he could definitely cure Hillary. Added to the large sum of money were demands for a goat, along with other ritual objects supposed to enhance the efficacy of the ritual cure.

Hillary's confidence in the man's claim to cure him of spiritual attacks was not surprising. Living with a disease the cause of which was supposedly unknown, it was productive to assume that juju (black magic) could cure him. On one of my visits, Hillary mentioned that he believed an unknown person might be causing him undue spiritual harm, disclosing, in addition, that he had awfully long and sweaty nights.

As the religious studies scholar Adam Ashforth observes in relation to post-apartheid South Africa: "When suspicions of witchcraft are in play in a community, problems of illness and death can transform matters of public health into questions of public power, questions relating to the identification and punishment of persons deemed responsible for bringing misfortune to the community, that is: witches" (2000, 1). In a similar vein, Hillary's engagement with the healer was informed by his belief that someone intended to harm him. Further, his reliance on the herbalist in this moment foregrounded a self that believed that the ritual had curative powers. Here, he suspended his Christian beliefs in his quest for a cure from a medicine man who would otherwise be considered as demonic and primitive in the African Christian imaginary.

Hillary's determination to engage the services of the herbalist was born out of his disappointment with medical results that diagnosed his condition as malaria. Did he have malaria? Was he telling a story to cover up the possibility of having contracted HIV? In my interactions with him, he never mentioned that he had HIV. I only believed what he said, which was that he probably had "chronic" malaria or was the victim of spiritual forces. Hillary's experience with the herbalist was short-lived. My suspicion that the native doctor might be a dupe was confirmed when Hillary's sister discovered that the herbalist connived with a neighbor to dupe him. With the herbalist out of the picture, Hillary looked elsewhere in search of an answer to his sickness. In his desperate quest, he sought the services of a Christian spiritual preacher-cum-healer in an isolated suburb on the outskirts of Accra. The healer, a woman in her sixties, was believed to heal people miraculously. Hillary claimed that he first heard about the miracle-maker on the radio. Listening to an advert that celebrated her powers to make the crippled walk again, to raise the dead, and to heal those beleaguered by incurable diseases such as HIV, he saw her as the final solution to his chronic condition. Furthermore, he was delighted that she was a Christian healer who performed rituals that also drew on non-Christian, animistic practices. Hillary, who attended church every Sunday with his sister, describes its service:

> This spiritual church is unlike any spiritual church that I have seen in Ghana. There's a lot of discipline. Members have to be at service on time, to avoid missing miracle hours. During miracle hours, the angels of God descend. At this time the doors to the church have to be shut. That way, the miracles will be more effective. I think the other goal is that we don't want other spirits inhabiting this space. It is not good for the miracles and us. We need the healing, so we have to be disciplined, which is why I leave very early to make it on time for miracle service. I am hopeful that whatever chronic disease is making me feel weak will end with this woman. They say she can even cure HIV/AIDS. I have seen people who have attested to the woman's credibility. Every time I go there, there's someone giving a testimony about how much better they feel. I am already feeling better after having been there twice.

Hillary self-styles in a manner that diverts attention from what I believed was the actual cause of his condition—seropositive status. While mentioning HIV/AIDS in this conversation, he did not directly claim that he had contracted the disease. Yet, it appears that his belief that the healer could cure persons living with HIV drove him there. By resorting to stories that reduced his condition to supernatural causes, he averted our suspicions of his seropositivity. These were, therefore, significant discursive acts enacted by Hillary. By drawing on a dominant discursive regime that often reduced an illness with an unknown cause to the supernatural, he concealed his condition, thereby averting ostracism. Hence, Hillary's public secret, his seropositivity, was safely kept. This deflection, I argue, relies on his performance of a self that he desired to mask. He lived amphibiously. Confused as I was by his terminal illness, I could not rule out the possibility that he was either under spiritual attack or was living with HIV. The fact that Kobby and other sasso believed that Hillary was experiencing spiritual afflictions did not help resolve my vacillation either.

Against this context, when Hillary admitted in the video that he was HIV positive, that revelation was truly directed at an NGO existing to meet the needs of persons living with HIV. Would Hillary have been able to tell Aidspan about his quest for a spiritual cure? Moreover, would he have been able to tell Aidspan that he was under spiritual attack? I claim that Hillary stood to benefit from Aidspan as someone afflicted with HIV at the time of the interview. Thus, Hillary's self-presentation in the video at once revealed how he struggled to navigate both African Christian and queer liberal identities. However, the clip elides how sasso

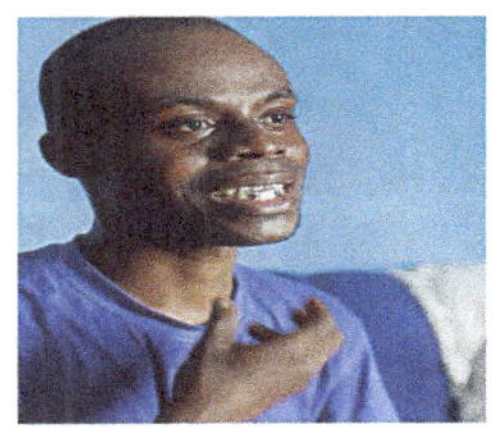

FIGURE 4. A still from the Aidspan video in which Hillary narrates his ordeal with HIV/AIDS. Source: Aidspan.

navigate both African Christianity and queer liberalism, reducing these sites of identification as polar opposites that constrict each other.

The African Christian Subject as "Victim" of Queer Liberal Modernity

I return to the Aidspan video to consider just how it circumscribes Hillary's self and the world around him. In so doing, I clarify how the video reinforces homophobia as one of the leading causes of HIV/AIDS among gay men in Ghana, thereby overwriting those complexities that work to produce their vulnerability in this neoliberal context. Hillary's narrative in the documentary stages a distinction I hope to make here, and to disrupt at the same time: African Christian subject as the product of African Christian modernity versus the queer subject as the product of queer liberal modernity. The former is rooted in the matrix of Christianity, colonialism, and commerce (see Pierre 2013, 5), and the latter is shaped by ongoing neoliberal and neocolonial ferment (Ferguson 2006; Agathangelou 2013).

The still in figure 4 is from the Aidspan video, which opens with the camera zooming in on Hillary's lips. He tells the viewer his name, his age, and his status as a person living with HIV. This is followed by a scene of the fishing harbor in Jamestown, dotted by canoes, with men fishing. Hillary immediately appears in another sequence on the beach, walking by some of the canoes with fishing men in the background. Wearing a light green T-shirt with violet stripes, he walks alone. The clip quickly returns to the scene in his living room, where the interview began.

Before disclosing his seropositivity in the video, Hillary proceeds with an anecdote about a friend who went to the hospital to get blood work done only to be confronted with questions and biblical counsel. Explaining why he did not seek health care at the onset of his illness, he mentioned a diseased friend who had to constantly contend with the unwelcoming looks and services of nurses at the hospital. Intended to capture the ignorance of health workers, who probably mostly identified as Christian, and who are pathologized in the narrative for their antihomosexual responses, the story teems with the kind of sentimentality that might incite a cause to rescue Hillary and gay men. Since health-care providers often castigated sasso at the hospitals, leading to interactions that ultimately discouraged them from accessing needed health services, Hillary expresses angst at the maltreatment of a friend of at the hands of the nurses. He asserts the following: "It was a common practice of the nurses expressed toward sasso whenever they went to the hospital to seek health care, even if it had nothing to do with receiving HIV/AIDs-related services."

Notwithstanding his own ailing condition in both contexts, Hillary demanded improved access to health care for MSM, for persons living with HIV (PLHIV), and for female sex workers (FSW), suggesting that such measures would help minimize fears among MSM. By drawing on biblical tropes, health workers not only elide the understanding that Christianity itself is a complicated echo of colonial and missionary projects, as Janice Boddy (2007) has suggested, but also heighten homonegativity. The insidious spread of what might be read as religious violence toward sasso is perhaps justified by the following assumptions held by health-care providers. Reliant on particular logics of Christianity, nurses who attended to sasso read their castigations as acts of redemption from the excesses of Western influences, of which homosexuality was often regarded as the most abominable. By quoting passages from the Bible to MSM, health workers pathologized sasso because they engaged in sexual practices that were "naturally" un-Ghanaian. However, in the process, they sought validation and legitimacy in the redemption of sasso from what they considered as the ills of queer liberal modernity and demonic Western practices.

Condemning sasso as sinners by referring to them as not part of the nation-state's official sexual identity—heterosexuality, that is—the health workers drew on Christian rhetoric to confine the likes of Hillary to zones beyond Christian modernity. In the latter formation, sasso are regarded as subjects contaminated by Western culture, in other words, decadent citizens. For instance, Ofori, a peer educator who worked closely with hospitals that provided services to MSM, conveyed his embarrassing ordeal with a doctor. "I was once scolded for being uncivilized and referred to as an animal by a medical doctor," he said. Painfully recounting his experience, he shared how the doctor unapologetically declared that "fire and brimstone would rain on me like it did to the inhabitants of Sodom and Gomorrah, that story from the Bible. I am Christian, too, and it's not like I am not struggling already with being sasso. Some of us try to do good stuff, too. In fact, for the most part we are often even better Christians than those who ring bells about how holy and perfect they are. I think it is frustrating when they say such things to us."

Not long before Ofori disclosed this story to me, the then moderator of the Presbyterian Church of Ghana, the Right Reverend Professor Emmanuel Martey, boldly and unapologetically referred to homosexuals as even worse than animals during the vetting of Nana Oye Lithur, a human rights advocate who promoted LGBT+ human rights, and the then director of the Human Rights Advocacy Center (HRAC), an organization for which Hillary was once a volunteer. The medical doctor's reliance on the Bible may entrench the notion that Christian modernity situates sub-Saharan Africa outside queer liberal modernity; however, Ofori's revelation says otherwise, given his struggle to overcome the unhealthy confrontations between both modernities. His experience exemplifies the tensions emanating from being both sasso and Christian.

Such health workers discouraged sasso from accessing health care. Hillary, for example, disclosed his reluctance to visit the hospital in a timely fashion as the result of the hostile environment engendered by health-care workers. Receiving news that he was HIV positive at a hospital where health workers heaped scorn on those with the disease made his discovery of his seropositivity even more traumatic than it might have been. In our interactions, Hillary recalled how MSM did not patronize health-care services for fear of being castigated by health workers who allowed their Christian worldviews to interfere with their duty to offer health care to sasso. Hillary's involvement in major HIV/AIDS prevention projects allowed him access to knowledge that other sasso did not have, and his revelations in the video position him as a queer liberal modern. In this schema, Christianity is rendered as the negative copy of queer liberal modernity, where modernity is indiscriminately pathologized.

The Queer Liberal Subject as a "Victim" of African Christian Modernity

When Dennis Altman, the pioneering Australian gay academic and activist, argued that "both affluence and political liberalism are required for a commercial gay world to appear" (1997, 421), he quite literally forgot the extent to which these processes occurred within particular configurations of racialized power and orchestrations of colonial capitalist modernity. Thus, we might ask, what was at stake for Altman when he made this claim? Did a nation's acceptance of "gay" identity signify the new fad that described one's modernity? For Altman, neoliberal modernity represented the enabling environment out of which the queer liberal body arose. However, his articulation of capitalism with gay identity conceals what the historian John D'Emilio (1983) described ten years earlier as capitalism's seductive relationship with gay politics. Arguing that the rise of gay identity was conceived out of the fraught bond that gay politics shared with capitalism, D'Emilio exposed the exploitative conditions that gave rise to gay identity, and how that very claim to identity perpetrated exploitative and oppressive structures. Altman's uncritical assertion that political affluence and liberalism were the stepping stones toward queer liberalism, then, displaces how the controlling discourses, images, practices, and regimes that made gay identity visible further disenfranchised and marginalized other bodies—specifically queers of color such as sasso.

For D'Emilio, the development of capitalism and its free labor system saw great swathes of people migrate into urban centers to look for employment. Thus, the enterprise of free labor significantly shaped predominantly existing heterosexual structures. This shift, among others, created an environment in which gay men and women came to interpellate themselves, drawing on capitalist modernity's ideologies. Altman's assessment, appearing more than a decade after D'Emilio's penetrative observation, however, elides the complexity of the history of political liberalism and the affluence required to nourish gay liberalism, particularly in postcolonial settings, where such relationships are even more complicated. It is in this historically fraught context that the Aidspan video functions, emphasizing how being tolerant of minorities is an integral feature of queer liberalism (Eng 2010). Hillary's expression of dissatisfaction at health workers in the documentary partly celebrates the position that queer tolerance is indicative of modernity whereas African Christian logics are cast backward.

Thus, African Christianity is perceived to be perpetually at odds with a more progressive Christianity that animates the West, where there are now a growing number of churches that consider themselves the citadels and sanctuaries of queer freedom by virtue of their endorsement of gay marriage and tolerance of queers. Once again, the complicated and problematic racialized histories that constituted Christianity in Africa, and their fraught relationship to colonialism and capitalism, are ultimately obscured by such constructions.

In the regime of queer liberal modernity, health workers' intolerance toward MSM is perceived as the corollary of their ignorance. Ambrose, a clerical worker, recounted his disappointing experience with a nurse to me. Apparently, he had contracted a sexually transmitted infection (STI) and was in dire need of antibiotics. Experiencing excruciating pain, he confidentially told the nurse that he suspected his condition was the result of having anal sex with some men in his neighborhood. Following that disclosure, the nurse drew other nurses' attention to him, revealing Ambrose's homoerotic engagements, a disclosure that was supposed to be kept a secret. Ambrose added that the nurse described his interest in homoerotic intimacy as a "demonic practice." For these health-care providers, Ambrose's infection was simply a supernatural penal sentence from God. Herein resided a paradox. While Ambrose required urgent medical attention, the health workers contrarily shared the view that he needed spiritual intervention.

Angrily recollecting this story, he wished he had had a bolder response to the nurses who embarrassed him without reason. For Ambrose, the health workers were "not only illiterate and petty, they were also pretty unqualified to be in such positions." "What makes me mad," he maintains, "is that my taxpayer's money feeds these ignorant workers." Ambrose's story is one of many accounts that sasso shared regarding their negative experiences with nurses. It is important to note that not all nurses in this context maltreat sasso. A nurse in the Aidspan clip, for instance, dismissed some of her coworkers for their negative attitudes toward sasso. "Every client that comes to a health worker must be treated with the respect and the individuality that the client needs," she said. "As a health worker, no matter your religious background, you should never impose your religious values on the client." This nurse's appearance in the video automatically designates her as a "good nurse." Perceived to be free from the trappings of African Christianity, she poses as a figure of reason, who, by sharing progressive views on the issue of homosexuality, gets configured as "modern" in the queer liberal sense of the term. Thus, ironically, sasso, as amphibiously modern subjects, critique health-care workers, whereas health-care workers generally look upon them as locked in vile sexual practices that require their redemption.

Another scene in the documentary features a medical doctor who reinforces the narrative of ignorance among Ghanaians. She launches an appeal for funds, hoping that such financial donations will help ease the woeful conditions incapacitating health-care delivery for key populations, including sasso.[8] Directed at global donors such as the Global Fund, Aidspan's primary donor, the request for financial assistance is intended to help minimize persisting ignorance around HIV and male homosexuality, as well as curb the spread of HIV/AIDS. By stressing that resources from the Global Fund will help quicken the pace of knowledge required to mitigate homonegativity and the spread of HIV, she shows how LGBT+ liberalization has yet to arrive in Ghana. The medical doctor's narrative, unlike the medical doctor who blatantly scolded Ofori with Christian religious epithets, reinforces Altman's view that political liberalism and affluence constitute the dispensation in which gay identity can appear (1997). Here, American dollars and European euros have to be pumped into HIV/AIDS programs and auxiliary projects from donors like the Global Fund to facilitate the enabling environment required for queer liberalism.

The documentary further imagines the ignorance and intolerance of health-care workers as the offshoot of Christianity without paying attention to the historically constituted contexts in which they reside. Here, Christianity of the African variety is interpreted as stifling its followers' ability to rationally and epistemologically embrace sexual minorities, who are perceived as decadent citizens in the epistemic and moral universe of Ghana.[9] There are two competing epistemologies here. The first is tied to African Christianity, which is perceived as backward. And the second is tied to queer liberalism, which is couched as progressive and civilized. Once again, the colonial-cum-racist binary is reasserted, masking the persistent interpenetration of these ideologies.

For sasso like Hillary, who work in HIV prevention and LGBT+ human rights organizations, the uncanny ties between these two frameworks shape those uneasy conditions that make amphibious subjectivity palpable. In particular, the collisions and collusions create the possibility and impossibility for amphibious queer self-making. Hence among sasso, LGBT+ is both an approximation *of* and *for* modernity in the context of queer humanitarianism. However, they, too, consider themselves to be "Christian moderns," to recycle Webb Keane's term (2007). For Keane, in postcolonial contexts that forced the embrace of Christianity, Christian practices continue to actively function as a key site of modernity-making and human emancipation. Extending Keane's argument here, it appears that health workers who evidently drew on Christian rhetoric to convert sasso at the health centers operated from an ideological standpoint similar to the one that nourished missionaries during the civilizing encounter (Keane 2007; Pierre 2013; Miescher 2005).

These health workers perhaps sought to disencumber sasso, that is, emancipate them from what they perceived as sexual contamination. The convoluted intersections of queer liberal and Christian modernities present questions about when, where, and how sasso emerge as new privileged subjects amid transnational neoliberal LGBT+ human rights organizing. On the one hand, like many Ghanaians, sasso endure the uncertain reverberations of neoliberalism, given their location in postcolonial contexts with fraught pasts. On the other hand, these pasts, animated by combined forces of Christianity, coloniality, and capitalism, shape and reshape their locations as vulnerable subjects. How, then, are the intersections between vulnerability and privilege in sasso lives to be comprehended? To what extent do the uneasy alliances, which are tendencies of neoliberal modernity in the postcolonial milieus, decrease sasso ability to comprehend the shifts in their lives? How do sasso deal with these transitions and tensions in a nation that continues to be racialized under rancid neoliberal regimes?

Interstitial Subjects: Sasso at the Intersections of African Christian and Queer Liberal Modernities

While on the surface, it appears that there are two competing frameworks of modernity, I intimate here that both African Christianity's and queer liberalism's articulations of modernity are Janus-faced constructs that spawn Janus-faced problems. I aver that "African" Christianity, as discussed previously, is purportedly sutured to "Western" Christianity, the latter being an iteration of Christianity that is at once deeply colonial, and now postcolonial and palimpsestic, because of its domestication and vernacular dynamism. Queer liberal modernity, on the other hand, is perceived to be in tandem with secular neoliberal democracy. Thus, in the secular framework of human rights that supposedly pervades queer humanitarian reason, Christianity betokens backwardness. And, in what might be conceived to be the bulwark of the homophobic state of reason, African Christianity, as it were, gay identity is primal and sub-animal, as echoed by the moderator of the Presbyterian Church of Ghana. Together, these articulations of modernity are at once epistemological and ontological, intermingling in a postcolonial landscape grappling with the pressures conceived by the unholy matrimony between neoliberalism and neocolonialism.

I argue, therefore, that the moderator's sentiments to the media be closely examined as the corollary of the uneasy transitions within a nation and a transnational world undergoing unprecedented transformation. As a Christian modern, the moderator, like the nurses sasso confronted at the hospital, can be figured as benefiting from the historical privileges Christianity promised its converts. In that regard, he, in the heteronormative order of things, emerges as a privileged subject. In the present context, however, the privileges accorded Christian modernity collide with neoliberal articulations of modernity, which, by "salvaging" sexual minorities simultaneously embed them in transnational queer liberal circuits. These uneasy transitions, especially in Africa in general, and Ghana, in particular, are evidenced by the pursuit of postindependent development agendas, which sought to accelerate liberal modernity.

The intensification of neoliberal economic practices in the eighties, for example, bespeaks the shifting terrains of sexual citizenship, wherein Ghana was officially enrolled in a global political economy through programs of structural adjustment and economic recovery. These programs significantly shaped the contours and directions both of African Christianity and those visions of democratization held by postcolonial African leaders. For these fledgling nations, aspirations for democracy, as Claude Ake (1996), the late Nigerian political scientist, reminds us, presented contested spaces for building the nation in a context reeling from the debris of a past of colonial exploitation. The continuing marginalization of postindependent nation-states in the global political economy is rooted in this history of unequal power relations founded by colonialism, slavery, capitalism, and racial apartheid (Rodney 1972).

The current anxieties around transnational LGBT+ human rights activism cannot, therefore, be detached from the conditions created by neocolonial liberal modernity. For example, sasso are embedded in LGBT+ human rights projects that attract vast amounts of funds that seek to reduce homophobia. These projects, supported by "queer dollars," however, elide other conjunctures that intersect to trigger antihomosexual violence. The execution of these projects masks and reproduces violent class inequalities and the harsh regulation of Ghana's economy by neoliberal institutions based in Euro-America such as the International Monetary Fund (IMF), the World Bank, and the European Union. Thus, sasso, supposedly the beneficiaries of these funds, emerge as vulnerable subjects and targets. It is clear, then, that the optimistic practices by transnational LGBT+ NGOs to rescue sasso, coterminous with the hardships suffered by the Ghanaian masses, intensify homonegativity (Berlant 2011).

To be clear, the remains of colonial Christianity and its concomitant neocolonial political economy can be seen in the vibrant surge in African Christianity, which currently vies for legitimacy by competing with queer liberal projects and attempts by the African nation-states to assert sovereignty and self-determination. The tensions from the competition to redeem sasso as both postcolonial bodies independent of queer liberal projects and as queer bodies to be liberated from the predations of the homophobic nation-state epitomize the nervous conditions that constitute neoliberal Ghana.

Subjectivity Remixed: Sasso at the Nexus of Nervous Modernities

The documentary further envisions queer liberal modernity as more respectable and proper, characterizing Christian modernity as both improper and inhumane to sexual minorities. For instance, the medical doctor in search of funding opportunities highlights Christianity as one of the major obstacles preventing queer liberation, depicting Christianity as a barrier to health-care access for key populations such as MSM. Elevating queer liberal modernity over Christianity in this paradigm of modernity effectively displaces the "coeval" existence of these modernities (Fabian 1983). Therefore, the depiction of Hillary's experience as synecdochic of the experiences of gay men in the video reinforces the image of a homophobic Ghana in need of a cure from LGBT+ human rights missionaries. In this imagery, too, health workers are featured as utterly intolerant toward sexual minorities because of their Christian evangelizing of MSM. Steven, a sasso who works as a peer counselor, once described to me his experience with a nurse:

> One day, I went to see the doctor because I contracted a sexually transmitted infection (STI). I had been to that hospital before and did not like the way the nurses treated me. Initially, I did not want to go to the same hospital, but my options for going to clinic are limited where I reside. Once I arrived, I could hear the nursing attendants giggling and whispering to each other. I knew they were talking about me. Based on the way I was dressed, in my skinny jeans and tight velvet shirt, there is no way these ignorant people were not talking about me. When it was my turn, one of them boldly asked: "So, when are you guys going to stop doing these things?" I responded by asking what she meant by that. And she said, "The kind of thing that you do that brings you here for us to inspect your anus. You guys are going to go hell. Do you read the Bible at all, young man?" I kept silent because of how embarrassed I was. There were other patients around, and these illiterates had the nerve to publicly disclose my private affair. Sometimes they don't respect privacy, these Ghanaian nurses. They need to be educated on the importance of confidentiality.

Like Ambrose, Steven conveys the challenges MSM confront. In retrospect, he regrets not being able to lambast the nurses for embarrassing and making him feel guilty. However, his ability to narrate his experience to me places him in a position that authorizes him to interpellate health workers as ignorant, insensitive, and naive. This can also be read as an act of compensation engendered by his queer liberal subject position, which gives him a framework to have thought about demanding that he be treated justly. The charges he brings against the nurses are informed by how the latter allowed their religious backgrounds to narrow their understanding and attitudes toward MSM. Moreover, Steven perceived them as both witless and "un-Christian": "If they claim to be Christian then they should love their neighbors as they love themselves and not kill them instead."

Toward the end of the Aidspan clip, too, Hillary quotes a verse from the Bible to justify how ignorance breeds death. He says: "For the lack of knowledge, my people perish." In its original form, this verse, found in Hosea 4:6, states, "My people are destroyed for lack of knowledge: because thou hast rejected knowledge, I will also reject thee, that thou shalt be no priest to me: seeing thou hast forgotten the law of thy God, I will also forget thy children."[10] That he cites the quotation in the clip reveals how his Christian subjectivity coincides with his queer liberal self. This entanglement reflects the workings of his multiplicitous self and the coeval existence of selves that are supposedly figured as perpetually in conflict in larger religious and liberal discourses.

The quotation also paradoxically foregrounds the extent to which particular ideologies related to missionization, such as those that emphasize the significance of Victorian sexuality, trigger health workers' hesitation at offering MSM medical services, leading, sometimes, to their death to HIV/AIDS. At the same time, the denunciation of health workers' homonegative attitudes by Hillary, Ambrose, Ofori, and Steven signals their participation in projects that attempt to expose the vulnerabilities that sexual minorities in Ghana face, such as their lack of empowerment and the absence of reliable and efficient health services. In that regard, they embrace the brand of queer liberalism that animates Aidspan's politics. Thus, their commitments do not imply a foreclosure of their identities, as both African Christian and queer liberal modernities make us believe.

Hillary's open identification as gay and the revelation of his seropositivity in the video makes him appear "progressive" compared to most sasso. Within this framework of tolerance, the latter are no different from the health workers, given their repudiation of the clip. Hillary, then, emerges as a modern subject in the queer liberal sense of the word. However, such a reading, judging from the negative responses to the video, disarticulates and threatens the subject locations of the sasso who demanded that the video be removed from circulation. Their displeasure with the video emanates from it diminishing their amphibious subjectivity by fixing them as gay. Thus, while sasso articulate amphibious subjectivity in the face of the increased visibility of same-sex politics and concomitant homophobia, Aidspan evades the precarious contexts of their subject positions, as well as their decision to have their public secret out and circulating in the public domain.

I have demonstrated that in Jamestown, Hillary refrained from employing *gay* as a term of identification by embracing *sasso* instead. In sexual health projects such as the ones facilitated by Family Health International (FHI) in Ghana, he deployed *MSM* to capture his identity. However, in BURJ-related projects that aimed to empower sexual minorities, he self-identified as gay. Hillary's embodiment of these myriad identifications crystallized in the following conversation that I had with him regarding to whom he reveals his work and sexual proclivities:

> I am sasso because that is the term the people in Jamestown understand. Gay is sometimes too negative. Once you say you are gay people immediately think you get fucked in the ass. Yes, I am a believer of gay liberation in Ghana; however, in Jamestown I feel that when I say I am sasso, I do everybody and myself great good. Just think about this. How many people in the community do you think will understand the term "gay"? It is very recent, and I didn't know it existed until recently. I say it only when I am around human rights groups and people who I believe have some level of education and tolerance for effeminate men. Also, when I did the SHARP project for Family Health International, we used the term "MSM," because the organization did not want the Ministry of Health thinking that it was imposing gay identity on Ghanaian homosexuals. Sometimes, one must know when, where, and how to be gay. My mother knows I am sasso. If she knows I am gay at all, she wouldn't tell me in my face that she knows I sleep with men. And my church members love me and prefer I do not say these things around them. They, too, know very well that I sleep with men, but they know that it is not their business to castigate me for doing what I do.

We glean an amphibious subjectivity from this excerpt. Openly identifying as gay when he deemed convenient, he nervously subscribed to "the gay international" (Massad 2007) and Altman's notion of the "global gay" (Altman 1997). For Hillary, *gay* indexes a modern sexual lexicon perceived as the byproduct of Western LGBT+ humanitarian projects and media influences on Ghana. These shifts and movements from one self to the other are not always easy for sasso. Reflecting on the discomfort emerging from these transitions, he declares: "I remember getting caught for making sexual advances toward a guy at the bar by my cousin. I was quite embarrassed by that, but quickly diffused it by making a joke out of it."

In this situation, his public secret, that is, his homoeroticism, came out in the open, yet he had to quickly cloak it. The contradiction that inheres in Hillary's narrative, therefore, reflects the uneasy entanglements of both Christian and queer liberal modernities, and his locations in them.

Blending and Bleeding Subjectivities: When LGBT+ Freedom Breeds Homonegativity

The queer of color critic Chandan Reddy (2011) and critical and queer literary studies scholars like Jodi Melamed (2011) and Lauren Berlant (2011) have amplified the fractious relationship between liberalism and the production of violence. For Reddy, queer liberalism, circulating under the banner of queer liberal politics, produced a brand of freedom that concurrently produced violence, which reinforced a "whitewashed" queer normativity that disenfranchised queers of color. Melamed perspicaciously argues that liberal projects ultimately represented and destroyed the lives of the victims on whose behalf they spoke. Lauren Berlant (2011) uses "cruel optimism" to capture the insidious character of liberal projects that claim to produce freedom. I contend here that, in a similar vein, projects such as the ones pursued by Aidspan, despite their optimistic intentions, "blend and bleed" sasso constituencies in differing degrees.

The sense in which I use "blend and bleed" is different from how Bryant Keith Alexander deploys it in his fascinating elucidation of performing queerness together with Black masculinities in pedagogical settings (2006, 4). While Alexander uses "blend and bleed" to capture diversity, I use it here to uncover how queer liberal projects' inclination to blend in turn homogenizes rather than attends to the historically specific circumstances of subject formation and those structures of power to which both their pasts and presents are sutured. It is such homogenizing that bleeds, my metaphor for vulnerability and violence, the populations that are often represented as their target. I argue that Hillary and other sasso are on the receiving end of such invidious projects. To echo Melamed, the representation of sasso as vulnerable queer subjects who live lives that are at the mercy of the homophobic nation-state paradoxically heightens their visibility and precarity.

By blending and bleeding, therefore, queer liberal projects sidestep how amphibious self-making occurs among the target population for whom they pursue such freedom and liberatory projects. For instance, I have argued that some sasso continue to practice Christianity, deriving succor from it in times when Ghana is hit by harsh neoliberal reforms such as conditions imposed on the nation's spending by the World Bank, the IMF, and the European Union. In the midst of these economic shifts, Hillary and Ofori, for example, drew attention to their appreciation for Christianity, often invoking a popular Ghanaian moniker that "it shall be well in Jesus' name." These sasso identified as Christian, but they also fiercely indicted health workers who imposed their Christian beliefs on MSM. The complexity of their relation to Christianity is constitutive of the violence faced by minority subjects. In the case of sasso, the ability to choose when, where, and how to be queer in order to overcome the violence exacted by African Christian and queer liberal modernities shaped and was shaped by their amphibious subject positions. In their moments of need, they often went to church, fasted, and prayed, and, if need be, raged at neighbors who drew on the repertoire of Christianity to shame and ostracize them.

An active member of the Anglican Church in Jamestown, Hillary often spoke about how much he loved his church and his role in his congregation. In the summer of 2012, when I visited him in Jamestown one humid evening, he recounted his passion for his church.

> I really love my church. I make it a point to attend choir rehearsals every Wednesday and Saturday. I enjoy wearing the colorful robes with kente stripes, and also performing on Sundays and other special occasions are activities I love. Almost everyone who goes to my church knows how I appreciate being in the choir. For example, I am known for my reliability, and, as a result, I have gained a lot respect in the church. Whatever I do outside of the church stays there. I am aware some of the members in the choir know that I am sasso; however, they still like me for who I am. Although I have been confronted by some of the church elders in the past, most have been less critical of me over the years. Sometimes I tell myself that the Anglican Church here in Jamestown is truly a rewarding space to be sasso, especially as most of the mothers here have sons who are like me and do sasso.

In this account, Hillary shines a light on his active involvement in church activities. In this conversation, he does not openly self-describe as gay; instead, he deploys the term *sasso* to shroud his homoerotic inclinations in the context of the church. Although some members of his church were aware of his homoerotic encounters, they did not engage in open conversations. Sexual and erotic languages were often enmeshed in a latticework of figurative and proverbial vocabulary, especially when they were understood to be nonheteronormative (Epprecht 2008; Ashforth 2000).

Hillary's ability to harmonize his passions for church and for LGBT+ activism—presumably incongruent—in a seemingly seamless fashion reflects his capacity for self-styling. Drawing on the amphibious resources at his disposal, such as the convoluted meaning of *sasso* as a verb, noun, and an adjective, as well as his knack of disidentifying with heteronormative practices, he both curtails and minimizes homonegative responses likely to be thrown at his queer subject position. Such disidentificatory (Muñoz 1999) acts are enforced through competent phallic practices such as fatherhood, pretentious conformity, and marriage, all of which make one appear heteronormative.

Constricting the extent to which Hillary amphibiously self-fashioned, the documentary represents the tolerance of LGBT+ human rights as a mark of modernity undermined by Christian modernity. Thus, it ignores how these modernities overlap, albeit fractiously, in Hillary's life. Hillary's friends were aware of his HIV status. And their knowledge of his status was silenced in their quest to avoid marking him. His Christian stature and sasso awareness of his intense religiosity heightened their desire not to remove the curtain that covered his seropositivity. Residing in a context where being seropositive is represented as the result of one's amorous sexual practices, sasso, as a community, effectively acted to save Hillary's image. Foster, for instance, recounts that "Hillary would have done the same for anybody else. We sasso know how our culture is. Sometimes, we are better off keeping it among ourselves. Of course, there will be that gossip, but we always look out for each other if need be." Foster's narrative highlights Gyekye's (1987) emphasis on the value of the community for the individual and vice versa. It is indeed a compelling example.

Hillary ultimately authored himself in a manner suited to negotiating the multiple conditions he traversed, some of which were stifling, while others were liberating. For Aidspan, his subject position clarified the predicaments of gay men in Ghana, such as their travails with HIV. How are we to grapple with amphibious becoming as a contested practice that allows for, and at times complicates and implicates, queer self-making in postcolonial Ghana? And how can an appreciation of the milieus in which these multiple selves are enacted allow us to fathom, in a complicated fashion, how sasso mediate international NGOs such as Aidspan, local human rights NGOs such as BURJ, spiritual healers, medicine men, and even the ethnographer (myself)?

I conclude this chapter by returning to Macharia's litany of complaint, which expressed discontent at the presence of a desert in the emerging field of queer African studies, a desert that hankers for an oasis teeming with conceptual and ethnographic wetlands derived from African scholarship. In this chapter, I concur with Macharia's demand, illuminating how African philosophy, like the worldviews of sasso, is ignored in much of queer liberal scholarship and queer liberal politics of liberation. And, although a rereading of Gyekye's notion of "amphibious personhood" is significant, it too is insufficient in attempts at "queering Queer Africa," to quote Ugandan feminist Stella Nyanzi (2014). Yet Gyekye's intervention does provide a framework through which to understand that Hillary inhabits a lifeworld scrambled by ongoing collusions and collisions between neoliberalism and neocolonialism.

Thus, how might the strategies adopted by Hillary and other sasso both exemplify Gyekye's idea of amphibious identification and show its inadequacy? How is

Hillary's relationship with Aidspan, his family, friends, the ethnographer, and the cultural ecosystem a reflection of amphibious subjectivity? How are we to make sense of how his life *queers* African philosophy, anthropological conceptions of gender and sexuality, and queer African studies? In summation, how queer is Hillary, if he is at all? Aidspan evidently scrambles the scrambled milieus that shape sasso processes of queer self-making. Whichever way we seek to understand the scenario Hillary's multiple selves present us, it is important that we account for how he transcends as well as muddles tropes of suffering and victimhood.

Hillary's navigation of selves in environments rendered nervous by the cumulative impacts of a past of European colonial and Christian domination, and the accumulating impacts necessitated by present neocolonial and neoliberal articulations of modernity, make him complexly amphibious. Familiar with the self that exceeded homophobic environments during fieldwork, I understood that Hillary was a fierce advocate for sexual minorities and LGBT+ rights. He challenged anybody who disrespected sasso. That same person was also uninhibited about disclosing his sexual exploits to me. In fact, it is Hillary who first introduced me to the idea that "the sweetness of homoerotic sex is in its secrecy." Hence, if Hillary's presentation in the video emphasizes his painful ordeal with being HIV positive, then the documentary submerges his microsociological relationships with friends, family, and the multiplex nature of his ontology and instead foregrounds Hillary as a victim.

Hillary articulates different selves to different individuals and organizations at different times in order to create and re-create himself when and how he deems fit. Such performances may be configured as politically driven, informing claims to both heterosexual and homosexual citizenships in milieus that are clearly divided on the issue of queer citizenship. They also enable queer self-fashioning among sasso in postcolonial Ghana in ways constitutive of becoming and unbecoming, in other words, the performance of what Stuart Hall refers to as an "unfinished closure" (1987, 6). Aidspan's imperative to reduce Hillary to his gay identity is tantamount to cutting out huge chunks of his life. As Taussig reminds us, "If it is the cut that makes the energy in the system both visible and active, then we should be aware of cuts in language, strange accidents and contingencies" (1999, 5).

The documentary slices out important dimensions of Hillary's life, neglecting the complexity of his subjectivity; in doing so, it makes visible that which is known but cannot be accounted for by the video—the public secret. The documentary, then, stages a paradox. It "beatifies" Hillary, and, in so doing, pathologizes the sociopolitical and cultural milieu that supposedly disenfranchises sexual minorities from engaging in queer self-making. Hillary emerges as a "saint," whereas the sasso who vociferously demanded that the video be pulled down emerge as "ungrateful sexual minorities," backward and no different from the homophobes who subject them to antihomosexual oppression. Finally, that sasso sanction the video by requesting that it be removed from the virtual public sphere not only enforces a claim to queer citizenship but also highlights the extent to which coevalness does not imply the absence of power based on race, class, gender, and one's location on the globe.

Sasso reactions to the Aidspan video reveal how a well-intentioned project can have negative consequences by representing and destroying the bodies that are the targets of human rights rescue missions. The clip may possess the potential to unveil some of the issues faced by sexual minorities—which it undoubtedly does—but the demands made by sasso that the video be removed from YouTube and other internet platforms reveal that the film did compromise their complex selves. The Aidspan exposure of sasso echoes Ashley Currier's point on the paradoxes of visibility and invisibility as they play out in LGBT+ human rights projects. For Currier, "Visibility and invisibility are not completely separable from one another analytically. Invoking public visibility also implicates those who are not visible and structures that generate visibility" (2012, 7). What work does visibility or invisibility do, and who stands to benefit or not benefit from structures that present opportunities and challenges to visibility?

Prince's unequivocal statement below, which is drawn from a phone conversation during the uproar triggered by the video, sums up my arguments in this chapter.

> Kwame, I don't understand why these people don't really get us. As for me, I think it is important that they recognize that if we say we are gay, we say so because sometimes it is nearly the English equivalent of sasso, perhaps because gay people are effeminate and not necessarily because they have sex with men. Of course, if having sex with men can be part of your gay identity, and you are able to throw both your effeminateness and who you have sex with out in the public together that is fine, I wouldn't shame you. Over there [by which he means in the West], it is OK to do that. In Ghana things operate differently, although these things have changed because of, you know, that alleged conference thing which happened in Koforidua about nine years ago, when there was an allegation in the media that some international gay organization had plans to organize a conference. Before, we could be sasso [effeminate selves] in public and do sasso [engage in homoerotic sex] with our boyfriends in our bedrooms, alleyways, public bathrooms, football fields at night, and even the bushes. Nobody dared to challenge us. These days, things are different, because to be sasso means to be an effeminate man who has sex with men. It means to be gay, and that can make people look at you differently. By that I mean it fixes your reputation, you are no longer sasso but you are gay. That, in a way, was just what that documentary video did to the sasso who it associated with Hillary. As for Hillary, he is big mouthed, and it is like he knew he was going to die and leave us with these troubles. What I am therefore saying is that it would be wrong to tell me to go tell my mother, my father, my brother, and my sister that I am gay. I believe that they all know that already, because I used to be called Kwadwo Besia while growing up in my village. Just as I am OK with hearing other sasso say they are gay, I believe it is their decision to make regarding when is the appropriate moment to say so. When we go to outdoorings, for example, the people we encounter mostly know what we do in our private lives. But when they see us in a video like that, what do you think they

> will say, especially when I did not want my face plastered on some video that I didn't know was going to be made public, especially to Ghanaians? The internet is a place where things are hard to disappear; these people should learn to respect us.

Prince's concern shines light on how the video commits violence against sasso. As I write this, the video is still accessible online, and, Aidspan, it appears, is not inclined to delete it. The video made sasso identities monolithic, flattening out the complex constitution of their subjectivity as self-identified effeminate men, leaving them gravely embittered because it emphasized their sexual proclivities. Prince's analysis of the video also clearly shows how it remains insensitive to the cultural parameters within which sasso operated as self-identified effeminate men. And as with Hillary, Prince's insightful observation is nothing short of a theoretical overture.

Extrapolating from Hillary's experiences, we can infer how and why sasso identify in a particular way at a given time, as they amphibiously navigate transnational LGBT+ human rights activism and its concomitant cruel optimism, often belied by homonegativity. Sasso response to the Aidspan video clip signaled their desire to remake themselves in an unprecedented situation in which homophobia and ostracism were anticipated. Moreover, the clip consolidated the stereotype that effeminacy was a denominator for gay identity, reinforcing the notion that gay men were more likely to be infected with or living with HIV, as could be surmised from Hillary's declaration. In Jamestown, assumptions about effeminacy are murkier and not clearly defined. The suburb is, therefore, a site of contradictions, where being an amphibious subject intermingles with African Christian, queer liberal, and epidemiological subjectivities, among others; this complexity was flattened out by a video bearing the title *I Didn't Want to Bring Shame on My Family: Being Gay in Ghana.*

4

The Paradox of Rituals

Queer Possibilities in Heteronormative Scenes

> You can't be a sasso and not be interested in an outdooring, a wedding, or a funeral, especially when they involve a sasso, their relative, or friend. These occasions are opportunities for us to get together and remind ourselves that life isn't too bad. That we are valued and loved. How would these events look without us? Think about it!
>
> —KISSI (MARCH 2014)

> But the constantly blurry, unfinished character of the birthday text is due not only to its palimpsestic nature but also to how its guiding metaphoric terms . . . literally and figuratively keep in constant motion.
>
> —OMISE'EKE NATASHA TINSLEY, *THIEFING SUGAR* (2010, 50)

> By no means unique to the Caribbean region, this fetishization of Carnival as the principal site of sexual possibility tends to foreclose—even in polite conversation—any other possibilities for an engagement with same-sex desiring communities.
>
> —LYNDON GILL (2018, 31)

In summer 2013, a few weeks into fieldwork, Kobby, my key informant, invited me to an *outdooring* (birth ritual/naming ceremony). It was held on a Saturday evening at Clubhouse. I was not expecting Kobby's invitation. On the day of the event, I was wrapping up my interviews with sasso when he asked me to join him. Truly delighted about the event, he noted that the outdooring would be very "sasso in character" because the couple whose child was being named are sasso. "They are also very popular in the community," he claimed, "because they are financially well off, and renowned for their industriousness." Kobby's description of the event and the cast of characters surprised me. I wondered how a seemingly heterosexual couple could be sasso, let alone have children of their own. Because Kobby's statement appeared utterly contradictory, I asked, "If they are sasso, then are they men who have sex with men or are they merely self-identified effeminate men?" Kobby replied, "No, they are a male and female couple. I know that sounds strange. However, the man is very feminine and the woman is very masculine. She was an outstanding footballer while in secondary school. Here in Jamestown, she is renowned because of her past career. Her husband runs his own business ventures in the community, which includes a provision store and a little restaurant around Clubhouse."

Not only did this revelation pique my ethnographic curiosity, but it also highlighted how sasso subjectivities and the linguistic conventions about the term *sasso* are fluid. Underscoring the fact that sasso do not self-identify only as effeminate men, this revelation also provided an opening through which to perceive both women who have sex with women and women who exhibit "masculine-looking" features as an integral part of the sasso universe. Kobby's description of the wife corroborated observations made by anthropologists Kathleen O'Mara (2013) and Serena Dankwa (2009, 2021) in their study of female masculinity in Accra. Jamestown, the context of my study, was a part of varied networks of female intimacies that competed and were entangled with heterosexual formations. And rites of transition such as weddings, funerals, and outdoorings made these networks possible. As Kissi describes in the first epigraph, these events are a defining feature of sasso life.

A few months after the outdooring, Kissi, a popular sasso who lived in Jamestown, invited me to participate in a birthday celebration. He was throwing the celebration to commemorate his thirtieth birthday. The event attracted a motley crew of individuals in Jamestown and beyond. Much like the outdooring, the birthday brought sasso together in a manner that paradoxically highlighted while simultaneously flattening such differences. The celebration also occasioned the unapologetic display of effeminacy, which wouldn't have been possible in other settings. At the party, sasso publicly discussed their engagement in homoerotic practices, admissions normally limited to their own circles. Bringing together a cast of sasso and nonsasso characters, the birthday party, like the outdooring, blurred distinctions established by gender, sexual orientation, ethnicity, and religious affiliation, among other identifications. In a manner reminiscent of Tinsley's (2010) observation in the second epigraph, Kissi's birthday was a "text" that not only invoked the palimpsestic character of the birthday party but also remixed it by infusing it with Ghanaian content.

Life transition rituals and the spaces in which they occur are themselves paradoxical settings that engender possibilities for queer self-fashioning, thus muddling the boundaries between heteroerotic and homoerotic desires and practices. In effect, the two rituals discussed here share characteristics with what the French folklorist Arnold Van Gennep (1961) calls "rites of passage." For Van Gennep, these are "rites which accompany every change of place, state, social position and age"

(Van Gennep 1960, 8; Turner 1969). And, as the religious studies historian Philippe Buc (2001) suggests: "Rituals are a complicated point of entry," allowing us access to the contradictory worlds that sasso traverse. Like the threshold or the door, rituals are the entrance and exits into worlds colliding and colluding coterminously.

My ethnographic observations of these Ghana-centered ceremonies flesh out the interventions by Victor Turner (1969) and Mikhail Bakhtin (1984), who theorize ritual and carnival, respectively. I outline how these ritual practices bring same-sex desire to life in apparently heteronormative spaces while amplifying the unimagined affinities between heteroerotic and homoerotic desire. I am interested, then, more in the rituals here than the theories offered by these white theorists. Like the anthropologist Lyndon Gill, who carefully highlights the fecund queer possibilities that yield from the carnival in Trinidad and Tobago, elaborated in the third epigraph, I, too, am interested in how nonnormative desire and intimacies are expressed in heteronormative domains that supposedly discipline nonheteronormativity. My reliance on the theoretical analyses of carnival and ritual offered by Turner and Bakhtin may appear to go against the grain of my investment in and preoccupation with African theorists, specifically Kwame Gyekye and his theory of "amphibious personhood." I turn to these white theorists merely to demonstrate how the ceremonies that animate this chapter not only breathe life into their abstract interventions but also anticipate their theorizations. In effect, the main characters in these rituals—Kissi, the sasso couple whose baby is christened, and the wider cast of sasso who actively engage in these events—bring vibrant meanings to the theories of liminality and carnival espoused by Victor Turner and Mikhail Bakhtin while simultaneously demonstrating the fleshiness of theory.

While the actual details of these ceremonies may appear far less important than what they signify, if one observes the broad outlines of these ceremonies, one is not likely to see any detail that looks appreciably different from other such rituals around the world. Indeed, these microdifferences, or the articulation of globally recognized similarities, matter here because they tell whole and complex stories. At a christening ceremony, for example, one is likely to see parents, grandparents, relatives, and friends all in attendance to welcome the child and commit them to the social community. And yet, with the outdooring and birthday celebration considered here, the principles undergirding them make all the difference, because the principles are outside characteristically heteronormative occasions and arrangements, including the spaces in which they are held.

I provide the general outlines of a typical outdooring among the Ga, then proceed to describe the space in which the outdooring I observed occurred—Clubhouse. First, I ask how sasso presence at Clubhouse mark it as a tangibly queer geography, and second, how the celebration makes visible those queer contours of the bar and the location in which it is nested. Like the outdooring and birthday analyzed here, I maintain that Clubhouse allowed for sasso subject formations to blur those boundaries between the sacred and the profane, heterosexual and homosexual, Christian and un-Christian, and so forth. Further, as Kissi indicates, one cannot wholly understand ceremonies such as outdoorings, weddings, and funerals without sasso. In fact, they are ubiquitous in sasso lives.

THE CONTOURS OF AN OUTDOORING

Indeed, the coordinates of a typical outdooring resemble Van Gennep's description of birth rituals as "ceremonies for the newborn child" which, he suggests, "involve a sequence of rites of separation, transition, and incorporation" (1960, 50). The outdooring ceremony is thus a ritual to welcome and initiate the newborn into the world of humans, and during the ceremony "not only is the newborn child considered 'sacred,' she is not even seen to exist until she has 'obtained the favor of all those present'" (Van Gennep 1960, 50). The term *outdoor* is used in Ghanaian parlance to signal the transition of the baby from the world of the yet-to-be-born to the world of the living, to paraphrase the words of the Ghanaian religious scholar Kofi Asare Opoku (1978). Here, it is important to note that the outdooring ceremony, much like christening ceremonies elsewhere in the world, is not typical among the Ga. Indeed, other ethnic groups in Ghana share some of the features or characteristics of this ritual.

Known among the Ga as *kpodjiemo*, which means "transitioning through" or "coming out of the door," the typical outdooring, according to Clare Korkor Fayorsey, unfolds as follows:

> The eighth day after the birth of a child, it is taken over to its father's *wekushia* or family house for the naming ceremony. A delegation of elders of the maternal line, that is both male and female relations of the baby's mother, accompany the baby to its father's *wekushia*. The baby is given to a renowned personality or elder of the family. This elder must have an admirable reputation because it is believed that the baby takes on the character of the person who names it. Thus, a baby girl is named by a woman and baby boy by a man. (1992, 25)

Indeed, the event I observed shared some of the characteristics Fayorsey (1992) describes. On the eighth day following the birth of a child, the newborn is outdoored at sunrise. Although the event I observed was held in the evening, it was the continuation of a ceremony that had begun in the early morning hours. The Ga are one of several patrilineal ethnic groups in Ghana, reckoning kinship ties through the male line, which explains why the event I attended was held in the compound of the house of the newborn child's paternal grandparent. As the Ga historian A. A. Amartey has observed, generally, four main figures participate in the event, including the paternal grandfather, two *otsiame* (linguists), and the godfather or godmother, depending on child's gender (1985). In the outdooring I witnessed, the otsiame, or MC, was a sasso, chosen specifically for his unrivaled oratorical gifts.

The setup for the outdooring itself was elegant, featuring canopies and gazebos that adorned the street snaking through the vicinity of Clubhouse. An open space, much like a compound or courtyard, was carved out for dancing and merriment, and, not surprisingly, all activities on the program gravitated there. The outdooring rerouted traffic, thus altering the meaning of the street and its signification to the community in that moment. The social interactions and differences that occurred there bore the characteristics of another kind of "middle passage," that space of transition which Victor Turner (1969) illuminates in his analysis of ritual in *The Ritual Process: Structure and Anti-Structure*. My intention is not to belabor Gennep's and Turner's formulations of liminality, but to show how the spaces of ritual, described by the latter as those intervening moments in the ordinary, are coterminously sites of contentment for sasso (Turner 1974, 273).

It is in the in-between domains of these ceremonies that communitas, which characterizes relationships between those undergoing the ritual transition process, occurs. I use *ritual* here rather carefully because of the various questions it generates in anthropology. I tend to accept Buc's warnings about the inadequacies of using ritual too loosely as a hermeneutic for assessing all social assemblages (2001). Hence, while I am especially mindful of its inadequacies in the context that I am examining, the kpodjiemo I observed engendered a kaleidoscope of subjectivities transected by ethnicity, gender, sexual orientation, age, religion, and class. The mishmash that ensued, to echo Bakhtin, was "a characteristic logic, the peculiar logic of the inside out, of the turnabout, of a continual shifting from top to bottom, from front to rear, of numerous parodies of travesties, humiliations, profanations, comic crownings and uncrownings" (1974, 11). These plays unfolded in the space of Clubhouse, which brought together people from all walks of life.

SITUATING CLUBHOUSE, PLOTTING AN OUTDOORING

I began this chapter by indicating that Kobby took me to Clubhouse for the outdooring. Clubhouse is a bar in Jamestown, located in an area also called "Clubhouse," largely because of its popularity. Clubhouse was a few blocks away from Wato, the rooftop bar situated at the intersection of Jamestown and the general post office, which sat on the fringes of the central business district (CBD). I conducted interviews with sasso at Wato because of its proximity to Tema Station, the major bus terminal in the city. Clubhouse had the undisputed reputation of being a suitable location for celebrations such as outdoorings, funerals, wedding receptions, and other revelries. That popularity surely explains why it was the site selected for the outdooring I attended.

Clubhouse, bar and area alike, attracts sasso from all walks of life, mainly because the owner brazenly embraces this varied clientele. Unlike other bars, where sasso felt obligated and pressured to act in line with the expectations of proper gender behavior, such as acting in a masculine manner, Clubhouse mostly accommodated sasso, encouraging them not to fear public reproach and retribution. Essentially, the bar served as a space in which the rules of hegemonic masculinity, inflexible gender ontologies, and Christological assumptions about propriety were suspended. Like the space of the carnival, to echo Bakhtin, Clubhouse functioned as a domain of play and mockery; in many instances, the sasso who gathered there made fun of heteronormativity (1984). It was not surprising that Kobby asked me to go out there with him, as he was of the conviction that it was a particularly comfortable space for sasso. The sasso who patronized Clubhouse did so in the company of their consorts, or "boyfriends." Together, they laughed, fought, engaged in intimate banter, and resolved tensions and problems, whether economic, familial, spiritual, or health related. Clubhouse also served as a therapeutic space where sasso could vent their outrage at the social, moral, political, economic, sexual, and religious restrictions on their lives.

Blurring the Sacred and Profane

First, Clubhouse—both the bar and the vicinity in which it is embedded—is imbued with an everyday ordinariness. Second, an occasion like the outdooring transforms this profane geography into a sacred domain. In short, Clubhouse serves as a useful ethnographic example of how the quotidian and the sacred interweave. At the end of a regular working day, Clubhouse is filled with bar regulars, consisting mostly of government employees and people employed in financial institutions and NGOs in and around the CBD, as well as people in the informal sector such as area fishermen. While most of these men identified as heterosexual, some clandestinely engaged in homoeroticism. There were the gentors, who quite frequently had discreet encounters with sasso. These men, as I have elaborated in an earlier chapter, held regular jobs, had a steady income stream, and were also mostly married to women in the community. On certain occasions, the sasso who patronized Clubhouse were also in the company of logs. The latter mostly resided in Jamestown or in neighboring suburbs and found Clubhouse a relaxing place to hang out and get free drinks from their sasso "boyfriends."

Insiders and Outsiders: Navigating Queer Self-Practice in an Indeterminate Space

Some Clubhouse patrons preferred to stay indoors, where they would not be seen from the street, to avoid being branded as un-Christian and uncouth for drinking alcohol. Most Ghanaian Christians reprimand people who patronize drinking bars, and from their perspective bar patrons are sinful. To these Christians, alcohol consumption is unholy and unwholesome (Acheampong 1996). Although sasso are often already pronounced guilty in this Christian moral universe, Clubhouse remained a safe space for them. Ishmael, a Clubhouse regular and a sasso who was self-employed as a graphic artist, describes this ambiguity.

> Almost all the sasso I know in Accra either go there or will direct someone else to go there because of how accommodating the staff are. There, we can fight, we commune, some steal boyfriends; in fact, we do so many countless things there. After church, some of us will occasionally converge there to grab a cold beer. I don't believe that drinking a beer makes one a sinner as many Ghanaians make it appear. No, it does not! Drinking in moderation is all one needs. If the uptight Christian thinks I am a sinner because I drink, then what will they do when they discover that I do sasso, that I enjoy having sex with men. I am sure they will say I will go to hell as a result. Such they will without hesitation. So, if I come to Clubhouse and you decide to call me a sinner, then it is up to you. Take your hypocrisy to your room. When I am there, I sit outside, that way I can observe all the juicy men who walk by. There are those who prefer to sit inside because they want to avoid as much as possible the prying eyes and the gossipy mouths of the residents who live around the bar.

Ishmael's story makes apparent that at Clubhouse, the Christian self is conceived as oppositional to the self that consumes alcohol, as well as oppositional to the self that engages in homoerotic sexual relations. Ishmael's nimble self-styling, however, exemplifies amphibious self-making, wherein he navigates among seemingly contradictory selves. While the indoor section of Clubhouse provided a cover for those patrons who sought to conceal their alcohol consumption, this inside-outside divide was by no means rigid. Indeed, clients occasionally spilled over from one section of the bar to the other. Further, it was clear that sasso preferred to while away their time outdoors. This afforded them a view of the men in the community who strolled up and down the street and sometimes trickled in and out of Clubhouse. For the most part, these men were well sculpted and built, perhaps because of their profession as pugilists or fishermen. Ayitey, one of the regulars at Clubhouse, remarked that some of the men who strutted along the street were readily available for "fast sex": "To make a move, just politely ask them over, and if you have some money buy them free drinks. Everybody likes a cold and chill beer when the weather is sizzling hot. After two or three bottles of Club Beer, plus a stick of spicy khebab, if you are lucky, you have your man for the day, two, or forever. The guy will do whatever you tell them to. It is like you have put them under a spell."

Ayitey's description challenges the idea that masculinity was reducible to acting manly. Having access to financial capital, they were able to maneuver their way easily around men. Ayitey owned a hairdressing salon which provided him the steady income that allowed him easy access to logs. That he was more financially independent than the logs shored up his masculinity despite his effeminate traits.

Although Clubhouse served as a crucial cruising spot for sasso, it was not safe. Kofi described how he was once attacked by an elderly man who issued homophobic epithets at him for being too loud and acting effeminately. In the moment of the attack, Kofi recalls that he "desisted from reprimanding him because he was an old man. He could literally be my grandfather. So, we had to show him some respect. In fact, at the time, we wanted to verbally attack him but that would have created some drama. Moreover, we did not want to create a scene because we respect the owner of Clubhouse." Kofi's confrontation highlights the fact that no "safe space" existed entirely; even Clubhouse could provide only limited security from heterosexual sanctions. Such realities did not prevent him and other sasso from patronizing the bar, perhaps because even though the gendered performances on display at the Clubhouse reinforced hegemonic masculinity, the space paradoxically enabled homoerotic possibilities.

There were occasions when sasso undertook hilarious performances that rehearsed the sexual positions of the logs and gentors they had sex with. Laughter was for them a crucial coping mechanism that allowed them to challenge the myth that all Ghanaian men were heterosexual. In his critique of how Christian propriety stifles the subject's ability to self-style, Mikhail Bakhtin elaborates on how laughter emerges as an important strategy for dealing with church symbols and rituals that inhibit the regeneration and renewal of the body. As Bakhtin notes: "Foolishness and folly, that is laughter, are directly described as 'man's second nature' and are opposed to the monolith of the Christian cult and ideology" (1984, 75).

Clubhouse not only afforded sasso the opportunity to deride Christian ideas on proper masculine behavior, etiquette, and alcohol consumption, but also was spatially a "vent for laughter." In this domain, to reiterate Bakhtin, "the material bodily principle linked with it then enjoyed complete freedom" (1984, 75). Sasso fashioned themselves freely in this space despite the occasional acts of resistance and reprisal they faced from sections of the heteronormative public. Clubhouse arguably allowed sasso the freedom to mock men who were passive in the situation of sexual intercourse yet exuded virility in the public sphere of Jamestown. In this geography, "ritual leveling and humiliation," to use Turner's (1969) phrase, occurred, as sasso exposed logs and gentors, who pretended not to have anything to do with them. In effect, at Clubhouse, sasso "outed" those men who preferred to hide inside their heteromasculine shells, revealing their public secret and flaunting it on the streets of Jamestown. There, sasso unapologetically expressed their effeminacy all the while deriding those gentors and logs believed to be masking their homoerotic leanings. In other words, they exposed the "true colors" of the men who clandestinely engaged them for sex while participating in the homophobic outrage directed at sasso in particular and the LGBT+ community in general.

Clubhouse as a Ritual Space: Transfiguring the Ordinary into Queer Possibility

The outdooring I witnessed with Kobby was not the first rite of passage to have occurred in the vicinity of Clubhouse. In fact, the space was normally filled with throngs of people attending events ranging from weddings to funerals every weekend. During these occasions, the area looked colorful, as guests attending events were decked in the most elaborate and sophisticated outfits. When we arrived,

Kobby stopped to say hello to a group of women sitting together at the bar, many of whom were considerably older. Drinking large bottles of Club Beer, a popular alcoholic beverage in Ghana, the women were adorned in beautiful white satin wrappers, sewn and decorated with pink-colored shells and cowries. They wore makeup that highlighted the contours of their facial features and lip glosses that highlighted their lips. Some donned the local, more modernized version of *kaba* and *slit*,[1] which, very fitting, revealed their voluptuous curves. Others wore outfits ranging from kente, African, and Holland wax prints to smocks and satin robes. Some of the women donned *asho-oke*, the striking Nigerian headgear widely in vogue in Ghana.

The women with whom Kobby interacted had doctored their skins with creams meant to lighten their complexions in a manner that pronounced their femininity. While skin bleaching is a common phenomenon in Ghana, it is particularly widespread among Ga women (Pierre 2013). The practice of skin bleaching, however, does not occur in a vacuum. As Jemima Pierre avers: "To understand the sociocultural politics of contemporary skin bleaching in Ghana, we have to grapple with the ways that global racial meanings, with ideologies of whiteness as power, 'constitute broad sociopolitical realms with control over the most intimate details of daily life in various localities'" (Pierre 2013, 110, quoting Burke 1996, 159).

To fathom why these women bleached excessively, then, will be to embed them in this matrix of global colorism and anti-Blackness, leftovers of colonialism and racial capitalism. Thus, they embodied a femininity that flouted the expectations of authentic, proper, and modest Christian womanhood while reinforcing notions of beauty rooted in anti-Blackness. I am aware that the management of the body in several Christian contexts in Ghana is ambivalently hinged to avoiding excessive material consumption. Christian women are required to be proper and virtuous, refraining from drinking alcoholic beverages in the public sphere and avoiding conspicuous consumption at all cost. In this framework, too, wearing too much makeup was acknowledged as an immodest way of conveying one's beauty. However, the women at the outdooring contravened this rule. By wearing makeup and bleaching, expressions of conspicuous investment in physical appearance, these women contradicted the social expectation that women should appear plain and modest.

As we walked among the outdooring guests, we ran into Kissi, who spiritedly gestured that we join him. For the occasion, he was decked in an outfit that attracted the attention of the crowd. He wore a beautiful white satin robe embroidered with colorful beads, bought during one of his business trips to Lagos. An orange hat and dark shades completed the look. Because of his stature in Jamestown, Kissi had a large following. At the event, Kissi served as the fashion police, evaluating the outfits worn by guests. Moreover, he unreservedly shared how most of the women at the event were sasso. Not bothered by the fact that guests might hear him, he declared: "Kwame, you see these women who are gorgeously dressed, and are acting like they have dressed up for men to pick them up, well you should know that they are our sisters. Do not be deceived, because they do sasso too." The ladies, unperturbed by Kissi's utterance, waved back at me to signal that they could care less about Kissi letting their public secret out in the open. After all, almost all the guests at the event were sasso, including the couple whose child was being christened. At events like this outdooring, comedies such as the one displayed by Kissi were integral to the ceremonial quilt and the "carnivalesque humor" undergirding such rituals (Bakhtin 1984, 15).

During the ceremony, Kobby and Kissi left to engage Prosper, the sasso in charge of organizing the outdooring, who assigned them various tasks: counting the number of guests, serving food, and receiving gifts. Kobby and Kissi's desire to play a role at the event demonstrates sasso support for each other and how the success of rituals like the outdooring was a significant matter to them. In the sasso world, it was presumed that sasso added a tinge of glamour and decorum to events like this one. The demand for sasso services resulted from the understanding that they possessed efficient organizational skills, were reliable and industrious in the face of pressure, and brought festive tones and color to the ritual.

The outdooring provided an important setting for amphibious self-styling. Since the couple whose newborn child was being named were sasso, the event paradoxically both conventionalized and rendered unconventional the hegemonic tropes of being a proper woman or man in postcolonial Ghana. Notably, in features and looks, the father of the newborn child was stereotypically effeminate, and the mother was stereotypically masculine. Together, they challenged the prevailing inflexible assumptions around gender and physicality, as well as such labels as LGBT+. How then do we comprehend the consummation of a queer heterosexual couple, especially when an outdooring ceremony continues to fortify the foundations of heteronormativity?

The Liminal Process and Culinary and Polyvocal Remixing

Besides flattening out ethnic, religious, and sartorial practices, the outdooring also functioned as a space where foods associated with different ethnolinguistic groups in Ghana were served. There was *jollof rice*, a dish originating among the Wolof people of Senegal, as well as *kenkey* and *banku*, predominantly Ga and Ewe staples. Those who preferred *fufu* and *ampesi* (boiled yams and plantains), originally Akan dishes, were treated to these. *Tuo-zaafi*, a dish known among the ethnic groups of Northern Ghana, was given to those who desired it. Arguably, the sartorial and culinary transections enabled the renewal and reintegration of multiplex ways of being and embodiment.

The MC for the event was Patrick, a sasso from Jamestown whose oratorical gifts were deemed unparalleled. In his role as the MC, he wove Ga, English, Twi, Hausa, French, and more to emphasize his polyglottic character. Ga is the dominant language spoken in Jamestown, yet Patrick code-switched during the outdooring in a manner that affirmed his linguistic prowess and dexterity. Just as griots do in other parts of West Africa, Patrick showed off his linguistic skills in the songs he sang and the appellations he rained on guests. This versatility reflected his desire to impress hosts and guests alike. Against this backdrop, if the outdooring was a site that evoked both antistructural and carnivalesque traits, Patrick's ability to speak in languages that were not indigenous to Jamestown made the outdooring ritual a canvas of linguistic ingenuity.

As the ceremony unfolded, sasso showered appellations on the couple for having their third child. Unquestionably, this extension of adulation was an acknowledgment of their being successful in the phallic race toward fatherhood (Adomako Ampofo, Okyerefo, and Pervarah 2009). I am aware of the ostracism and stigma associated with childless women here. Thus, I do not intend, whatsoever, to let my analysis discriminate against women's reproductive success. I aver, however, that the moral economy of patriarchy rewards men who accumulate procreative capital by fathering children biologically. The chorus directed at the couple, nevertheless, emphasized the phallic capital of the husband, seeing as the newborn was his third child.

The MC intermittently interrupted the chorus from the crowd, politely demanding that the shouts and accolades be accompanied by money and gifts for the couple. In this moment of jubilation, the crowd reveled in the fact that an effeminate-looking man and a masculine-looking woman were introducing their third child to the world. And since self-identified effeminate men are regarded as "failed men" because of their effeminacy, I believe the event was a celebration of the couple's win in the phallic competition for children. Following these dramatic cultural enactments, the MC invited the couple into the center of the ceremonial space, asking them to dance together. Sasso and guests at the event moved to the dance floor to express their support. The song track of the event consisted of gospel, R&B, hip-hop, hip-life, and hi-life. The tapestry of unlikely musical and melodious compositions magnified the antistructural nature of this space (Turner 1974; Deflem 1991).

To climax the outdooring, the newborn was brought out of hiding, where he had been kept for seven days with his mother. The guests greeted and embraced this moment with loud shouts and ululations, accompanied by claps and standing ovations. The baby was clutched in the bosom of his mother, who stood next to her husband. Before the couple stood an elderly man. As per tradition, it was the duty the oldest surviving male in the paternal family to name the child. This involved invoking incantations that assured the child of protection in a world animated by humans and supernatural forces and relatives and nonrelatives. Born to a nonnormative heterosexual couple, the baby, following the naming ritual, was "thrown into a world" populated by sasso and members of Jamestown. Here was a world in which the nonnormative and normative, citizens and dissidents, transgressive and compliant, appeared seamless, and yet they were also simultaneously competing presences and copresences.

The outdooring culminated with the naming of the newborn child. In Ghana, newborn children are named after the day on which they were born, not the day of the celebration of outdooring. And since the child was born on Monday, he was named Kwadwo, or Kojo, which, as I discussed in the first chapter of this book, translates as "calm male child." Additionally, he was assigned an ancestral appellation. Among the Akan of Ghana, a newborn is exposed to various objects which belonged to deceased family members; the choice made by the newborn identifies them with one of their ancestors. It is precisely this rite that incorporates the newborn into the world of the living—their family, in particular. The same case can be made of the Ga, who, given their proximity and interactions with the Akan have over time embraced aspects of Akan customs.

The outdooring ceremony described renders untidy those neat distinctions between heterosexuality and homosexuality, yet it also establishes differences between them, especially as they are sites at which the newborn child is gendered. Thus, while the outdooring might be ultimately read as creating a space of impossibility because it potentially constricts sasso subjectivities, its carnivalesque and liminal characteristics inevitably create just the opposite: a space of possibility. There, amphibious subjectivity became tangible.

RIVAL GEOGRAPHIES: BIRTHDAYS AND QUEER SELF-MAKING

Like the outdooring ceremony, birthdays are celebrations that teem with contentment and joy for sasso, even in the face of homonegative onslaughts waged by the state, church, and sections of civil society. Thus, the spaces created by these events constitute "rival geographies" that allow sasso to bond and renew their connections despite the adversity and uncertainty created by a state hell-bent on criminalizing being LGBT+. The Black feminist historian Stephanie Camp (2002), drawing on Edward Said's notion of "rival geography," demonstrates the extent to which the enslaved on plantations in America created geographies that rivaled the rigid and dehumanizing spaces constructed by slaveholders. Said had originally used the term to capture anticolonial resistance to colonial occupation (Said 1978). Riffing off of Said, Camp observes that enslaved men and women "together, but differently, took flight to the very woods and swamps that planters intended to be the borders of the plantation's 'geography of containment'" (2002, 535). The spaces in which the celebrations I discuss here occur are similarly rival geographies. In fact, they vie for a presence that sasso orchestrate in the shadows of heteronormativity.

I attended Kissi's birthday party one hot Friday evening during the harmattan season just as the thick gust of fog hovering over Jamestown was succumbing to the cool breeze coming from the ocean. Kissi was known in the community for his entrepreneurial virtuosity. He managed a boutique in the heart of Jamestown called Splendid Expressions, which also served as a base for sasso in the same way Terry's shop, discussed in chapter 2, was a haven for sasso seeking refuge in Accra. Kissi's shop was housed in a shipping container on the fringes of Salaga market in Swalaba, a subdivision of Jamestown. The profits from his business enabled him to display his wealth, especially during events such as weddings, birth ceremonies, funerals, birthday celebrations, and popular cultural events in and around Accra.

"A Decorated Donkey Cannot Be an Ass": Sasso as Sartorial Subjects

Kissi often decked himself out in perfectly tailored clothing made by other sasso and tailors known to him in the vicinity of Jamestown, where customized clothing was quite affordable compared with those exorbitant prices charged in the upscale and expatriate areas in Accra. Kissi's sartorial sensibility was unmatched among sasso. A self-described fashionista, he prided himself on introducing elaborate, flamboyant styles that appealed to sasso and nonsasso alike, although most sasso could not afford them.[2] In response to my question about his fascination with fashion, he answered:

> Kwame, as humans, dresses are the houses we live in. The body needs a place to stay, and clothing is the house. The decoration of your house speaks volumes about your personality and your location in the community. You may come from a place like Jamestown. However, what you wear can make you stand out even if you're not rich. I may come from a place that is regarded as a low-income community. However, whenever I am in that dress and I show up at that wedding event with another guest living in, say, an upscale area in Accra, I am unmatched.

While I was fascinated by Kissi's unqualified obsession with clothing, I was equally spellbound by his thoughtful understanding of the place of clothing in the world, particularly in a setting like Jamestown. I was taken especially with his rejection of the local aphorism that "a decorated donkey is still an ass."

> My problem with people who think that they have it all is that they assume because you are poor you can't do what they can do. I disagree. I think that a decorated donkey is not always going to stay an ass. They can become a beautiful horse too. My point is that they will appear different once you dress them up [laughs]. It takes people like me courage and time to appear gorgeous. I have worked hard, I have traveled around, and I know what is tasteful for me. I believe that I have earned what I do. What I like may differ from your preference. And, even if we appreciate the same thing, the manner of our appreciation will be differently expressed. So, of course, I am convinced that a decorated donkey is definitely not an ass.

Kissi's position here undoubtedly reflects the fact that the sartorial tendencies of sasso evoked the *multivocality of drag*, which describes the extent to which sasso draw on clothing not only to draw attention to their effeminate selves, but also to flatten out class hierarchies while simultaneously reproducing hierarchies of gender and sexuality. This being the case, it is vital to acknowledge that Kissi's sophisticated sartorial sensibility did not preclude his desire to shore up his position in the sasso community and Jamestown. Arguably, it solidified his status in this time and space.

For his thirtieth birthday, Kissi dug deep into his financial coffers to fund his celebration. Bedecked in a custom-made long-sleeved white shirt that highlighted the contours of his torso and wrapped in skinny pants with kente patterns, Kissi reveled in his knack for merging elaborate, vernacular-styled fashion with Euro-American styles. On his Facebook page, he regularly uploaded pictures of himself or his associates bedecked in fancy outfits. His ultimate plan for the birthday was to festoon himself in thirty different custom-made outfits to mark the celebration: "I am still sweet sixteen," he began, "but being thirty means I can look back to measure my accomplishments. Thirty solid years of hard work require investing resources into making thirty custom-made attires." He added, "Don't you agree, Kwame?" To this I simply smiled.

THE LIMINALITY OF THE AMPHIBIOUS BODY AND LOCATION

Kissi's birthday was a celebratory event that not only elevated his status but also offered him an opportunity to interact with reputable members in the community whom he invited to the party. As at the outdooring, the food and drink showcased Kissi's social capital. Five big deep freezers containing an assortment of alcoholic and nonalcoholic beverages, both locally brewed and imported, were stationed at the entrance of the event. The display of merriment at Kissi's birthday party magnified his worth to the invited guests, many of whom were residents of Jamestown or neighboring suburbs. Organized by a sasso, the event dissolved those social hierarchies designed to delegitimize sexual and gendered expressions, identifications, and subjectivities. I use *delegitimization* here to describe how Kissi created spaces that both contested and upturned the clean and tidy categories that operated under heteronormativity. Thus, the birthday party presented a rich ethnographic example of how normative (nonsasso) and nonnormative (sasso) bodies converged to blur those lines of difference officially constructed as making them distinct, lines that are defined by their effeminacy. In a manner resembling Omise'eke Tinsley's description of birthdays organized by the mati of Suriname, Kissi's "birthday party loudly, unmistakably" (2010, 54) happened for fun, especially for the sasso in attendance. In sum, the event engendered a rival geography that contended with heteronormative practices while also exposing its frayed edges.

If I regard the birthday event as a rite of passage, it is also a site at which the carnivalesque was undoubtedly staged. Brisk and provocative dances by sasso to music of various orientations clearly reflected the jubilation that animated the space. The canopies under which the hosts sat were staged like gazebos, designed with decorations reminiscent of festive events like Mardi Gras in New Orleans and the Afro-Caribbean carnivals organized annually in the Caribbean and its diaspora. Held at night, the party space was decorated with lights reflecting multiple colors, and ushers escorted guests into the scene and barred the uninvited from the space. In this circumscribed space and time, the grandiosity of the party (quality), coupled with the number of invited guests (quantity), effectively cemented Kissi's social status in Jamestown.

Unanticipated Hierarchies: The Reproduction of "Capitals" in Queer/Liminal Spaces

Among sasso, the acquisition of economic, symbolic, and social capital was highly coveted. One's degree of nearness to wealth seemingly bespoke one's nearness to whiteness, what I refer to as racial capital. The number of *obronis*—white bodies—that circulated around sasso was significant, for such associations could minimize the effects of homophobia, as was the case with Terry, the sasso with a white husband in England. Racial capital marks a particular kind of social capital, which, as the anthropologist Jemima Pierre reminds us, is integral to the forms of "racecraft" that find expression in postcolonial spaces (2013, 5).

I believe that the penchant to acquire white racial capital is motivated by the desire among sasso to assuage the adverse effects of effeminacy in this precarious sociocultural milieu.[3] That sasso have access to particular forms of capital illustrates the extent to which their effeminacy presents them with opportunities and challenges simultaneously. For example, Kissi was in a long-distance relationship with an older German man called Walter who had visited Ghana some years back as a tourist. Walter often sent Kissi money in order to enhance his standard of living in the broken economy that defined Ghana's neoliberalized landscape. On the one hand, Walter shored up Kissi's racial capital; on the other hand, his effeminacy robbed him of the capital tied to being masculine. These various forms of capital therefore convoluted Kissi's navigation of the landscape. His access to whiteness and wealth occasionally fortified him against the onslaught of homonegativity and poverty. As with Ghanaians in general, whiteness symbolized privilege, comfort, and class mobility for sasso. Frantz Fanon puts it aptly: "You are rich because you are white; you are white because you are rich" (1967, 34).

Using money remitted to him by Walter, Kissi enrolled at the Goethe Institute in Accra, where he embarked upon learning German. It was his goal to be able to speak German by the time he and Walter got together. In fact, several sasso in Jamestown observed Kissi's enchanting experience with Walter, who showered him material resources few sasso could imagine. For them, Kissi's lived reality was undeniably one that resembled a Disneyesque fairy-tale, a dream come true.

On several occasions, Kissi dreamed of a future in which he would be entirely free from the capricious socioeconomic conditions Ghana wrought. Noting that "latching onto a white boyfriend expedited the process of escaping Ghana as an effeminate man who faced gender, social, moral, and economic adversities," Kissi proceeded to acknowledge that, at all costs, one could benefit from "swallowing the bitter pill if they needed a way out of Ghana." Kissi planned to settle down with Walter in the future, but that plan was thwarted when their long-distance relationship dissolved. After the breakup, Kissi experienced severe bouts of depression, regretting moments in which he felt he could have preserved his relationship with his "white sugar daddy" by abiding by his rules and meeting his needs, even if they seemed at times unreasonable.

The negotiation of interracial relationships by postcolonial subjects reinforces colonial relationships; however, such interactions need to be understood against the backdrop of suffering and resignation triggered by neoliberal and neocolonial regimes. Sasso like Kissi live in these precarious contexts. For these men, options to escape the vagaries of the economic, sociocultural, and sexual conditions are either minimal or nonexistent. In effect, Walter was Kissi's "savior," as it were, providing him with the startup capital required to set up his boutique. The money enabled him to travel to nearby Nigeria, Benin, and Togo to import clothes to fill his boutique. Moreover, he imported clothes into Ghana from China, relying heavily on both Chinese and Ghanaian traders who did business there.

Embodying and Disembodying Colonial Memories

The birthday celebration instantiates an example of Ghanaians' palimpsestic existence, a legacy left behind by colonial rule and Christianity. In that regard, Kissi's celebration of the event, along with the space where the event was held, resurrected memories of a past whose effects continue to play out in the present moment. For the purposes of the birthday, Kissi arranged for the delivery of customized birthday invitation cards from China. My invitation card arrived just a few hours before the event that Friday evening. Present at the event was a videographer, who shot the ceremony from beginning to end. This arrangement was part of Kissi's plan to showcase his financial stature in the community. In Ghana, contracting the services of a videographer is an expensive gesture, which means that Kissi's ability to video his birthday party illustrated, as he later told me, "a show-and-tell."[4] Furthermore, he maintains: "I want to make people happy, I am all about happiness as you know, and organizing this party is one way to do so. People in Ghana live in miserable circumstances. A good birthday will definitely make one smile. It will make them heave a sigh of relief."

The birthday celebration was held in the remains of a colonial enclosure in the middle of Jamestown, a few blocks away from the James and Usher Forts. What used to be a colonial, slaveholding, and mercantile post was transformed into a "generative" space. Being a historic space where African bodies experienced "death" (Brown 2010), the space was transfigured into a domain for the celebration of "life." In other words, the birthday ceremony temporarily brought life and jubilation to a site of former ruin and devastation—death. In stark contrast to the weddings that mostly white people conduct on former plantations in the American South, which desecrate and efface Black death, Kissi's birthday celebration recuperated the space in a manner that amplified the continuing presence of Black life in the ruins left behind by colonization and slavery. In a speech delivered during the event, Kissi claimed:

> My birthday is a celebration for everybody. We don't have to worry about who we are. We are here and we are going to live. Have fun, eat, and enjoy yourselves. Life, as they say, is short. We should enjoy life just like everybody else. Nobody should sit on your happiness, for an unhappy life is clearly not worth fighting for. To live is to be happy even if you are sasso. In fact, I think we are some of the happiest people here in Jamestown. Imagine this community without us. Just imagine! I thank God for adding another year to my life. Hopefully, we will all have long life and prosperity in the years to come.

Embodying aspects of Christian, Ga (Ghanaian/African), and colonial modernity, the birthday celebration is a paradox. It permits sasso to bond, while reinserting itself in sasso lives as a colonial relic. It showcases the continuation of Euro-American and Christian traditions which have been reproduced by sasso. The domestication of this ceremony, however, does not simply reduce it to a local affair. Indeed, it is undoubtedly a ritual and festive performance that coextends with transnational and global currents and meanings in a space that is palimpsestic. Hence Kissi's birthday arguably endogenizes Western understandings of the birthday by blending it with traditional celebrations of life. In so doing, the birthday also brings together unimagined and presumably inharmonious constituencies, that is, heteronormative and nonnormative subjects who together danced the night away.

The Outdooring and Birthday Celebrations as Antistructural and Carnivalesque Performances

Rituals, like carnivals, enable role reversals and role-play. During a ritual, such as an outdooring, sasso effectively undertake key roles, the goal of which is to ensure the success of the event. Moreover, during rituals, the suspension of normative rules implies that structural norms and mores will be reshaped and circumvented. For Victor Turner, rituals occasion "anti-structure," conceiving spaces where subjectivities are both forged and challenged (1974). Turner further elaborates antistructure as "a generative center" which allows for the possibility of what he terms "liminality" and "communitas" (Turner 1974, 273). Communitas, emphasizes Turner, "does not merge identities; it liberates them from conformity to general norms" that constitute an orderly society, or what he describes as "ordinariness" (1974, 274).

Undoubtedly, Turner's notion of the normal—in other words, structure—is analogous to Bakhtin's formulation of the officialdom instituted by church and state, the very formations that persistently attempt to undermine the transformative potential of the carnivalesque (1984, 45). I argue that the outdooring space (in the same vicinity as Clubhouse), the ruins of colonial/slaveholding posts, the people who populated it, and, finally, the events that occurred there "sent," to reiterate Turner, "various dangerous ambiguities . . . since the classifications on which order normally depends are annulled or obscured" (1974, 273). Indeed, there was temporary antinomic liberation from "behavioral norms and cognitive rules" (1974, 273).

These freedoms resonate with Bakhtin's observation during carnival time that the bodies and selves that otherwise would have been constricted by officialdom become unencumbered and free. For Turner, these shifts mark "fixed points" during the ritual at which transformation occurs (1974, 274). I refrain from assuming that these points are fixed, arguing instead that they are composite spaces that consist of layers of social, religious, spiritual, economic, and political meanings. These spaces inform the processes that contour them just as the processes contour these spaces. For instance, the outdooring shapes the meaning of the street and vice versa. Kissi's birthday shifts the meaning of a structure which was originally erected to accommodate slaves and later became a medium security prison. It is in these ambiguous shifts that amphibious subject formation manifests. During these events, sasso were reminiscent of the bondpeople about whom Stephanie Camp writes in the plantation south. "Bondpeople, who had their own plans for their bodies," argues Camp, "violated the boundaries of space and time that were intended to demarcate and consolidate planters' patriarchal power over plantation households" (2002, 535). In a similar vein, sasso violated those norms of heterosexual society and normalcy by entertaining themselves in these spaces without fear of reproach.

Like the Bakhtinian carnival, both the birthday and outdooring occasion a moment in which "life is subject only to its laws, that is, the laws of its own freedom" (1984, 7). Hence, rituals and carnivals present antistructural openings that enable sasso to cultivate practices of the self that are distinct from their lives in the realm of the mundane, defined by the varied social contexts in which they are nestled. Yet, it is important also to note that these two spheres entwine uneasily, and "created during carnival time [or ritualized time] a special type of communication impossible in everyday life" (Bakhtin 1984, 10). The temporary suspension inured by ritual festivities presents opportunities for sasso to reforge their identities. The anthropologist Lyndon Gill, speaking to carnival in Trinidad and Tobago, sheds light on how they not only allow for the expression of desire but also are themselves sites of nonnormative sexual possibility. These occasions are undoubtedly moments where queer bodies in a nation-state insistent on policing dissident sexualities forge citizenship and belonging beyond the parochial and often oppressive framings of official citizenship.

Similarly, the space of the rituals discussed in this ethnography blurs the boundaries between heteronormativity and homonormativity. In effect, they enabled travesty, and it is precisely these transgressions that allowed for the "the renewal of clothes and the social image" (Bakhtin 1984, 81). Laughter was recognized as transgressive, blasphemous, and derogatory in the space created by the officialdom of the church. If the spaces enabled by carnivals simultaneously generated laughter, then these ceremonial events and the spaces in which they occurred afforded sasso an opportunity to obscure and mock heteronormative boundaries. Spaces like Clubhouse, then, served as sites at which sasso mocked men who wore the social image of heteronormativity during the day, all the while being intimate with sasso at night. Such acts of derision are reminiscent of the indecent gestures and the disrobing that Bakhtin emphasized was characteristic of celebrations such as the feast of fools, which is "a grotesque degradation of various church rituals and symbols" (1984, 74–75). Similarly, a space such as Clubhouse and the ruins where Kissi celebrated his birthday were sites at which Christian propriety and mores were degraded and challenged unabashedly.

In *Rabelais and His World*, Bakhtin states:

> Life is shown in its two-fold contradictory process; it is the epitome of incompleteness. And such is precisely the grotesque concept of the body . . . contrary to modern canons, the grotesque body is not separated from the rest of the world. It is not a closed, completed unit; it is unfinished, outgrows itself, transgresses its own limits. The stress is laid on those parts of the body that are open to the outside world, that is, the parts through which the world enters the body or emerges from it, or through which the body itself goes out to meet the world. (1984, 26)

The rituals analyzed in this chapter illuminate the two-fold contradictory process that Bakhtin describes. They are moments that block the foreclosure of bodies and performances that depend on the body in order to have life. The outdooring ceremony and Kissi's birthday are queer geographies that call into question the understanding that heterosexuality is fixed, Ghanaian, African, natural, and normative. They reveal that these neat and tidy placeholders are merely incomplete. During these celebrations, "the unfinished and open body (dying, bringing forth, and being born) is not separated from the world by clearly defined boundaries; it is blended with the world, with animals, with objects" (Bakhtin 1984, 26–27).

PART THREE

Becoming and Unbecoming Amphibious Subjects in Hetero/ Homo Colonial Vortices

5

Palimpsestic Projects

Heterocolonial Missions in Post-Independent Ghana (1965–1975)

> Sometimes, Kwame, I think Ghanaians are some of the most hypocritical people I know. The most hypocritical being those Ghanaians who go to church. When it is corruption, they don't talk. When men abuse women, they don't talk. When it is politicians stealing from them, they won't talk. When pastors tell them lies and steal their money, they won't talk. But let it come to homosexuality. That alone will get them so angry. What is wrong with Ghanaians and homosexuality? As a sasso who goes to church and believes in the Bible, which I think is a wise book, I have never for the love of God understood why Ghanaian Christians are terrified by LGBT+ issues. They are OK with everything wrong, except homosexuality, which, mind you, is not wrong.
>
> —FOSTER (AUGUST 2014)

In October 2019, Mr. Moses Foh-Amoaning, the executive director of the National Coalition for Proper Human Sexual Rights and Family Values (NCPHSRFV),[1] expressed outrage at efforts by the Ghanaian government to incorporate the Comprehensive Sexuality Education (CES) program into national educational policy. The coalition declared on various media platforms that six years was a particularly young age to introduce concepts about sex and gender to children. In fact, they were critical of a module in the program titled "being male and female," which, in their opinion, was an "active strategy" to normalize LGBT+ presence in Ghana. Joining in the homophobic chorus was the then president of the Ghana Pentecostal and Charismatic Council, Paul Yaw Frimpong-Manso, who called the policy "comprehensive satanic engagement."[2] This was not the first time the coalition had expressed outrage at the LGBT+ issues in the country. Since its founding in 2013, the coalition has waged a campaign against what it calls "the LGBT+ problem in Ghana."[3]

Some members and allies of LGBT+ human rights organizations in Ghana took to Twitter and Facebook to express umbrage at the coalition while simultaneously mocking them.[4] That something as fundamental as a policy intended to widen the existing curriculum on sex and gender triggered a moral debate was interpreted as ridiculous by critics of the coalition. Indeed, the backlash against the backlash echoes Foster's rather penetrative suggestion in the epigraph that Ghanaian Christians will malign homosexuality and remain silent on issues that affect them directly on a daily basis—corruption, domestic violence, economic underdevelopment, and so on. Foster's apprehension at the anti-LGBT+ positions taken by the coalition illustrates two key points that are highlighted in this chapter. First, how anxieties around allegedly nonnormative sexual and gender formations work to consolidate the heterosexual nation. And second, how the backlash at the increasing visibility of LGBT+ human rights politics by formations like the coalition resurrect anxieties expressed by Christian organizations toward polygamy at the dawn of Ghana's independence.

The coalition's outrage exemplifies the organization's attempts to engage in smear campaigns against the LGBT+ community in Ghana. For example, the invasion of the LGBT+ Rights Ghana office in February 2021, which drew global attention to the state of LGBT+ issues in Ghana, vividly captures the central role the coalition plays in policing sexual citizenship. Shortly before the office was invaded, a ceremony had been held to celebrate its opening on January 31, 2021.[5] Widely publicized on Facebook and attended by high-profile foreign dignitaries like the Australian high commissioner to Ghana and the Danish ambassador to Ghana, the ceremony created a fanfare that attracted mixed reactions on social media in particular and Ghanaian media in general.

Affronted by the fact that an LGBT+ office was not only inaugurated but was openly called LGBT+ Rights Ghana, members of the coalition and politicians demanded that the ruling New Patriotic Party (NPP) government close the organization. In the ensuing days, members of Ghana's National Security raided the LGBT+ Rights Ghana office, locking it up.[6] For the coalition, Westernization is to blame for the LGBT+ presence in Ghana, the same Westernization that introduced Christianity, Western education, Western forms of government, Western economic practices, Western development aid, and so on.

In this chapter, I examine letters exchanged between the Christian Council of Ghana (CCG) and Christian Aid (CA), a Christian humanitarian organization based in Britain, between 1965 and 1975 to illuminate the historical contexts anticipating the coalition's homophobic vitriol. In a move to normalize monogamy in post-independent Ghana, the CCG, with financial support from CA, established the Committee on Christian Marriage and Family Life (CCMFL) in 1961 to "promote positive Christian teachings on sex, marriage, and family life."[7] Although the CCMFL projects were nationwide, in this chapter, I focus on the committee's projects in the Volta Region, Ghana's easternmost region, bordering Togo, to explicate how heterosexualization and heteromonogamy were construed as necessary for Ghana's advancement into modernity.

Here, I generate a series of questions fundamental not just to this chapter but to my project overall, namely: How did heteromonogamous projects consolidate heterosexuality as Ghanaian? How are colonial/Christian missionary projects to liberate Africans from atavistic polygamous practices analogous to contemporary queer liberal activists' attempts to rescue LGBT+ citizens from violent homophobic regimes? Lastly, how is the coalition a palimpsestic iteration of the Committee on Christian Marriage and Family Life (CCMFL)? The sense in which I use *palimpsest* here aligns with Ella Shohat's description of time as "scrambled and palimpsestic, in all the worlds, with the premodern, the modern, the postmodern, and the paramodern coexisting globally" (1998, 20). Hence, I assert that the environments in which LGBT+ humanitarian projects unfurl are defined by multiple publics, subsumed under colonial (European) and customary (indigenous) publics. These publics are palimpsestic not just because they normalized heteromonogamy but because they anticipated the homonegative reactions against LGBT+ visibility in Ghana. If the palimpsest is "a parchment on which writing has been partially or completely erased to make room for another text," or a document with "faint traces" of something that was, then the NCPHSRFV, which opposes homosexuality in the contemporary moment, has traces of the CCFMFL projects.

SITUATING THE CHRISTIAN COUNCIL OF GHANA

The Christian Council of Ghana (CCG) is an organization comprised of a membership of "twenty-six member churches and three Christian organizations."[8] Its members currently comprise Orthodox, Protestant, and neo-Protestant denominations. The new Protestant formations include the Pentecostal and Charismatic churches. Established on October 30, 1929, by five churches, the CCG includes the African Methodist Episcopal (AME) Zion Church, the Ewe Presbyterian Church, the English Church Mission (Anglican); the Presbyterian Church of the Gold Coast (Ghana), and the Wesleyan Methodist Church. The Orthodox and Protestant members of the council differ doctrinally and liturgically; yet, under the banner of the CCG, they have historically supported Christian marriage and family life. They have also recently been outspoken against the liberalization of same-sex sexual politics in Ghana. Leading members from Catholic, Protestant, and the new wave of Pentecostal denominations have participated in the condemnation of homosexuals. Most denominational leaders have also relayed their dissatisfaction with what they regard as the government's apathetic stance, warning it to refuse any funding and donations granted by organizations in the West that support gay marriage and rights.[9] In a book bearing the same title, Paul Gifford has described this new wave of Christian denominations in Ghana as constituting "Ghana's New Christianity."

Gifford's (2004) apt framing highlights the vexed composition of Christianity and Christian practices in postcolonial Ghana, under conditions sometimes contested by Protestant and Pentecostal churches. These churches are conceived as being radically opposed to Orthodox churches, which in Ghana comprise Catholic, Anglican, Presbyterian, and Methodist. Despite such fissures, the CCG remains an organization that fosters interchurch partnerships between Orthodox, Protestant, and Pentecostal denominations in Ghana. The core mission of the CCG is to "search for unity and to work with members on issues of social concern and be the voice of the voiceless in society."[10] While the organization serves as the face of Christianity in Ghana, it also plays a crucial political role for the Ghanaian government, offering advice on issues of social, political, moral, economic, and cultural significance. Not only does the CCG advise members of government but it also holds them accountable for social and political issues affecting Ghanaians; some of the organization's leaders are also key members of the Council of State, one of Ghana's most respected political advisory institutions. In this chapter, I speculate that the normalization of heteromonogamy under the watch of the CCG's subsidiary, the Committee on Christian Marriage and Family Life (CCMFL), deepened the CCG's relationship to the nation-state.

CIVILIZING MARRIAGE: ELIMINATING POLYGAMY FROM THE "HEART OF DARKNESS"

At the dawn of Ghana's independence, the country inherited discourses on the naturalness of the Christian nuclear family and compulsory monogamy. As Angela Willey argues, discourses on proper marital conventions, tied to Victorian values, emphasized "the institution and regulation of heterosexual monogamy . . . as essential to the superiority of 'Christian nations' over 'Polgygamic races'" (2006, 532). The assumption that polygamous societies were inferior justified Christian and colonizing Europeans' pursuit of civilizing projects that cemented Christian heteromonogamy. What I capture as a heterocolonial project, which is the melding of colonization with heterosexualization, crystallized European culture as the bastion of civility in several African contexts. Hence, African sociocultural formations that did not conform with European cultural forms were immediately racialized as atavistic (Tallie 2019, Ray 2015; Epprecht 2008).

As the Africanist historian T. J. Tallie provocatively notes, among the Zulu of colonial Natal in the moment of the colonial encounter, polygamy and vernacular practices like *ilobolo* (bridewealth) emerged as sites for the construction of racial difference. These cultural practices and formations served as justification for Europeans to distinguish themselves as superior while regarding Africans as inferior. This distinction solidified Eurocentric assumptions about African difference. In meticulous detail, Tallie pointedly notes: "Whether or not indigenous

African women themselves saw polygamy as a means of negotiating their position in an agrarian society mattered very little to settlers. In newsprint, missionary pamphlets, and travel literature, Natal's settlers consistently depicted women as oppressed by barbarism of their men—particularly through *ilobolo* and polygamous marriages" (2019, 19).

The racist logic that African polygamy was an institution that oppressed women is overturned in the terse anthropological essay entitled "Sexual Inversion among the Azande," by the British social anthropologist E. E. Evans-Pritchard. In the ethnography, Evans-Pritchard describes how polygamy presented women (and men) with the opportunity to create erotic and intimate connections. Providing insights into the intricate intersections between polygamy and homosexuality among the Azande in precolonial Sudan, Evans-Pritchard observed that these practices shifted with the appearance of Europeans. "Male and female homosexual relationship," argues Evans-Pritchard, "seems to have been common among the Azande in past times. Between males it was approved in the bachelor military companies. Between females it is said to have been a frequent, though highly disapproved of, practice in polygamous homes" (1970, 1428).

The male homosexuality observed by Evans-Pritchard among the Azande is attributed to two factors. First, the Azande were a highly a militaristic culture with military organizations made up of married men and "bachelor companies, some of whom would always be living in barracks at court, to take boy-wives" (1970, 1429). Second, there was a shortage of women of marriageable age, leading to the phenomenon of "boy marriages."[11] Even in the days before the arrival of Europeans, homosexual relationships were commonplace in Azande culture. To buttress this point, Evans-Pritchard not only cites other scholars to suggest that it would be misplaced to theorize that homosexuality among the Azande was introduced by the Arabs,[12] but also provides compelling evidence on the entwinement of polygamy and lesbianism. I cite his explanation at length here:

> It can be said generally that a woman who is one of three wives would not sleep with her husband more than some ten nights a month, one of six wives more than five nights, and so on. One of the many wives of a prince or of an important commoner in the past might not have shared her husband's bed for a month or two, whereas some of the dozens, even hundreds, of wives of a king must have been almost totally deprived of the sex life normal in smaller homes. Adulterous intercourse was very difficult for a wife in such large polygamous families, for the wives were kept in seclusion and carefully watched; death on discovery, or even on suspicion, would have been the penalty for both the wife and her lover. It was in such polygamous families, Azande say, that lesbianism was practiced. (1970, 1431)

By providing an example of how polygamy became a fecund domain for the unfolding of female homoeroticism, I am not disputing the fact that polygamy, like monogamy, was patriarchal at its core. Rather, I suggest that polygamous practices yielded opportunities for queer intimacies and desire in ways that made polygamy not only antithetical to monogamy but antithetical to the heterocolonial intent at the core of colonial expansion. And as Tallie's (2019) and Evans-Pritchard's (1970) historical observations suggest, the anxieties generated by polygamy reinforced European attachment to heterosexuality and the racialization of polygamy.

Polygamy may not have been the only institution that unsettled European colonial presence; indeed, the presence of female-headed societies, cultures where women played significant roles in the public sphere, also troubled the colonists. As the Nigerian anthropologist Ifi Amadiume spells out in her *Afrikan Matriarchal Foundations* (1987b) and *Male Daughters, Female Husbands* (1987a), respectively, the Western categories of gender and racial difference displaced native logics and interpretations in ways that gravely affected the crucial roles women played in community and nation-building. Situating the foundations of African matriarchy in Egypt, Amadiume goes a step further to perspicaciously unsettle its demonization in Western epistemology. Evidently, the existence of female-headed societies questioned as well as threatened parochial constructions not only of gender and sexuality but also of the family that colonizing Europeans brought with them to Africa. In view of this, the eventual elimination of the coexistence of matriarchal and patriarchal formations may have been key to the redefinition not only of gender and sexual difference, but also of racial difference. Within this trope, patriarchy distinguished Europeans from Africans, reinscribing a fixed and immutable view of gender and sexuality all the while furthering racial differentiation. Thus, in this formulation European patriarchy was construed as "modern" as opposed to a "primitive" African patriarchy.

Meanwhile, some scholars have outlined how African marital formations, unlike those established by Christian missionaries and colonists, did not rely on rigid notions of gender and sexuality. The phenomena of "male daughters" and "female husbands," which Amadiume (1987b) observes among the Igbos of Nigeria, as well as the androgynous practices quite common to African spiritual formations, demonstrate the rigidity of precolonial gender and sexual representations. Italo Signorini's ethnological examination of the phenomenon of "friendship marriages," or *agɔnwole agyalɛ*, among the Nzemas of southwestern Ghana is notable (1973). Calling it "marriage between two persons of the same-sex," Signorini shows how practices of friendship between men unsettled hetero-monogamous notions of marriage institutionalized under Europeanization and Christianization. Friendship marriages emphasized the contiguous character of heterosexual and "same-sex" marriages among the Nzema. Heterosexual marriage was made stable by the friendship marriages, revealing the fluidity of marital unions and the institutions that orchestrated them. In the wake of Europeanization and Christianization, these fluid marital formations and erotic subjectivities were racialized as backward, deeply anchoring white heteropatriarchal monogamy as an advanced marital form.

This representation of monogamy as natural and normal was supported by race-scientific discourses spewing out of phrenology and craniology in the eighteenth and nineteenth centuries (Willey 2006; Newman 1999). The phrenologist Lorenzo Fowler, in his book *Marriage: Its History and Ceremonies; with a Phrenological Exposition of the Functions and Qualifications for Happy Marriages* (1847), offers grand unscientific narratives on how the composition of the skull and the size of one's reproductive organs determined a successful monogamous marriage. Fowler proceeds to unequivocally argue that the more proportioned one's reproductive organ, the better suited the person was for monogamous marriage. Fowler's sexological extrapolation, it goes without saying, circulated as scientific fact in a moment in which Black bodies faced dilemmas incited by their hypersexualization and criminalization. These pseudoscientific assumptions were cathected onto Black bodies to justify the legitimacy of the inflexibility of racial difference. The paradoxical role science played, then, in solidifying racial and sexual differentiation is significant. As the historian Rudi Bleys argues, "The growing impact of science has often been seen as liberating, not least because it opened perspectives for a more secularized vision of the world. Yet it also implied far-reaching reification of sexual desire in fixed identities, just as it crystallized cultural difference in racial identities" (1995, 2).

Differentiating Black bodies from white bodies, Fowler's pseudoscientific phrenological formula legitimized the fiction that Black bodies were unfit for monogamous marriage, while normalizing modes of racial and sexual difference as immutable. Indeed, as Bleys (1995) suggests, the liberal posture of science was connected to its violation of non-Western bodies, and to be specific, bodies of African descent. A few decades later, toward the end of nineteenth century, the imperial ethnologist Sir Richard Burton drew on superficially articulated cultural difference based on pseudoscientific discourses to divide the world into "sotadic" and "non-sotadic" zones (Burton 1885). Drawing from his travels through Asia, the Middle East, and Africa, Burton arrived at the conclusion that the sotadic zone was comprised of geographies where sodomy was rampant, and the nonsotadic zone was where heterosexuality was practiced. Burton's thesis that topography shaped sexual desire significantly influenced Western conceptions of sexual desire and gender representations in the non-Western world. The sotadic zone, imagined as tropical, apparently accommodated "sexual inversion." In other words, same-sex behavior, specifically male-to-male sexual behavior, was believed to be rife in geographies found in the sotadic zone (Burton 1886; Bleys 1995). Although the entirety of Africa's tropical topography fell outside of the sotadic zone, the continent's assumed nonsotadic tendencies were racialized as hypersexual heterosexuality in Burton's racialized sexual schema (1886). Evidently, the construal of gender and sexual formations in Africa in the Euro-colonial imagination circumvented customary constructions of those very formations, which were undermined by the introduction of colonization and Christianity.

Colonial and Customary Publics as Sites of Gender and Sexual Contestations

I want to emphasize here that the various heterocolonial projects executed by Europeans were incomplete precisely because of the presence of "customary publics,"[13] which, on occasion, colluded or collided with hegemonic colonial publics (Ekeh 1975; Ray 2015; Tallie 2019). The Nigerian political scientist Peter Ekeh, in his essay entitled "Colonialism and the Two Publics in Africa: A Theoretical Statement," distinguishes between the "primordial and the civil publics" (1975, 92). Ekeh argues that there are two public realms in Africa and that they have different moral imperatives. "The primordial public is moral and operates on the same moral imperatives as the private realm . . . whereas the civic public is amoral and lacks the generalized moral imperatives operative in the private realm and in the primordial public" (1975, 92). In the primordial public, there are "sentiments, and activities, which nevertheless impinge on the public interest," and the civic public is "historically associated with the colonial administration . . . which has become identified with popular politics in post-colonial Africa. It is based on civil structures: the military, the civil service, the police, etc." (1975, 92). Ekeh's distinction matters for how I historicize the ways in which gender and sexual difference unfolded as sites of contestation during colonial rule. What he terms primordial and civic publics, I maintain, inflected practices and articulations of gender and sexuality while inducing shifts in the moral compasses that governed these formations. Unlike Ekeh, however, I am interested in the distinction between "colonial" and "customary" publics. Drawing on Ekeh's formulation, I argue that the colonial public was wedded to European sensibilities while the latter, that is, the customary public, found its home in indigenous African practices and ways of being and becoming.[14] Not only did these publics have sub-publics subsumed within them which variously competed for legitimacy depending on what was at stake, but they also unevenly interpenetrated each other in ways that produced serrated sociocultural, politico-economic, and spiritual qua religious geographies that complicated notions and practices of gender and sexuality. The tensions around gender and sexuality then and now are in large measure tied to the ontological alignments and misalignments yielding from the collusions and collisions between these publics and their ancillary publics.

Against this backdrop, the racial projection of hypersexuality onto the Black body, arguably a by-product of the colonial public, beckoned colonial and missionary projects intent on saving African women and men from indigenous practices like polygamy (Tallie 2019; Ray 2015). In particular, the hypersexualization of the Black female, as the treatment of Saartjie Baartman reveals, articulates European fantasies about the Black woman's body.[15] As the Black feminist Deborah McDowell argues, the Black female in Western cultural imaginaries has always "embodied both lack and excess (and excess as lack)" (2006, 298). McDowell further illuminates how, for example, the black female buttocks emerge as "the most synecdochical signature of the black female form" (2006, 306). But the Black female body, at once racialized as expressing sexual insatiability, is also constructed as the victim of a native culture that enchained her to the presumed violence of polygamy and indigenous patriarchy. To center the paradoxical figure of the Black female body here is to unpack how colonial management, which drew on scientific racism and the elevation of Christian morality, established and magnified empire's reliance on the institutions of science, religion, and capitalism to enforce and naturalize monogamy. It is precisely this management that produced the vexatious publics, namely the colonial and customary publics, that animated African women's worlds.

The effort to save African women, integral to the civilizing and Christian missionary enterprises, involved white women. Trained in the vocation of importing logics and practices of propriety, these women were integral to the architectures of colonialism and imperialism (Willey 2006; Stoler 1995; Boddy 2007; Ray 2015). In *Civilizing Women: British Crusades in Colonial Sudan*, Janice Boddy (2007) provides historical detail on how indigenous women in the Sudan had to be coded as uncivilized in order for their colonization and civilization to be justified. Noting that native women were compelled to embrace whiteness and Euro-American Christian virtues of womanhood, Boddy highlights how the institutionalization of Victorian notions heightened native women's vulnerability while minimizing their agency during the colonial encounter. Enfolding Sudanese women into colonial management schemes prompted their forceful adoption of colonial selfhood (2007).

There is a clear path from the efforts to rescue African women from polygamy and other invidious indigenous practices in the aftermath of independence to current attempts to save homosexuals in Ghana by LGBT+ human rights organizations. While the former, I insist, anticipates the latter, it also historically occurs against the backdrop of a post–World War II moment in which the impending death of British colonialism coincides with other unanticipated forces to exacerbate the crises of the nuclear family. Moreover, the reverberations yielding from these rescue missions amplify how reactions against LGBT+ visibility politics in Ghana are more the result of the tensions engendered by the collisions between the colonial and customary publics in the contemporary moment.

UNANTICIPATED REVERBERATIONS: COUNTERCULTURAL MOVEMENTS IN POSTWAR EUROPE AND SHIFTING SOCIAL STRUCTURES IN POSTCOLONIAL LANDSCAPES

The ascent of Christian monogamy in postcolonial Ghana inevitably coincides with a diminishing Christianity, the rise in secularization, and a decline in nuclear family values in Europe. Imagined as the natural and moral basis for the creation of the family, monogamy was unabashedly constructed in postindependent nations as healthier and better suited for achieving modernity.[16]

The ideologies around monogamy, such as its civility, naturalness, and moral purity, sustained the notion that parents and children in monogamous, nuclear households were much fitter and more closely knit than in polygamous families. Evolutionary language justified the advantages that monogamy had over polygamous unions. Exempted from such problematic claims, for example, was what kind of opportunities the so-called patriarchally insidious institution of polygamy afforded its supposed victims. African women, for instance, formed intimate female bonds, as described by E. E. Evans-Pritchard among the Azande of precolonial Sudan.

To be clear, this ideology was proliferated through outlets regulated by organizations such as Christian Aid (CA) and the Christian Council of Ghana (CCG) against the backdrop of countercultural movements in Europe and the United States, mostly arising in the fifties and sixties and continuing well into the seventies.[17] When in the 1950s, countercultural movements opposing colonial rule and imperialism began to question the sociological, political, and ideological status quo of imperial European nations after the Second World War, the shifts propelled by these movements also influenced the logics of Christianity and ideas about marriage and family. With the demise of British imperialism imminent, formerly colonized peoples began to migrate to the metropole in large numbers from the Caribbean, Africa, and South Asia to seek education and economic opportunities.

Campaigns were waged by the civil rights movement in the United States, and countercultural formations such as the antiwar movement, women's rights, sexual rights, and anti-apartheid and anticolonial organizations triggered sociopolitical paroxysms around the world from the sixties through the seventies. In Britain, the countercultural movement spurred by the "British invasion," which fostered an antihegemonic popular cultural ideology animated by such bands as the Beatles, the Kinks, the Rolling Stones, and the Who, also strengthened the movement against mainstream status quos.[18] The cultural reverberations that these British bands produced were, indeed, transatlantic in character. Arriving on the shores of the United States in the mid-sixties, the Beatles were received with much enthusiasm.

During this period, racial politics in the United States became explosive, with the assassinations of key political figures and leaders of the civil rights movement such as Malcolm X and Martin Luther King Jr. The rise of the Black Power movement, among other sociopolitical movements, along with the flowering of rock and roll and pop music (and much later, punk music) shifted the political tenor of the moment.[19] Adding to this were the Stonewall Riots and gay and lesbian uprisings in New York City and other US cities. This was also the moment during which Britain decriminalized homosexuality, leaving its former colonies stuck to colonial-era constitutions that criminalized homosexuality (Kaoma 2009). These legal strictures, then, became the basis for the naturalization of heterosexuality in postcolonial nations, which continued to espouse and implement laws left behind by colonial administrations.

Evidently, the countercultural currents animating the British Atlantic had ripple effects on former colonies and nations fighting for independence. The forties and fifties saw the beginnings of what Martinican psychiatrist Frantz Fanon captures as "a dying colonialism" (1967). Occurring at a time characterized by post–World War II anxieties, these movements began to shift the mainstream sociocultural, moral, and religious landscapes which had long defined Euro-America. Inevitably, this was a fertile period for the New Left, an intellectual and activist movement which emerged in Britain (Oglesby 1969).

Interrogating mainstream white supremacist, colonialist, capitalist, fascist, and masculinist ideologies, the emerging intellectual currents nourished ideological alternatives that engendered antiracist, antifascist, antiwar, antimasculinist, anticapitalist, and antinuclear positions.[20] More important, the imperatives of these emerging formations had sociological, religious, and moral implications, some of which included the disruption of Christianity and its ideas about monogamy and the nuclear family, which, in turn, challenged normative understandings of race, class, gender, and sexuality in postwar Britain. If the monogamous Christian family was on the verge of collapse in Europe, postindependent African nation-states ultimately emerged as sites where Christianity and the dying monogamous family could be rescued. The achievement of modernity became the alibi for the pursuit of these projects.[21]

In a manner reminiscent of Evangelical Christians' desire to salvage heterosexuality in contemporary Africa, Christian humanitarian organizations like Christian Aid, at the turn of independence, collaborated with their local counterparts in Ghana, the Christian Council of Ghana (CCG), to establish the Committee on Christian Marriage and Family Life (CCFML). Together, these organizations pursued projects that strengthened Christian monogamy and nuclear family values in the aftermath of independence.

SITUATING CHRISTIAN AID: POSTINDEPENDENT AFRICA AND THE RISE OF CHRISTIAN HUMANITARIANISM

If the countercultural movements in Euro-America had both overt and covert linkages with anticolonial reverberations under way in Africa and Asia, then some of the impacts of these connections can be seen in the handful of African nations that achieved independence in the fifties. On the eve of Ghana's liberation from colonial rule, for example, Kwame Nkrumah, the first president of Ghana, declared that "independence would be meaningless, unless connected to the total liberation of the African continent" (1965, 40). Achieving independence on March 6, 1957, Ghana steered the anticolonial qua decolonial bandwagon, which emphasized total liberation of the African continent from European imperialism. As the first nation in sub-Saharan Africa to wrestle itself from the shackles of British colonial rule, Ghana emerged as the vanguard of independence for other African nations south of the Sahara, whose anticolonial projects were animated by sociopolitical uprisings on both sides of the Atlantic.

Incidentally, the sixties represented a watershed moment of anticolonial success, as over thirty African nations gained independence from their European colonizers (Cooper 2014; Ake 1996). This period also witnessed the emergence of Christian organizations which sought to rebuild a devastated Europe. In Britain, organizations such as the Oxford Committee for Famine Relief, popularly known as OXFAM, and Inter-Church Aid (ICA), which was later to be known as Christian Aid in the early sixties, were established to offer aid to victims of the Second World War and its reverberations throughout Europe. Christian Aid's outreach combined Christian teachings with family planning methods as a healthy way of rehabilitating vulnerable populations.

Thus, in its formation, Christian Aid declared its goal "to help European refugees who had lost everything."[22] Functioning much like Oxfam and Save the Children, Christian Aid was established in 1948. To some degree, Christian Aid can be characterized as "first generation" humanitarian organization, to use David Korten's typology (1990). Operating under the banner of Christian reconstruction in Europe, Christian Aid claimed "not to evangelize, but to alleviate suffering for ordinary people no matter what their faith."[23] As a member of the Disaster Emergency Committee (DEC), Christian Aid was one of few organizations operating under the British government in the postwar era to respond mainly to emergencies occurring during civil wars and in the aftermath of catastrophes and natural disasters—famines and earthquakes (Jones 2014). The organization began to focus on postcolonial nations in Africa, Asia, and the Middle East in the fifties. In Africa in particular, their projects, which included the establishment of kindergartens, educational programs addressing family planning methods and contraception, and significantly, the effort to institutionalize monogamy, formed part of its renewed vision to "combat poverty." With the appointment of Janet Lacey as Christian Aid's president in 1952, the organization's mission to address poverty in the developing world was ostensibly linked to questions that bordered on the idea of the family and marriage. It is unsurprising that the Christian Aid projects in Ghana throughout the sixties and seventies were executed with African marriage and family as the key locus of change.

As part of the organization's goal to end poverty, it also emphasized the need to support medical facilities that offered family planning and contraception services, as well as workshops for Christian youth. Between 1965 and 1975, Christian Aid and the CCG collaborated on projects that circulated ideas about the necessity of monogamy and the nuclear family for happy and healthy children. In the racist projects of the nineteenth century, monogamy was deemed unsuitable for Africans, but with the death of monogamy in postwar Europe, postcolonial nations like Ghana became fertile grounds for replanting the seeds of this institution. There, the adoption of the nuclear family qua monogamy was in line with

FIGURE 5. Poster advertising Christian Aid Week. Source: http://www.christianaid.org.uk/aboutus/who/history/.

fostering the progress of the nation. Having embraced the nuclear family model as the mark of modernity, the postcolonial nation-state participated in a project supported by Christian Aid to salvage Western Christian ideals in Africa.

Proliferating and Consolidating Christian Monogamy and Family: The Role of the Committee on Christian Marriage and Family Life (CCMFL)

The CCG's Committee on Christian Marriage and Family Life (CCMFL) was established on February 26, 1965, as part of the council's vision to promote the virtues and values of Christian marriage among families in Ghana.[24] The CCMFL's subsidiary, the Volta Region Committee on Christian Marriage and Family Life, was created to encourage Ghanaian Christians to both embrace Christian values and uphold monogamy, not only as a tenet of a healthy Christian life, but also as vital to the nation's development. Together with representatives from the Ministry of Health and other governmental organizations, including "homemakers, doctors, teachers, pastors, social workers, and administrators," the project encouraged Ghanaians to abandon polygamy and other aspects of indigenous culture that presumably hindered achieving a healthy marriage and family life.[25]

Without a doubt, the CCMFL projects reinserted Britain into the most intimate aspects of Ghanaians' lives in the postindependent moment, as donor support mostly came from Ghana's former colonial power. Moreover, at the time, the Volta Region Committee on Christian Marriage and Family Life was the only such regional committee that foresaw the execution of Christian practices and virtues for marriage among youth and adults. The committee's stated goals included the following:

- To aid youth and adults in development of true Christian Attitude toward marriage in both its physical and spiritual aspects.
- To aid those individuals whose marriages are proving unsuccessful.
- To aid couples in matters of family planning and problems arising from sterility.[26]

It is apparent that the goals set by the CCMFL set aside former racialized constructions of monogamy, which was historically perceived to be doomed to fail among hypersexualized Africans, for whom such practices were deemed unsuitable. Over time, the CCMFL added two additional objectives, aimed at assisting individuals to be "better adjusted members of their families" and "to prepare young people for well-adjusted, satisfying adult lives whether single or married."[27] Part of the committee's responsibilities included organizing the Christian Home Week every year, during which event the committee delivered its goals and objectives to attendees, several of whom were teachers and youth from member churches. This two-and-a-half-week program also involved meetings with pastors in districts around the country. As noted in the 1966 secretary's report, one of the key objectives of these district meetings was to highlight teenage problems and crises confronting the nation.

The CCMFL leadership also feared that the country's youth were at the mercy of the pangs wrought by the sociocultural transformations unfolding in the wake of Ghana's independence. Hence, the organization developed projects targeting youth, the population that would enable the progress of Christian marriage and family life. In particular, students were to be introduced to the basic principles that undergirded Christian relationships, such as refraining from premarital sex and using contraception in the event of premarital sex, so as to prevent teenage pregnancies. The CCMFL invited participants to lead workshops in which youth were given specific suggestions in a guide to help them navigate those difficult situations in their own lives.[28] The guide also contained a list of events to be undertaken during Christian Home Week, at which leaders from the CCMFL played an important role by steering participants on what to do and what not to do in their local denominations and communities.

The youth-centered projects undertaken by CCMFL extended beyond its campaign to prevent premarital sex and unwanted pregnancy, to organizing programs that provided young people with the practical information they needed to navigate the rapidly modernizing landscape of Ghana. In these programs, too, youth were educated on sexual abstinence, approaches to Christian living, and having a healthy sexual relationship within marriage, all under the supervision of mentors appointed by the church. These programs were undoubtedly sites for the incubation of heteromonogamy as a practice that cultivated those "refined" habits necessary for modernity.

Supporting CCMFL: The Role of Christian Aid

The first director of CCMFL was Mrs. C. F. Paton. In charge of projects executed by the committee, Mrs. Paton regularly corresponded with leading officials of Christian Aid seeking financial support to sustain the Christian marriage and family life projects in the country. The CCMFL's reliance on Christian Aid resulted from their lack of financial resources for the various projects they undertook. One of the earliest exchanges between Mrs. Paton and Miss Janet Lacey, the director of Christian Aid, is a letter dated May 20, 1965, in which a demand is made to Christian Aid to withdraw an application initially sent by CCMFL to support medical work in the Volta Region. In the letter, Mrs. Paton requests instead that Christian Aid fund an "earlier project, listed in the 1965 Project Book of the World Council of Churches." The project, writes Mrs. Paton, deals "with education in personal relationships and Christian Marriage, or to put in another way, the fight against promiscuity, gonorrhea and the resultant sterility. It is one of the Home and Family Life projects approved for Africa and is already operating."[29]

European education, combined with Christian teachings on marriage and personal relationships, is prescribed in the letter as the antidote to the promiscuity so deeply entrenched among Ghanaians in the postindependent moment. In a pre-HIV/AIDS era, the pathological rendering of Ghana as a place where unhealthy sexual practices and relationships exacerbate venereal diseases such as gonorrhea is used to justify Christian Aid's urgent intervention. Although Ghanaians, and particularly Ghanaian women, are imagined as the victims of diseases like gonorrhea, what is not underscored is the fact that they are victims of age-old and persistent tropes constructing Africa as the continent of hypersexuality and disease.

Besides the demand for funds to assist with combating promiscuity, gonorrhea, and their resultant sterility, Mrs. Paton requested assistance to construct medical centers in Accra. These medical centers, if completed, would provide family planning services for prospective and married Christian couples. Stressing the need to address such issues as infertility in her letter to Miss Lacey, Mrs. Paton points out that "we quite realize that infertility cannot make the dramatic appeal which freedom from hunger projects can, but on the personal and social levels sterility is an urgent matter and one in which a Christian medical unit can help best to treat the anxiety symptoms associated with it."[30] In a separate section of the same letter, she writes: "Their work in the Volta Region follows roughly the same lines as that in the rest of Ghana: conferences for teachers and Teacher training students on a Christian altitude [*sic*] to sex and how to impart this; trying to promote pastoral care of married couples; a medical advice center at Ho for married couples . . . this will offer help on infertility and contraception."[31]

Essentially, the requests for funding were not only to enhance the quality of life for married couples but also to provide resources for teachers to transfer knowledge about Christian monogamy to students in schools as well to educate them on the significance of family planning.

The conferences organized by CCMFL provided opportunities to train participants to help them educate true Christian families on the virtues and responsibilities of family planning and contraception. Mrs. Paton's request for funding to pursue projects that centered on Christian marriage was a defining feature connecting the CCMFL to Christian Aid. On another occasion, the secretary of the Volta Region Committee on Christian Marriage and Family Life, Mrs. Vivian Hazel, a Ghanaian woman who represented the interests of CCG, served as the CCMFL's liaison with Christian Aid, appealing for funds and grants to support projects in Ghana. The grants provided by Christian Aid helped to organize workshops that encouraged Ghanaians to embrace monogamous lifestyles and adopt birth control practices. By entrenching monogamy as the index for modernity, these projects fortified the idea that Ghana was primarily heterosexual.

ON THE NECESSITY OF CHRISTIAN MONOGAMY FOR A "HEALTHY AND HAPPIER" NATION AND SEXUAL CITIZENSHIP

In a conference address to delegates at the Conference for Teachers on Christian Marriage and Family Life in the Volta Region, the Reverend Samuel Buatsi exhorts participants to be wary of the vagaries of traditional elements of Ghanaian culture such as polygamy and emphasizes how it stalls progress.[32] Advocating instead for Christian marriage, he distinguishes it from polygamy, maintaining that it is sanctioned by a divine authority. Turning specifically to youth, he cautions that "most members of the younger generation have begun to find themselves . . . at the crossroads of the old and the new."[33] The reverend calls on youth at the event to understand that preparing themselves for Christian marriage, that "life-long, exclusive union and fellowship of one man with one woman," will allow them to deal with the rapid shifts in Ghana.[34]

Circulating Heteromonogamy and the Nuclear Family: Let Us Plan for Happy Healthy Children!

The widely distributed illustrated pamphlet *Let Us Plan for Happy Healthy Children!* was published in 1966 by the CCMFL. Focusing on the significance of Christian marriage for post-independent Ghana, the illustrated pamphlet contained step-by-step instructions for building a happy family. A manual for heterosexual marriage, the pamphlet anticipates the anti-LGBT+ themes of the National Coalition for Proper Human Sexual Rights and Family Values (NCPHSRFV). The pamphlet asserts that monogamous homes are healthy and happy because they embrace effective family planning strategies and eventually lead to the planned birth of children. In a letter dated September 21, 1966, to Miss Janet Lacey, Mrs. Vivian Hazel enclosed a copy of minutes from their meetings and the report from the Synod of the Evangelical Presbyterian Church, pamphlets published in English and several local Ghanaian languages on the medical advice center, and information on the need for happy healthy families.[35]

The front page of *Let Us Plan for Happy Healthy Children!* features a hand-drawn picture of a husband, his wife, and their four children standing next to a bungalow. The image on the front cover ostensibly conveys a modern Ghanaian family. The characters in the picture appear in what can be read as traditional Ghanaian attire, and the children are distinguished by their neatly trimmed hair. Indubitably, the pamphlet is set on imagining a nation built on monogamy, in which nuclear family households embrace methods of familial care that are healthy for both family members and the nation. The model of the Christian family was believed to be the palpitating heart of the nation, propelling it into modernity and ensuring that families kept up with national progress. In this picture, polygamy was ultimately antithetical to Ghana's modernity.

The pamphlet includes a set of questions concerning family planning, a necessary condition for the proper love, care, and security of children, as well as for a warm and happy home. In this environment, too, children would be equipped with "character and training for life."[36]

The pamphlet also outlines the consequences of bad family planning, such as having too many mouths to feed, too many school uniforms to buy, too many extra rooms to build, and so on. In other words, large families were perceived as draining the family financially and thus producing stress on individual members. The consequences of such arrangements were likely to afflict the children, whose prospects for becoming responsible citizens would be compromised. Monogamy and the nuclear family were set against this dire portrait of polygamous family practices, which were not only financially ruinous but also "backward."

The information and overarching argument implied by the title *Let Us Plan for Healthy Happy Children!* run parallel to the argument in Reverend Buatsi's apology for monogamy, "that it made for happier families." Through *Let Us Plan for Happy Healthier Children!*, the CCMFL motivated Ghanaians to visit medical centers around the country that had been set up for the purpose of providing advice to married couples. These were called Medical Advice Centers. Doctors and nurses who specialized in the field of family planning staffed these facilities, providing information on Christian ways of self-care and pamphlets outlining the basis of healthy lifestyles.[37] The endorsement of these centers by the Christian Council of Ghana gave them credibility, all the while inspiring women to seek the services that they provided. There was also a section that gave the times and locations of the centers to motivate prospective couples to receive free medical assistance and counseling services on the usefulness of contraception. Family planning strategies were constructed as central to the survival of the nuclear family. The adoption of contraception, for example, modernized the nuclear family, making it more admirable. The acceptance of contraception by Christian families here was also supported by Protestant churches. And the Anglican Church, unlike the Catholic Church, had no qualms about contraception and family planning.

The CCMFL, therefore, faced very few obstacles in its pursuit of services that centered on family planning and adoption. Mrs. Hazel documents the progress and success of some of these projects in a letter to Christian Aid also dated September 21, 1966: "On behalf of the Volta Region Committee on Christian Marriage and Family Life, the Chairman and I wish to thank the British Christian Aid, most sincerely for supplying all the grant that was requested for our project. The work in the Volta Region is well under way. The need and interest is so great that that our problem is to know what projects should be given priority."[38] In the letter's closing, she adds: "I will be sending you my annual report and other material later, to give you an idea of what the committee is trying to accomplish. It is hoped that it will prove worthy of your support, and that you will deem it wise to continue your assistance in this project [for the] first few years in existence."[39]

In the letter, it is evident that the CCMFL continued to ask for assistance from Christian Aid in order to sustain its projects on building healthy Christian families. Mrs. Paton's correspondences with Miss Lacey, during which she asked for support for a project on the importance of the Christian family, is in a long line of exchanges between CCG and Christian Aid. In the intervening years, Mrs. Hazel, who took over from Mrs. Paton as the director and liaison, continued to keep in touch with Miss Lacey and Mr. Dudbridge, the secretary of Christian Aid. The CCMFL notified Christian Aid on any challenges or changes to the projects pursued on the ground in Ghana. Since the CCMFL had to submit annual reports on CA-funded projects in Ghana, the ties between the two organizations continued to grow, especially during the period when the project on Christian marriage and family life was undertaken. It is therefore not surprising that the Christian Council of Ghana today remains one of the most ardent members of the coalition that seeks to preserve the "proper family" values in the campaign against the liberalization of LGBT+ visibility in Ghana.

PALIMPSESTIC PROJECTS: FROM HETEROMONOGAMY TO HETERONATIONALISM

Arguably, the leavings of these projects constitute the palimpsests that inform the background against which LGBT+ politics occur today. Hence, I suggest that sweeping criticisms describing African Christianity and Africans as homophobic need to be more critical of and attentive to these histories and how they reincorporate themselves into sasso lives. Sasso also rewrite these histories in ways that complicate the construction of African homophobia and the reduction of African sexualities to heterosexuality. Moreover, we need to show how emerging LGBT+ human rights movements in Ghana are both affected and shaped by these complex histories.

I return to Foster's provocative point in the epigraph that introduces this chapter. First, it compels a rereading of the archive in ways that undermine the problematic construction that Ghana is a heterosexual nation. Second, it illuminates how "culture" and "tradition" are often deployed to condemn the pursuit of LGBT+ rights. The invocation of "tradition" in the debates on homosexuality in postcolonial Ghana is unlike the deployment of "tradition" in debates on temporality, whereby tradition is often pitted against "modernity." I argue that there is a simultaneous conflation of tradition, culture, and time in these arguments. Paradoxically, heterosexuality is not easily or neatly temporalized or recognized as merely existing in the past, because such an interpretation would offer proof that a variety of genders and sexualities have always existed in what is now known as postcolonial Ghana. The conflation works for a heteronormative nation-state bent on having the appearance of being modern in civilizational, colonial, and racialized terms. To this point, I quote Jacqui Alexander at length here; she suggests that this conflation is conveniently

> either intentionally invoked, disavowed, or muted as part of the repertoire of strategies deployed by different interests within or related to the state. Put differently, tradition and modernity have been used to designate specific temporalities, but they are themselves practices that are constituted through social relations that are interested in their purchase, and thus in that process move them into ideological proximity to, or distance from, one another. Since they do not operate simply as linear distinctions neatly demarcating a transition from one historical moment to another, or as categories that are merely fixed and inert, the question is not so much whether they matter but *how* they have been made to matter in matters sexual, what meanings have been affixed to them, who deploys them, and to what ends. When do "traditional" (hetero) sexual discourses get valorized within "modern" neo-imperial formations, and why? How do they come to be positioned as critical to the project of modernity? Does heterosexualization occupy a civilizing nexus in the neocolonial state's imperative of distancing itself from tradition in order to be counted as modern, that is, "civilized," and accorded the benefits of modernity? (2005, 193)

If anything, the ongoing onslaught of homophobia against the LGBT+ community, to which sasso are integral, happening in Ghana as I write this book invites us to not only return to the historical foundries in which were forged the ideologies and practices maintaining that homosexuality is un-African, but to also contend with the wreckage that heterosexuality's marriage to Christianity and racist/colonial notions of modernity continues to leave in sasso lives in particular and the LGBT+ community in general. The public outrage at LGBT+ activism in Ghana not only confirms Foster's point that Ghanaians are hypocritical but also articulates the selective if not convenient amnesia that becomes manifest when issues on homosexuality become the topic of the moment. Why not against corruption or violence against women or issues of poverty? Why are tradition, culture, and modernity not invoked on these issues, which affect a great majority of Ghanaians? Moreover, an often-missed point in the debates is how they reinscribe the tensions arising from the colonial/postcolonial versus customary/postcustomary publics.[40] What if we were to situate these debates in the histories of the contentions between the publics that continue to forge the frames of the heterocolonial nation-state—the colonial and customary publics? I, therefore, read Foster's criticism of Ghanaians not merely as a statement that is made in passing but as an intellectual diagnosis arising out of his observations of the increased visibility of the liberalization of same-sex politics and concomitant homophobia, and how this politics misses some vital historical points. Having links to several LGBT+ NGOs that interface with sasso constituencies on a regular basis and being a self-identified ardent Christian, Foster reveals the hypocrisy that belies the archive, and by this, I mean the fact that the archive can be problematically read to justify the heterosexualizing tendencies of the nation-state. The heterosexual anxieties around LGBT+ human rights politics epitomize the reverberations of heterocolonialism.

6

Queer Liberal Expeditions

The BBC's The World's Worst Place to Be Gay? *and the Paradoxes of Homocolonialism*

> Scott Mills walks through the slum, carrying buckets of water, visiting LGBT+s who live in hiding. Intermittently, Mills expresses his fear of homophobia in Uganda, wondering if he is going to survive at all. His fear of homophobia occurs against the background of his experience in London, where we see a sequence with Mills among his friends talking about how easy it is for them to be gay there. Accordingly, they discuss how the UK has become increasingly open-minded about gay identity. To get an insider view of homophobia, we are taken from London to Portsmouth, Mills's hometown, where the succeeding sequence shows the narrator interacting with a Ugandan gay asylum seeker. The man is described as a persecuted gay man who fled Uganda for the UK in order to protect his life. The Ugandan gay man reveals his travails in Uganda, especially with the police and his family, which disowned him. Comparing his experience to the gay asylum seeker, Mills utters: "This is a million miles away from what I went through." And in the background, we see the Union Jack, waving in the wind. The remainder of the documentary is sprinkled with scenes in which nongay Ugandans, including clergy, politicians, and some members of civil society, express homophobic sentiments. We also see sequences in which homosexuals share their stories about being victims of homophobia and fearing for their lives in the unpredictable climate created for sexual minorities.
>
> —SCENES FROM *THE WORLD'S WORST PLACE TO BE GAY?* (2011)

On May 17, 2014, Bring Us Rights and Justice (BURJ),[1] a local human rights NGO based in Accra, collaborated with the US and Dutch embassies in Accra to celebrate International Day Against Homophobia (IDAHO) for the first time in Ghana.[2] The event was held at the US embassy, a heavily securitized building located in Cantonments, one of Accra's affluent suburbs. Accorded the responsibility for organizing the event, BURJ received financial support from the US and Dutch missions in Ghana. IDAHO attracted sexual minorities from across Accra and other parts of Ghana, including constituencies of sasso, some of whom were either partially connected to or fully employed at BURJ.

Eight years before the celebration of IDAHO, in 2006, it was alleged that an unknown international LGBT+ organization had attempted to organize a conference in Ghana's Eastern Region. Knowledge about this alleged conference triggered the indignation of the Ghanaian public. The Ghanaian journalist Haruna Atta dubbed it "the conference that never was"; news about the conference incited a moral panic which drew the attention of the NGOs that now address LGBT+ issues in Ghana. In the journalistic exposé, Atta asks:

> So how/where did the story originate to have so gripped the nation as to invite a public statement from the government and condemnation from religious, social and traditional groups? The culprit, it seems, is all of us: the media. Isn't this something worth investigating by the National Media Commission? How could false media reports have created such an [*sic*] panic situation in Ghana at home and in the Ghanaian Diaspora? But true or false media reporting, one thing has been settled unequivocally in this sexual affair: it is now quite clear that Ghanaians do not have the stomach for gays and lesbians![3]

Atta's article marks 2006 as a pivotal moment in the public discourse on homosexuality in Ghana by underscoring one of the first public debates on the subject. Politicians, members of the clergy, and civil society leaders were embroiled in the ensuing controversy in ways that amplified anxieties around the subject of homosexuality in the country. This period, arguably, coincided with the pursuit of LGBT+ human rights activism by organizations including BURJ, the West Africa Program to Combat AIDS and STI (WAPCAS), and the Centre for Popular Education and Human Rights, Ghana (CEPERHG).[4] The celebration of IDAHO in 2014 was anticipated by the shifts caused by the increasingly widespread conversations on LGBT+ human rights pursuits in Ghana.

A centerpiece at IDAHO was the screening of the BBC's *The World's Worst Place to Be Gay?* The documentary first aired on the BBC's Channel Three in 2011 and was released on YouTube in 2012. Focusing on homophobia in Uganda, the documentary features the British DJ and TV personality Scott Mills, who chronicles the "precarious" circumstances in which sexual minorities live their lives. Mills's documentary reinforced what Manthia Diawara (2010) describes as the "humanitarian tarzanism" that underwrites documentaries on Africa, and about Africans, produced in the West. In other words, the film rehearsed representations about Africa immediately familiar to Western audiences, and despite its political tone, trafficked in a form of white saviorism all too familiar in LGBT+ human rights discourses about Africa.

The objective of this chapter is twofold. First, I illuminate how BURJ exemplifies NGOs that arose in Ghana in the last two decades of the twentieth century, providing an ethnographic portrait of the disagreements among BURJ employees in the wake of IDAHO.

Second, I highlight how the screening of *The World's Worst Place to Be Gay?* at IDAHO illuminates the vexed connections between racism and queer liberalism in postcolonial Africa and the nettlesome and conflicting environments in which African NGOs like BURJ reside. On the one hand, these organizations, in their activities and practices, seek to address LGBT+ human rights as an important human rights concern. On the other hand, however, the contexts in which they are nestled are animated by an uncertainty that compels these organizations to veil their pursuit of LGBT+ human rights projects for fear of exposure.

Arguably, BURJ's employees express an amphibious disposition analogous to the self-making practices of the sasso in this book. Not only an LGBT+ human rights organization, BURJ, like many NGOs founded in the late 1990s and early 2000s, began as a human rights NGO with a primary focus on gender issues. Here, it is important to signal a key difference in the politicization of gender in the context of the neoliberal international. In sub-Saharan Africa, the neoliberal wave orchestrated by projects of structural adjustment and economic recovery deployed gender as a political language to mainstream women into the public sphere. Against this backdrop, organizations like BURJ were committed to projects focused on gender mainstreaming upon their founding. LGBT+ human rights is a recent addition to BURJ's list of human rights interventions. Here, I contend with the question: does BURJ participate in homocolonial projects while simultaneously seeking to address the homophobic onslaught faced by queer Ghanaians?

SITUATING BRING US RIGHTS AND JUSTICE (BURJ) IN HISTORICAL CONTEXT

The rise and eventual prominence of Bring Us Rights and Justice (BURJ) in Ghana did not occur in a vacuum. Like many Ghanaian and African NGOs, BURJ's emergence and eventual prominence can be linked to the increased neoliberalization of Africa in the early eighties, typified by state deregulation. The years that intervened between the waves of independence in Africa to the eighties witnessed a litany of military interventions and governments that crippled the growth of postcolonial African nations. These years were followed by a slew of Western interventions that sought to rescue developing nations. The Ghanaian feminist and gender scholar Takyiwaa Manuh notes that this "long period of militarization and nonrepresentative government and increasing disenchantment with the state contributed to the spread of NGOs and their occupation of the space for independent action" (2007, 131). This period also coincided with the appearance of neoliberal pursuits in Africa in general and Ghana in particular, with the introduction of a wave of colossal political economic programs intended to help African countries recover.

One key feature of the neoliberal apparatus was its investment in state deregulation. To paraphrase the anthropologist James Ferguson, this implied the decentralization of state sovereignty (2006). It is therefore not surprising that neoliberalism reproduced the neocolonial apparatus left in the wake of colonialism's demise.

Of course, former colonial states no longer imposed rules on ex-colonies; non-state organizations and actors with their roots in the West now did the bidding of ex-colonial nations. The transnational organizations that emerged in the late seventies and early eighties expedited the globalization of neoliberalism through various interventions in a postcolonial world that had inherited the excesses of colonization (Ferguson 2006; Ake 1996; Pierre 2013). Organizations like the World Bank and the International Monetary Fund (IMF) arose during this period, implementing the Structural Adjustment Program (SAP) and the Economic Recovery Program (ERP). The projects executed under these programs demobilized state monopoly over their economies, introducing divestments that created an opening for the establishment of NGOs (Igoe and Kelsall 2005; Ake 1996). In many parts of Africa, development projects during this period coincided with efforts to resolve gender inequality within development itself.

The Latin American feminist and critical development studies scholar Sonia Alvarez describes the magnified shifts in transnational projects on women that required NGO interventions as the period of the "NGO boom" (1999). To be clear, the rise of NGOs in the non-Western world was accompanied, as it were, by intensified neoliberalization. As I have pointed out already, the transnationalization of governance and sovereignty, which required that NGOs compete for power and legitimacy on the stage of global politics, further disenfranchised nations in the so-called developing world.

The NGO boom marked a moment where "gender" entered public and political discourse. As Takyiwaa Manuh argues: "The language of gender serves to address some of the imbalances that have come in with or have been accentuated by imported economic and political structures" (2007, 131). For Manuh, NGOs invested in gender advocacy emerged in response to the structural readjustment of violence introduced by projects executed under SAP and ERP. It is unsurprising, then, that the gender mainstreaming movement began in the last quarter of the twentieth century. This shift coincided with the emergence of projects that tackled the consequences that the collusion between neoliberalism and neocolonialism had on women. I maintain that the emergence of gender as a placeholder for women is linked to these ripples.

In Ghana, in particular, the emergence of several feminist and legal organizations, such as the International Federation of Women Lawyers (FIDA) and the Women and Juvenile Unit of Ghana (WAJU; now called the Domestic Violence and Victim Support Unit [DOVVSU]), further mainstreamed gender issues as primarily women's issues. The founders and members of these organizations not only pioneered advocacy for women but also waged a campaign that addressed the multiple barriers confronted by women and girls as a result of the intersectional challenges induced by their marginal locations in the educational, economic, health, and other sectors. Collectively, these organizations wielded immense pressure on the Ghanaian government to legislate a domestic violence bill, a feat that transformed the landscape for women in Ghana.

The demands by these organizations included the revision of statutes in the national constitution that undercut the rights of women. At the time, human rights efforts predominantly focused on struggles for the rights of women, a cause that brought together women from a variety of backgrounds. Clearly, in the late 1990s and early 2000s, the fight for the rights of sexual minorities, unlike women's rights, was invisible in the human rights advocacy agenda. The founder of BURJ, Madam Ama Brew Hammer, together with feminists like Ama Ata Aidoo and later Takyiwaa Manuh, Dzodzi Tsikata, Akosua Adomako Ampofo, and Audrey Gadzekpo, among many others, spearheaded the demand for radical constitutional shifts.[5]

The events generated by the push for the implementation of a domestic violence bill drastically shifted the rhetoric on women's rights, resulting in an outgrowth of NGOs and activist organizations. The confluence of these formations sparked the process that led to the passage of the domestic violence bill. As Takyiwaa Manuh (2007) noted in the United Kingdom's Department of International Development (DFID) report, the "much awaited" Domestic Violence Bill (DVB) was enacted in early 2007, following years of undaunted demonstrations by women across the country. The successful passage of the bill was heralded as one of the most significant legal feats to tectonically shift Ghana's sociolegal landscape, opening up a space for broadening human rights issues into other sociopolitical and cultural spheres.

THE PAROCHIALIZATION OF GENDER UNDER NEOLIBERALISM

Neoliberalism's approach to gender in postcolonial Ghana in particular and Africa in general is distinguishable from its approach to gender in the Global North. In the Global South, neoliberalism advanced a gender campaign that compelled governments to engage in a politics of gender mainstreaming, which amounted to aggressive efforts to include women in the public sphere; a different approach unfolded in the West. In the Global North, gender extended beyond the idea of gender as women to gender as a social construction and an identity existing on a spectrum. Conversely, in sub-Saharan Africa, neoliberal strategies to include women reinforced those violent gender binaries that currently haunt LGBT+ human rights pursuits in postcolonial Ghana. In other words, neoliberalism, the political economic regime that institutionalized gender politics in Africa as a project invested in intentionally incorporating women into the sphere of the political, shaped the contexts in which the current anxieties around LGBT+ human rights pursuits occur.

The passage of the Domestic Violence Bill in Ghana anticipated the founding and establishment of Bring Us Rights and Justice (BURJ) by Madam Ama Brew Hammer in 2008. As a human rights NGO, BURJ has since been involved in addressing human rights issues and social justice advocacy projects in Ghana, ranging from class, access to justice and health, domestic violence, mental health, gender violence in schools, and workplace discrimination, to mention but a few. In sum, BURJ was conceived in a climate shaped by transnational organizations responding to larger social and economic problems in Africa. It is also important to note that the current anxieties around homosexuality, which defines the terrain in which BURJ pursues its LGBT+ activities, are the consequences of the "whack-a-mole politics of rescue" of SAP and ERP. The desire to rescue women, subsumed under gender mainstreaming, narrowed the focus of gender issues, and the consequences of this parochial approach are evidenced in responses to LGBT+ issues in Ghana (Currier 2012; McFadden 2011; Alexander 2005; Biruk 2020).

INTRODUCING BURJ

By the time I joined BURJ in September 2013, Madam Ama had just been appointed the minister for Gender, Children, and Social Protection. Currently, the organization is known for prioritizing human rights by pursuing legal actions against the violations of and infringements on citizens' civil rights and liberties by both the state and civil society. Madam Ama's rise to prominence was helped by her active participation in the late 1990s and early 2000s in feminist and legal organizations that waged multiple advocacy campaigns to compel the government to enact a domestic violence bill. The demands by these movements included the revision of statutes in the Fourth Republican Constitution to address issues of women and gender. Deeply embedded in these activist reformist projects, Madam Ama consolidated herself in the NGO domain and women's movement as one of Ghana's most influential activists and lawyers. Madam Ama's work in wide-ranging areas drew attention to BURJ from both local and global human rights arenas.

Since BURJ began executing programs that cater to sexual minorities, survivors of gender-based violence, people living with HIV/AIDS, and so on, it has received considerable funding from organizations in the Netherlands, the United Kingdom, the United States, and Belgium, among other Western nations. The organization's links to Northern donors, with whom it obviously shares paradoxical relationships, reinforce Ashley Currier's observation of the messy terrains in which the growth of the LGBT movement in countries like Namibia and South Africa played out. Currier writes: "Donor funding and relationships with international LGBT movement organizations facilitated Namibian and South African LGBT activists' networks with activists elsewhere in Africa, buttressing their international visibility. Thus, LGBT movement organizations were not entirely beholden to Northern donors and LGBT activists; instead, they were able to use these resources in ways that benefited a growing African LGBT movement" (2012, 20–21).

Similarly, BURJ is embedded in networks that allow activists and staff within the organization to participate, for instance, in international conferences on human rights in general and LGBT+ human rights issues in particular. Additionally, the organization is notable for a popular internship program it runs, which attracts interns from countries like Australia, the United States and Canada, Europe and parts of Asia, and Latin America. Occasionally, an intern will come from a country in Africa.[6] The internship program began with the inception of BURJ and has been running in conjunction with foreign missions in Ghana. On BURJ's website, there is a section that directs interested internship applicants to consider interning there. This is accompanied by a full description of the endeavors undertaken by the organization and a monthly internship fee of $150.[7] Upon admission, international interns conduct research, write publications, and actively engage in human rights outreach and campaigns and the various projects executed by BURJ.

In the main, BURJ, like many NGOs, especially those that focus on marginalized groups in postcolonial Ghana, illustrates Cal Biruk's observation that "NGO practices serve socially significant functions such as making a person legible through their citation of acronyms or categories like LGBTQI, often through activities that assume Euro-American notions of self as an autonomous thing to be confessed, named, or worked on, in notable contrast to scholarly renderings of African personhood as a state of becoming rather than being, and as ongoing achievement" (2020, 480).

NGOization therefore reinforces Westernization. And like the Christian missionary efforts that anticipated them, these organizations have agents and institutions, both local and nonlocal, that parrot particular notions of modernity. BURJ's LGBT+ human rights projects are subsumed under its "Access to Justice; Social Inclusion; Legislation and Policy Reform; Health; Government Accountability; and Community and Institutional Strengthening" pursuits. Besides the LGBT+ community, BURJ focuses on other target groups that include "persons with disabilities, including mental disabilities, women and girls, and prisoners."[8] BURJ, therefore, has a wide-ranging mission that, at the time of my ethnography, was expanding.

Claiming to be strictly nonpartisan, BURJ's human rights projects have included addressing socioeconomic inequality, discrimination, domestic violence, women's rights, mental health rights, and sexual and reproductive health rights. The section on sexual and reproductive health rights encompasses projects that focus on access to health for key populations, which include men who have sex with men (MSM), women who have sex with women (WSW), survivors of gender-based violence, female sex workers (FSW), and people living with HIV/AIDS (PLHIV).

BURJ employees are beholden to its vision "to become a respected human rights organization, both within Ghana as well as globally." Thus, the organization has minimal presence in other West African countries like Gambia, Senegal, Liberia, and Sierra Leone. While it is unclear whether it addresses issues affecting sexual minorities in these countries, what is clear is that BURJ's increasing interest in LGBT+ human rights issues and homophobia in Ghana is evidenced by the publication of what is arguably Ghana's first LGBT+ empowerment manual. The publication is intended for sexual minorities such as sasso. In the work and activities for sexual minorities undertaken by BURJ, sasso identities became subsumed under LGBT+. Thus, the "amphibious" pursuit of LGBT+ empowerment programs places the organization on the map of queer liberalism.[9] It is not surprising that IDAHO was organized under the auspices of the organization because of its prominence both locally and internationally on human rights issues. During preparations for IDAHO, I uncovered that some BURJ employees disagreed with the organization's increasing interest in LGBT+ human rights pursuits.

Knotted Micropolitics in LGBT+ Human Rights Advocacy

At the top of BURJ's hierarchy and functions are the director and the executive board, who steer the organization's major projects and activities. The executive director of BURJ during my time in the organization was Mr. Richard Owusu, a twenty-four-year-old man who took over from Madam Ama Brew Hammer. Born and raised in Accra, Richard, before joining Madam Ama Brew Hammer at BURJ, had earned his first degree from the University of Ghana. It is unclear whether Richard self-identified as sasso, although he secretly disclosed to me and several queer staff, most of whom were interns from Western countries, that he was gay.[10] Before assuming his position as the executive director of the organization, Richard closely worked as an assistant to Madam Ama. Here is an excerpt from a 2013 conversation with him:

> Madam Ama entered my life while I was in high school. Or should I say that I entered her life in high school. She has since mentored me by giving me the tools I needed to become a human rights advocate in Ghana. My burning desire to pursue human rights activism in Ghana, which is not limited to gender, LGBT+ human rights, but also includes the working poor, and other vulnerable groups, was all instilled in me by her. Growing up, I never envisioned myself working in an outfit like this; it was only when Madam Ama "adopted" me as part of her family that I became quite involved in activism and to take this human rights topic seriously. I know that as a self-described feminist in Ghana, Madam Ama has a reputation that sometimes endangers her. You know Ghanaians and what they think about feminism. Many think that it is not African and that it was brought here from Europe or America. But Madam Ama, like other notable Ghanaian feminists, resisted that narrative. Founding Bring Us Rights and Justice was definitely part of changing that story, which is why I became so attached to her inclination for social justice and the pursuit of human rights at BURJ.

Richard's investment in BURJ is inspired by his close relationship with Madam Ama. Following his appointment as the executive director of BURJ, Richard wanted to take the organization to new heights. Several projects occurred under Richard's leadership, some of which included education, research, advocacy, advisory, and monitoring. BURJ, periodically in 2012 and regularly in 2013–2014, pursued several projects concurrently. These projects spanned gender-based violence (GBV) in schools, a remand prisoners program, LGBT+ human rights, reproductive and sexual health, and access to justice for the marginalized.

These various endeavors are overseen by the director and the technical projects manager of the organization, Amanda Yarney, who was in her early thirties at the time of this ethnography. Like Richard, Amanda obtained her degree in political science at the University of Ghana. Before joining BURJ, she worked with Commission of Human Rights and Administrative Justice (CHRAJ). Programs involving human rights cases fell under the supervision of the director of BURJ's Human Rights Clinic, Akosua Agyapong, a thirty-two-year-old woman with a degree from Accra Polytechnic (now known as the Accra Technical University). Akosua was not a trained lawyer but coordinated a cohort of lawyers who served as counselors at the clinic. The organization also ran the popular Pro-Bono Lawyer Network (PBLN) program, with participating lawyers offering free legal services to vulnerable populations that lacked access to information about their human rights. These and other various activities run by BURJ propelled the organization into the limelight of human rights advocacy in Ghana.

My presence in the organization lasted for a year. During this period, I observed that the non-Ghanaian interns who were queer and mostly white occasionally asserted their LGBT+ identification without reproach from the organization's nonqueer Ghanaian members. In addition to the white queer interns, there were three other queer Ghanaians in the office, most of whom chose to be discreet about their queerness. However, during projects that focused on men who have sex with men (MSM), it became apparent to me that there were queer Africans in the organization because of how the MSMs interacted with them.[11]

There was constant dissonance among employees on LGBT+ issues. There were staff members who identified as "allies," thus accepting of interns and staff who self-identified as LGBT+. Also present in the organization were those employees who remained silent on BURJ's commitment to LGBT+ human rights. Some of these employees elected to not participate in projects that focused on sexual minorities, claiming that to be involved in LGBT+ projects would be to accept homosexuality, and such a position was incongruent with their religious affiliation as Christian. The dissension among the organization's staff on LGBT+ issues became apparent when Akosua, the human rights coordinator and staunch ally of the LGBT+, shared the following observation with me in 2014:

> I have been working at BURJ for over five years now. During my time here, I have always ensured, as the person in charge of running the human rights unit within the organization, that everybody is recognized as a rights-bearing citizen irrespective of their age, sexual orientation, gender identity, ethnicity, creed, class, you list them. Although BURJ started as an NGO that addresses women's vulnerable positions in Ghana, that interest has been widened to include other vulnerable groups. Maybe when Madam Ama established the organization she did not envision that it would grow to address LGBT+ human rights issues. I know that there are some colleagues who do not like the turn we have taken, which is addressing LGBT+ rights. They are the religious ones who claim we are doing something wrong. Their concerns aside, they know they have to survive. They know in order to survive you need a job.

> So, if there are grants that are being offered by international LGBT+ human rights NGOs to run LGBT+ human rights projects in Ghana, we apply for them. Those grants bring us the money that sustains them. You can disagree with the fact that we engage in LGBT+ human rights campaigns, but you have to do it because life in Ghana is hard and your job is good. Those who don't like the fact that we understand gay rights to be human rights are free to leave or stay. It is what it is.

Akosua's claims suggest that Madam Ama Brew Hammer established BURJ, first, to address the vulnerable positions of women in Ghanaian society, and then, with the passage of time, added other vulnerable groups, of which the LGBT+ community is the most recent addition. Although LGBT+ concerns have now been incorporated into the human rights framework adopted by BURJ, the pursuit of LGBT+ issues often occurs in tandem with sexual and reproductive health rights. It is within the organization's framework to improve access to health for key populations, which includes men who have sex with men (MSM), female sex workers (FSW), survivors of gender-based violence (SGBV), and people living with HIV/AIDS (PLHIV) that LGBT+ issues are addressed. I speculate that to avoid conflicts, the leadership of the organization subsumed LGBT+ issues within the larger framework of access to health and justice to avert being viewed as an LGBT+ organization in a country hesitant to recognize LGBT+ rights.

Despite the underlying dissension triggered by the place of LGBT+ human rights in the organization, BURJ continued to underscore the importance of improving access to health for sexual minorities. This included men who have sex with men (MSMs), most of whom were sasso. BURJ received a large grant from the funding pool called STAR-Ghana in 2013 to conduct research in five regions of Ghana among sexual minorities, most of whom were believed to have limited access to health care.[12] The research, called "Improving Access to Health Care for Key Populations and the Survivors of Gender-Based Violence," was approved by the Ghana Health Service (GHS). It was intended to create better health services for MSM, including sasso. I participated as the principal investigator for this project and witnessed the micropolitics among BURJ staff regarding the distribution of funding and the moral implications of offering services to homosexuals. Through these projects, LGBT+ issues were intermittently addressed, much to the dismay of a section of BURJ's staff. The debate about whether queer rights should become integral to BURJ's human rights program, I intimate, was possibly the corollary of the economic suffering caused by neoliberal forces that ran roughshod over Ghanaians and the ascent of a brand of Christianity that seemed to be competing for sovereignty with the nation (Biruk 2020; Quayson 2014; McFadden 2011; Hoad 2007; Gifford 2004).

The research project implementation required that employees work closely with sexual minorities, whether or not they agreed with their sexual dispositions, as well as with other marginalized and vulnerable groups. The project expected BURJ staff to collect data from MSM, female sex workers (FSW), and persons living with HIV (PLHIV). There were lingering disagreements among staff on the LGBT+ focus of the project.

The dissension engendered by BURJ's pursuit of projects related to the LGBT+ community was one part of the story. But the prevailing contentions and dissatisfaction among employees were also linked to economic disparities between high- and low-ranking staff. It was clear to some employees at the nonmanagerial level that wage gaps existed between them and the managerial staff. Low-ranking officials constantly mused over their measly monthly wages, which they insisted failed to buffer them from Ghana's worsening economic conditions.

Among the employees, in particular those who kept their queer identities a secret, including Kobby, projects that focused on improving access to health for sexual minorities came with benefits that kept them afloat in Ghana's indeterminate and harsh economy. The income from such projects enabled Kobby to support his mother and sister. Largely because of their familial obligations, he had to delicately balance himself between the NGO world, which promoted LGBT+ rights, and a family that espoused heteronormative values. In the process, he faced the scorn of family members, who accepted the financial support despite rejecting what came with that support: the increased visibility of same-sex politics and human rights advocacy for sexual minorities in Ghana.

Similarly, a number of BURJ employees expressed moral objections toward LGBT+ projects, but enjoyed the income generated by those projects. These employees, in a manner akin to the nurses and health workers at the hospitals who vilified sasso, opposed LGBT+ human rights politics and BURJ's pursuit of it. They regularly resorted to citing biblical passages to justify their moral stance against homosexuality. As one such BURJ employee, Clement, once suggested during a meeting to discuss the parameters of a public health project geared toward MSM:

> At the very least, we as an organization should know that we live in a country where homosexuality is unacceptable. Ghana is predominantly a Christian nation and our Christian moral values challenge us to be firm in our opposition to vices such as homosexuality. I work in an organization that seeks to bring recourse to the vulnerable and in no way argue that homosexuals need to be penalized. I think the organization's attachment to LGBT+ human rights is coming in the way of my own understanding of human rights, but of course, I can't condemn why we are pursuing it. We just have to understand that it is an illegal thing. It is as simple as that.

Clement's statement stages a crucial scenario, which is the extent of the collision of African Christian and queer liberal modernities in an organization supported and funded by Western donors that fuel queer liberalism. In fact, the expression of these antagonistic moral sentiments and commitments should not only be understood as a consequence of Ghanaians' fear of a dying morality but also be tied to the steady suffering and resignation in this neoliberalized nation. Ultimately, these dissensions, together with other lingering tensions, defined the backdrop against which IDAHO was organized.

Who Attends International Day Against Homophobia (IDAHO)?

With preparations under way for the celebration of IDAHO, BURJ witnessed an exchange of phone calls and e-mails with the two foreign diplomatic missions involved, the American and Dutch embassies. For the purposes of the event, Richard formed a four-member committee, including myself. The other members were two doctoral students from abroad, one of whom was a white intern and the other of Ghanaian extraction. Except for the white intern, all four of us remained surreptitious about our sexual identities, and understandably so, as I have already indicated. As part of the preparation for the event, BURJ held a meeting to discuss IDAHO's logistics. At the meeting, a section of the staff vented their disagreements with BURJ's increasing investments in the pursuit of LGBT+ advocacy.

Moral concerns around homosexuality and low wages were raised by some staff members, several of whom suggested that an NGO advocating for human rights should not financially disenfranchise its staff. For example, there were complaints that the director and the executive board received salaries that were not commensurate with their qualifications. The IDAHO preparatory meeting, therefore, served as the grounds on which staff like the senior technical officer (STO) and the director of the Human Rights Clinic vented their disagreements with BURJ's involvement with IDAHO. These employees shared the view that these diplomatic missions exploited BURJ to promote an LGBT+ agenda, challenging the original goals of the organization, which initially excluded LGBT+ human rights.

The suggested venue for IDAHO was the US consulate in Accra. Richard announced that since the event would be supported by the Dutch and American diplomatic missions, it was BURJ's responsibility as a local organization to mobilize persons and groups who self-identified as LGBT+. Those employees who decided to attend the event, some of whom self-identified as sasso and some as LGBT+, were given several responsibilities at the event. Since the event was held to celebrate IDAHO, the term *LGBT+* superseded *sasso*. In fact, never during the program was *sasso* deployed. At the preparatory session, it was suggested that the program begin with the screening of a documentary, which was to be followed by a panel discussion. At this time, the documentary to be screened was unknown to the organization, as it was staff at the US embassy who chose which documentary to show during the celebration.

Some BURJ staff began to question the organization's involvement in the celebration of IDAHO, asking, Is BURJ an LGBT+ human rights organization? Is it the mission of BURJ to secure LGBT+ rights in a country in which same-sex activity is criminalized? Is BURJ not engaging in a crime by clandestinely pursuing LGBT+ human rights, by celebrating IDAHO? The senior technical officer, Amanda Yarney, tabled these questions, which invited disagreements from Richard.

It would be tempting to interpret the differences expressed at the meeting as a mark of homophobia and BURJ employees' irrational apprehension about

IDAHO. I suggest that we look at the disagreements that arose that morning as offshoots, the causes of which are unclear to the outsider. For example, if the wage difference between Richard, who furtively self-identified as queer, and his subordinates were to be considered in the context of employees' objections to celebrating IDAHO, we would read the scenario differently. If Amanda's repudiation is read as the outcome of the employees' grievances and dissatisfaction with BURJ's celebration of IDAHO, then that adds another twist to the dissension. Also, some employees felt that they held the same educational qualifications as Richard, for which they deserved a better remuneration than they were currently receiving. Arguably, this dissatisfaction shaped why BURJ employees responded to IDAHO in the manner in which they did. Akosua Agyapong, the human rights coordinator in charge of running the Human Rights Clinic, had this to say after the IDAHO event:

> You know, Richard [the executive director] should remember that we both have the same qualification. So, if he expects us to work on such an event [IDAHO], he better pay us well. If he had a master's degree then maybe I would understand why he gets more than us. But, for now, he holds the same qualification as me. Also, I have no quarrel with IDAHO. No! Far from that! My concern is about the benefits that doing this collaboration with these embassies will bring to us all in this NGO. I think that it is easy for Richard to mobilize us to do this, but he's forgotten that not all of us are like him [by which she means gay and well off]. I think he should know that we will give our consent to participate in these events only if we are also content with how much we get at the end of the month.

To be clear, Akosua's apathy toward IDAHO is connected to her receiving what she regards as a paltry salary not commensurate with her qualifications. Specifically, she said that "my monthly wage is not commensurate with my duties as the human rights coordinator of the Human Rights Clinic at BURJ." Akosua insisted that to participate in the organization of IDAHO "added another line of responsibility to a job for which I get very little compensation." Thus, in her opinion, IDAHO had less to do with her moral position and more to do with the incommensurability of her monthly salary with her college qualifications.

Another reason for the hesitation was the lingering perception among several employees that Richard, who was much younger than his subordinates, was immature and was rude and disrespectful. Richard's age prompted some employees to conclude that he could be their boss, but never their coequal in age. When Richard was out of sight, Kobby would criticize his amateurish behavior by calling him a "square peg in a round hole" who "acts like a child. When we undertake projects and he sees men he's interested in, he acts like a chicken without a head. What kind of human being lives in the world like that? He has to be careful the kind of people he does that with, especially as some of these guys just do it for the money and are also more likely to blackmail you if you fail to give them what they want. I just hope that he's careful about his proclivities before he loses his job."

Sulley, the office manager, reinforced Kobby's sentiment by suggesting that Richard was clearly not ready for the position. Pointing to the fact that Richard secured the position of the executive director because of Madam Ama, he says:

> As a matter of fact, the founder gave him the position because of his bootlicking and sycophantic demeanor. He went and told on the immediate past director, which was why she was fired, for being inefficient and making a mess at the organization. But you know this is not the first time he has done that. He was also the founder's pet, being commanded to do what she wanted to do. So even if we ask for a raise, whenever he goes to see the founder, he cowers before her, failing to put our demands for a raise to her. All he cares about is himself, his friends and consorts. In fact, he is really someone who we can't trust. Because he gets all the money, too, he has become proud and disrespectful. Today he has an iPhone, tomorrow he has a Samsung Galaxy, what kind of human rights are we practicing if the leader is so self-absorbed and cares less about us, his subordinates?

It is evident that employees like Sulley and Kobby complained about Richard's immaturity. However, a select group of BURJ's employees, including the international interns, were of the view that he had the relevant skills and qualifications required to manage the organization. They shared the belief that Richard shifted the orientation of BURJ upon assuming the directorship early by incorporating LGBT+ human rights. Amidst the dissatisfaction and disaffection shown by some of the employees, BURJ's accountant, Vincent, was one of few in the organization who had a favorable view of Richard. For Vincent, "Richard has single-handedly transformed the organization to everybody's surprise. When Amanda was in charge, the interns were so miserable. They would come to the office and sit down idle. They were given no responsibilities. But, as you know, these guys [interns] are paying so much to come and experience doing human rights work in Ghana. But Amanda did not care, and BURJ was just going down the drain. But Richard changed all of that."

To be clear, opinions about Richard wavered. For instance, when knowledge about his sexual proclivities entered the conversation, the views about him became even more hostile. Some staff, aware of his homoerotic engagements, shrouded their knowledge in secrecy. By cordoning off their awareness of the director's queer proclivities, some staff preserved their contract with BURJ, as they feared any exposure of Richard's homosexual leanings might undermine their jobs. In a similar vein, queer Ghanaian employees had to operate under the paradigm of "don't ask don't tell" out of fear of becoming targeted by those BURJ staff who disagreed with LGBT+ liberalization.[13] These various tactics, adopted by both queer Ghanaians and their nonqueer Ghanaian counterparts, albeit in dissonance with the organization's goal to decriminalize same-sex sexuality, were conducted to safeguard BURJ's stability.

Unforeseen Entanglements: Amphibious Organizations and Homocolonial LGBT+ Humanitarianism

Evidently, amphibious self-making was palpable in the everyday activities of the organization. The queer Ghanaians in the organization navigated BURJ amphibiously. Although Richard would on occasion remind employees that despite their knowledge of his intimate life, he was the person in charge, he carefully navigated his queer identity in ways that did not interfere with his identity as a Christian with strong roots in the church.

Thus, Richard was often wary about the uneasy sexual and cultural climates in which he served as the face of BURJ. The tittle-tattles around homosexuality arose only when employees complained about delays in monthly wages or felt that they were not getting the bonuses promised them by Richard at the end of the year. For them, gossiping about the sexual leanings of the executive director in his absence represented a way of dealing with his "bossiness." Gossip, for the employees, was a way of asserting power and control, and to also cushion the consequences of working under what some presumed was a despotic leadership style. The deployment of gossip here shows just how homophobia was integral to the mechanics of BURJ. It was part of the latticework of an organization that fought homophobia in its various projects.

The disagreements among the staff on LGBT+ politics were mainly internal. On occasion, some staff explicitly expressed moral sentiments about the projects that focused on sexual minorities. They would sporadically either jocularly or seriously make a laughingstock of Richard. For example, Kweku, the man in charge of information technology at BURJ, knew about Richard's sexual proclivities without sharing how he came by such information. Having worked in the organization since its founding, Kweku knew a lot about the organization and its entrails. He once hinted at Richard's homosexuality in a conversation to me as follows: "I think he should be careful not to be caught having sex with a man, because he is the director of a respectable organization, and such an act might bring shame to the organization. If he goes around getting fucked in the asshole if he's caught in doing so all of us will be fucked up as well. We will lose our jobs and people will know that our boss was getting fucked in the ass."

Kweku's homophobic sentiment here privileges the organization's outward presentation as a respectable entity. He feared that Richard's sexual proclivities might jeopardize the organization's reputation as well as the employees working in it. In effect, Kweku expects the executive director to have a "modicum" of respect. While he does not directly share this with Richard, because he is his boss, the fact that he articulates this view reveals the dissonance in the organization about homosexuality and LGBT+ community. Kweku's concerns form the part of the background against which the disagreements shared before IDAHO were expressed. These various views amplify the fissures in the organization regarding LGBT+ human rights discourse and the organization's collaboration with the US and Dutch embassies.

In large measure, some employees were of the view that BURJ was either compelled to collaborate or that the executive director could not turn down the offer because of his fear of white people. Some members asserted that projects involving homosexuals contradicted their Christian moral values. On IDAHO, these staff did not show up at the American embassy.

IDAHO: The Event

Thirty members of the LGBT+ community attended IDAHO. Some of the LGBT+ members in attendance self-identified as sasso. In attendance, too, were the chief superintendents from the Ghana Police Service and diplomatic officials from the American and Dutch embassies, among other invited persons. Not all members of the executive board were present at IDAHO. For instance, the STO, the director of the Human Rights Clinic, the accountant, and other low-level employees absented themselves. However, five employees, including Richard and the international interns, were present to coordinate the program. The BBC's *The World's Worst Place to Be Gay?* was the centerpiece of IDAHO, which was followed by a discussion panel constituted by some leading members of Ghana's human rights community.

Audience members had various interpretations of the screening. Asked by the director what they thought about the documentary, most described the situation in Uganda as unfortunate and terrible. One attendee who self-identified as gay made the following remark:

> I cannot believe Africans are doing this to Africans. We are doing to ourselves what the colonial white people did to us, because of a religion that was used to punish us and to justify our place as people without culture, without history. I am not sure what else to make of the documentary only to describe how awful Africans treat each other. In Ghana, the situation is no different, but at least we manage to make it work for us as queer people. I think in a way that the documentary tells me that the LGBT+ community in Ghana is better off. My question is: are we going to get better or get worse? I am not sure or certain about that.

The response from this attendee speaks to the uncertainty animating the LGBT+ and sasso community in Ghana. There is evidently a sharp condemnation of Africans, a position that reechoes the documentary's condemnation of Ugandans and their government. Interestingly, however, the statement that Africans' treatment of homosexuals parallels how white colonists treated Africans is quite crucial. This analogy historicizes, in a fundamental way, the layers and intersections of oppression by highlighting how racism and homophobia entwine in rather uneasy ways. That white supremacy is categorically entwined with heterosexual supremacy is explained by the attendee in a way that the documentary itself fails to do.

Immediately after this remark, Anthony, a sasso in the audience, shared his concerns about the lack of historical understanding portrayed in the documentary and the wrongful generalization of African homophobia. Anthony questioned the veracity of the documentary and whether the BBC had attempted to do any historical research before producing the documentary and releasing it to the public. They also proceeded to ask the director why they thought the documentary was relevant for the celebration, as opposed to an African-centered documentary like *Dakan* (Camara 1997) or *Woubi Chéri* (Bocahut 1998), which refuse the tropes of African homophobia.

> I am a little confused about this documentary. It lacks some important historical facts and I also disagree with the idea that Uganda is the world's most homophobic place. Just recently, I read on the internet that a gay couple was brutally beaten in Germany. In South Africa, they are raping lesbians in order to cure them of lesbianism. Can you imagine that? Yet, South Africa is celebrated as one of the most tolerant nations to embrace LGBT+ people but the violence lesbians face there, especially Black lesbians, is unbelievable. This is why I disagree with the documentary on a core level. I mean I don't doubt that homophobia exists in Uganda, homophobia is there. But these white people always want to exaggerate things when they happen in Africa. Why aren't they talking about South Africa? Why aren't they talking about gays in Germany? Why aren't they criticizing sharply the evangelicals that spread homophobic messages? These people [evangelicals] support churches in Ghana too. Why don't they deal with those problems first before they can finally draw the conclusion that Uganda is homophobic? Now I think BURJ should have asked these questions too. They could have even chosen to show *Dakan* by Mohamed Camara or the Ivorian documentary called *Woubi Chéri*, which were all released in the mid-nineties. These two documentaries present a different narrative distinct from this BBC production, which repeats the same story that Africans are terrible people without any historical context. BURJ staff I know why you showed this documentary, but we have to let the white people here in the room understand that homophobia is not just an African problem but a problem for everybody, including them.

Anthony's response to the documentary is informed by his position as a longtime activist in the sasso community with a critical passion for history. At the time of the screening, he was completing a master's degree in African studies at the University of Ghana's Kwame Nkrumah Institute of African Studies, where he was writing a thesis on colonial interpretations of gender and sexuality. Anthony's critique of the documentary thus arises out of his own activist and intellectual work, which have been critical of how international NGOs in Ghana disrupt LGBT+ human rights activities being conducted by local organizations and their constituencies. It is, therefore, unsurprising that he rejected the wholesale description of Uganda as the world's worst place to be gay. In fact, his critique points to the racism embedded in the documentary, and how BURJ is complicit in producing such racism because it is supported by the American and Dutch embassies, respectively. Offering examples of homophobia in places advanced in LGBT+ human rights rhetoric as quintessential meccas for LGBT+ individuals, Anthony undermines that rhetoric by suggesting that homophobia is everybody's problem, thus refusing to racialize it.

Anthony is rather unequivocal in his opinion that the documentary reinforces racist narratives about Africa as backward, dangerous, and primitive while drawing on liberal nomenclature. His reading is critical not just because it reflects the dissonance among the staff at BURJ but because it illuminates those strings and conditions that tie BURJ to the American embassy, the mission whose staff elected to screen the documentary. Evidently, Anthony's observation underscores how NGOs like BURJ have to carefully tread the treacherous landscapes of aid giving and donor support orchestrated by Western-based organizations. Because BURJ is an organization whose activities are occasionally supported by the Dutch and American foreign missions in Ghana—donations that both enable the execution of human rights projects and serve as the source of income for BURJ employees—the organization's existence always hangs in the balance.

BURJ, as an organization, including its staff, is embedded in what I describe as an LGBT+ human rights industrial complex that paradoxically creates opportunities for engaging in queer politics while at the same time constraining local organizations that attempt to carefully tread minefields of uncertainty. That the American and Dutch missions in Ghana, as Anthony's perceptive observation illuminates, pay inadequate attention to local realities and the shifting and nettlesome landscapes in which those realities play out, puts BURJ, its staff members, and its LGBT+ and sasso constituents in a precarious situation. The rigmarole preceding the celebration of a typically Western-originated event like IDAHO invokes the tensions, conflicts, and pressure points that the increased visibility of LGBT+ human rights politics incites. I am of the view that organizations like BURJ, while invested in creating safer grounds for sexual minorities, get entangled in the matrix of the neocolonial and neoliberal apparatuses that reproduces the image of Africa, as I have argued elsewhere, as "the heart of homophobic darkness" (Otu 2017).

Thus, the paradoxical location of BURJ epitomizes the organization's amphibious location within a transnational LGBT+ human rights framework that racializes Africans while claiming to rescue its vulnerable LGBT+ citizens. I argue, then, that *The World's Worst Place to Be Gay?* is a homocolonial trope. It is homocolonial precisely because it calcifies images and representations of Africans by ignoring the complexities that constitute the background against which the LGBT+ communities which are the target of interventions play out. Anthony is, therefore, right to point out that documentaries like *Dakan* and *Woubi Chéri* would have been better suited to the celebration, especially as they are more representative of such complexities.

Despite several debates and controversies that IDAHO brought to the foreground, I acknowledge that organizations like BURJ have created spaces and opportunities where conversations on queer politics and discussions on the future of LGBT+ rights in Ghana have occurred. Although they do not boldly identify as an LGBT+ human rights organization, the fact that they engage in LGBT+ human rights projects has fostered an environment for new LGBT+ human rights organizations to evolve.

Sasso who formerly worked with BURJ have, since the completion of this ethnography, founded or established LGBT+ organizations, which unlike BURJ focus primarily on liberalizing queer visibility in Ghana. I touch briefly on some of these organizations in the conclusion to this book. Especially notable among these new organizations are Priorities on Rights and Sexual Health (PORSH) and LGBT+ Rights Ghana,[14] both of which share a holistic commitment to all things affecting queer people and nonheteronormative subjects in Ghana. There is also the SOLACE Initiative, "a non-governmental organization committed to working for the promotion and protection of the human rights of all persons specifically Lesbians, Gay, Bi-Sexual, Transgender and Queer (LGBTQ+) people in Ghana."[15] Most of these organizations have emerged between the last five to seven years. Their existence is indicative of a rising tide of queer Africans seeking to queer Africa by engaging in activist efforts for queer constituencies arguably more robust and intentional than predecessors like BURJ.

Conclusion

Queering Queer Africa?

> Queer Africa is much more than Michel Foucault and Judith Butler. It is lazy to always start our queer African narratives with either this French philosopher or his American compatriot. Departures to Jeffrey Weeks, Denis Altman, Gilbert Herdt and Peter Aggleton still fit into western hegemony over queer studies. Sprinkling the menu with Audre Lorde, Sonia Correa or Serena Nanda is a commendable effort but not nearly enough.
>
> —STELLA NYANZI, "QUEERING QUEER AFRICA" (2014, 65)

The contentions generated by queer politics and the desire for queer liberation in postcolonial Africa compel one to ponder what the horizon looks like for queer subjects in Africa. The recent rise in Christian heteronationalism in Ghana, evidenced by attempts among some members of Ghana's legislature to criminalize LGBT+ identities and activities, bespeaks the treacherous landscapes that queer African activists traverse daily in the contemporary moment. Moreover, they underscore the future of queer political pursuits and the challenges and possibilities they will yield for queer subjects. Like "the color line" in the United States of America, which W. E. B Du Bois (1903) famously described in his book *Souls of Black Folk* as "the problem of the twentieth century," might Africa's problem in the twenty-first century be the problem of the queer line? As I finish this book, for example, Ghana's speaker of parliament, Alban Bagbin, is relentlessly waging a campaign that will usher in the passage of an anti-LGBT bill in Ghana. At a gathering of politicians, members of the clergy, and the Muslim fraternity, the speaker unapologetically confirmed his support for a bill that he claims will preserve Christian marriage and family values. At the event, Mr. Bagbin publicly stated that "the LGBT+ pandemic is worse than COVID-19."[1] This Christian heteronationalist assemblage, as it were, calls into question the constitutional provision that mandates the separation of church and state. In this book, I have demonstrated how the forging of this ideology needs to be situated in the larger heterocolonial project that antedated Ghana's independence. By turning to African philosophy, in particular, Akan philosophy, I have attempted to problematize the claim that homosexuality is un-African.

In a provocative essay in the radical queer African anthology edited by the South African queer scholar Zethu Matebeni entitled *Reclaiming Afrikan: Queer Perspectives on Sexual and Gender Identities* (2014), the Ugandan gender and feminist scholar Stella Nyanzi unapologetically opens with a warning on how not to study queer Africa. The injunction implicit in Nyanzi's invocation brazenly calls on queer African scholars and non-African queer scholars interested in queer African subjectivities not to always capitulate to Euro-American theoretical framings when there is a bountiful wealth of knowledge and information brimming with so much energy on the continent. This knowledge is life since the lives lived by queer Africans amount to knowledge par excellence. Hence, for Nyanzi, "to queer "Queer Africa," one must simultaneously reclaim Africa in its bold diversities and reinsert queerness" (2014, 65).

In this project, I was drawn to the Ghanaian philosopher Kwame Gyekye's theory of "amphibious personhood" not because of its theoretical richness but because it provided me with a language to illuminate self-making practices of sasso, the bodies whose experiences animate this book. To understand amphibious personhood drawing on sasso lives and to understand sasso engaging with the theory of amphibious personhood exemplifies what it means to employ Africa to think "queerly" in a world interminably adumbrated by universalizing Western tendencies that bleed African/Queer bodies both experientially and intellectually.

I explored how sasso worlds are entangled with larger worlds. I approached the subject as a self-identified queer Ghanaian confronting the same historic and ethnographic dilemmas and scenes that form the backdrop of sasso lives. Unlike sasso, however, I am an anthropologist based in the West, enjoying the uneven benefits of queer freedom oft undercut by anti-Blackness, anti-immigrant sentiment, and increasingly virulent homophobia, transphobia, and queerphobia. Some might ask: who am I to write a book on sasso? My response would be that sasso worlds are worlds that commingle with other worlds. These worlds are scrambled by a colonial history that molded contemporary Africans into the subjects that they are today, or, in Lisa Lowe's words, "the connections, relations, and mixings among the histories of Asian, African, and indigenous peoples" (2015, 2). The increased same-sex visibility politics and homonegativity amid changing Christian and uneven neoliberal geographies of exclusion and privilege are altering the meanings and conventions of sexual citizenship in neoliberal Ghana. I make a key theoretical intervention by demonstrating how and why sasso are amphibious subjects trudging precarious terrains.

WHERE DO WE GO FROM HERE?

As a queer ethnographer conducting queer ethnography in a context that yields ambivalent responses to all things queer, I have rediscovered myself through my interactions with sasso in ways I could never have imagined. The sasso whose worlds entangled with mine in the process of this ethnographic journey—for example, Hillary and Kissi, all of blessed memory, and Kobby, who now resides in the United States—shaped my understanding of knowing where, when, and how to be sasso in this uncertain context. Having embraced me within their fold and accepted me as part of the sasso community, these sasso were, indeed, subjects who logically engaged with their worlds, nourishing me with ideas and experiences on which the ethnographic and philosophical foundations of this book are erected. I can never say enough about how much influence they have had on me not merely as interlocutors but also as teachers and theorists whose sharp and penetrative insights have allowed me to plot the various ethnographic and theoretical coordinates of this book. What I dare say here is that these sasso led me to discover the amphibious subject. In fact, they championed the cause that compelled me to imagine myself as an amphibious subject.

I participated in the lifeworlds of sasso in Jamestown, a low-income suburb of Accra, to understand how their lives questioned the tenuous politics of LGBT+ visibility. As amphibious subjects, their way of being in the world and becoming sexual citizens raised questions about the impacts of the Global North–based identitarian politics on their lives. The activities of LGBT+ human rights organizations heightened existing laws that criminalized homosexuality. Sexual minorities such as sasso, whose livelihoods depend on selling food, hairdressing, tailoring, working in health care, advocating for human rights, and doing HIV/AIDS outreach, were disproportionately affected by these transitions. Amid the shifts impelled by same-sex visibility politics in Africa, as well as the reactions against these shifts, sasso continue to adopt amphibious strategies in order to navigate the limits of the contested politics of queer self-making. As amphibious subjects, their lives also reveal that the epistemic collusion between the state and LGBT+ human rights organizations was total, yet yielded implications that were articulated differently (Massad 2007).

The contours of this book compel us to reexamine Africa, as a discursive and ontological space, and sexuality and race-making as processes that are entwined with the multiplex dimensions of Africa both as trope and as "reality." My insistence on exploring the place of sexuality and race in neoliberal Ghana brings to bear not only the impoverished analysis of race in Africa, but also the extent to which sub-Saharan Africa, that crucible of racialization and of racial difference, remains invisible in race studies. Thus, like Jemima Pierre (2013), who deploys race-craft to capture articulations of race in postcolonial Ghana, I argue that race in Africa needs to be conceived of as linked to racial projects in the African diaspora. These projects are scenes of power that on the surface appear benign yet have invidious consequences, what David Theo Goldberg (2008, 1) terms "racial neoliberalism." If transnational human rights activism historically began in the guise of civilizing and Christian missionary complexes (Otu 2017), which are racial projects that cemented white supremacy, then we need a transnational/transgeopolitcal and transhistorical analysis of Blackness and of the politics of rescue announced by these projects in the present context. These shifts are reminiscent of what Jacqui Alexander captures evocatively in her reminder to us that

> in the linear technology of time, tradition displaces the neocolonial and modernity displaces the neoimperial as preferred terms. Since both neocolonial and neo-imperial states work, albeit asymmetrically, through colonial time and simultaneously through Christian neoliberal financial time—organized under the auspices of global capital interests and lending agencies such as the International Monetary Fund and the World Bank—our task is to move practices of neocolonialism within the ambit of modernity, and to move those of colonialism into neocolonialism, reckoning, in other words, with palimpsestic time. (2005, 215)

The workings of the neocolonial, the neoliberal, and the neo-imperial become palpable when one observes the shifts wrought by the increased visibility of LGBT+ human rights politics on sasso and LGBT+ communities nestled in the neocolonial formation known as Ghana. Foregrounding sasso experiences, for example, through the globalized racial framework that Pierre (2013) calls for, as well as Alexander's conceptualization of the techniques of racist/imperial time, allows us to also consider how queering queer Africa can be a useful theoretical intervention. A race-based framework that explores Black/African people's relationship to desire and intimacy has been limited to the African diaspora, which is conceived as that fraught geopolitical context where racial formations persist. Would a race-based analysis of the queer liberal politics unfolding in Africa writ large and Ghana in particular allow us to see the manifold ways in which racialization functions to undercut Black/African lives? The accounts I have offered here respond to Pierre's frustration by illuminating the coeval presence of racial projects that occur in African and its myriad diasporas. They shed light on the extent to which "white saviorism" enacted through LGBT+ human rights activism not only perpetuates whiteness as the solution to the world's ills, but as a superior state of being. Therefore, this ethnography on sexual citizenship is simultaneously an ethnographic inquiry on race, and the extent to which neoliberal formations, by proliferating discourses and epistemes of freedom, liberation, and emancipation, engender vulnerability and marginalization.

Sasso participation in these formations is freighted by a tension deserving of analytical attention. Not merely plugged into NGOs such as BURJ, which interacts with embassies like the American and Dutch foreign missions in Ghana, sasso are embedded in global and local circuits of sexual citizenship and race-making. And with the social media boom, with interfaces such as Facebook, Instagram, and Twitter, sasso more and more are becoming global in ways that minimize the vernacular label *sasso*, which is rarely deployed on these internet-mediated platforms. How are we to imagine sasso as new privileged subjects who are also burdened by heightening homonegativity and a neoliberal ferment that continues to create economic peril in the postcolonial nation-state? In what ways should we fathom sasso amphibious subjectivity as at once unsettling normative systems and consolidating them? For instance, how does their presence in Ghana emphasize the failure of heteronormativity, whereby such failure is generative? Sasso experiences permit us to interrogate heterosexual and homosexual citizenships as forms that limit their ontological existence in neoliberal times. Furthermore, their lives, by shedding light on the story of race-making and sexual citizenship-making in postcolonial Ghana, also reveal the extent to which these are contingent processes that are also deeply historically situated and expose the connections between the nation-state and LGBT+ human rights politics.

Hence, rather than concentrate merely on critiquing the invisibility politics tied to state-sanctioned homonegativity, we must explore how turns to visibility and liberation have violent undemocratic legacies. The Egyptian feminist Nawal El-Saadawi, responding to Western feminists' perspective that veiling is oppressive, reminds us that "veiling and nakedness are two sides of the same coin" (1997, 140). Extending El-Saadawi's reading further, it is apparent that the increased visibility of LGBT+ politics in sub-Saharan Africa nourishes unprecedented invisibility for sexual minorities. Thus, visibility, as sasso lives suggest, can be dangerous, especially when it is framed within the ideological architecture of freedom and liberty—projects and designs that have long been antithetical to Black and queer lives. The queer theorist of color Chandan Reddy (2011) makes this connection apparent when he suggests that Western notions and practices of freedom have always consistently required violence, foregrounding the entanglement of liberation and violence.

Ethnographic inquiries, development and public health NGO interventions, and theoretical formulations need to question the persistent racialization of all issues in Africa. In the case of this study, the idea that queer liberalism epitomizes the zenith of a country's development is a crucial assumption that needs to be unsettled. As we interrogate the evolutionary myth that queer tolerance is the new civility, we should equally be attentive to how parallel organizations founded by local activists straddle the thin and uneven geographies of neoliberal human rights environments. For example, since I completed this fieldwork, several local organizations have emerged in Ghana that attend specifically to LGBT+ human rights issues, especially in the area of public health and social justice.

Several organizations stand out. They are Priorities on Rights and Sexual Health (PORSH), established in 2015, which is run by a sasso, and LGBT+ Rights Ghana, which is led by one of the most outspoken self-identified gay men in Ghana, Alex Donkor, who has a strong online presence and following.[2] There are also now organizations like the SOLACE Initiative, Rightify Ghana, Courageous Sisters Ghana (CSG), and Alliance for Equality and Diversity (AfED),[3] all of which have emerged since the completion of my ethnography. The emergence of these organizations demonstrates the urgency of LGBT+ human rights at a time when the heteronational state together with organizations such as the National Coalition for Proper Human Sexual Rights and Family Values (NCPHSRFV) launch aggressive anti-LGBT+ campaigns in Ghana. As I complete this book, there are efforts to enact laws that criminalize not only being LGBT+ but also engaging in LGBT+ advocacy.[4] In spite of the unfolding homophobic trepidations and onslaughts, these LGBT+ and their allied organizations have revolutionized their outreach by actively utilizing social media applications like Facebook, Instagram, and Twitter, providing them with a global audience and following. Both PORSH and LGBT+ Rights Ghana are not only committed to sasso, but also to trans rights and the rights of intersex people.

Unlike BURJ, PORSH and LGBT+ Rights Ghana staff are a mix of sasso and self-identified LGBT+s with allies that work with them. They have solid networks with health officials in designated hospitals who provide services for sasso if need be. These health officials, unlike those in other hospitals, do not draw on Christian tropes to refuse service to sasso or embarrass them. The emergence of PORSH and LGBT+ Rights Ghana are therefore effective examples of how sasso are beginning to enter the world of LGBT+ human rights organizing and politics on their own terms. Representing a generation of young Ghanaian queer women, men, nonbinary, and trans folk who are advocating for their visibility and rights, thus undermining the violence of a homophobia rooted in heteronationalism and concomitant Christianity, these organizations have made outstanding progress. Not only have they attracted international attention, but are also run by members who boldly claim LGBT+ identification or regard themselves as allies.

While their appearance on this stage is tricky, I contend that their approach to LGBT+ human rights from below has had transformative potential, especially as they are familiar with and knowledgeable about the complexity of the worlds in which sasso are nested. PORSH has attracted young Ghanaians by actively reaching out to them and providing them with critical human rights language to start a movement. If mainstream LGBT+ human rights projects, as I have revealed in this book, form part of race-liberal orders, then as Melamed indicates, their universalizing overtures are sometimes resisted and overcome by "subjects, epistemes, and cultural formations" that they have produced (2011, 47). PORSH and LGBT+ Rights Ghana are undoubtedly a logical response to the increased visibility of LGBT+ human rights projects, ambivalently refusing to be assimilated, formalized, or obstructed by those LGBT+ human rights projects that are ancillaries of race-liberal orders. To be clear, these are organizations that determine their own representation, involving sasso and members of the LGBT+ community in Ghana.

I hope that this book has opened, or will open, a vista through which to explore the consequences on sasso of the unimagined entanglements between LGBT+ human rights politics and state and religion-sanctioned homophobia in neoliberal Ghana. Indeed, here are communities that are not merely amphibious, but constantly embroiled in projects that at once validate and invalidate their humanity and existence in a neoliberal world. These formations equally enforce modes of governance and power that punctuate queer self-making in neoliberal margins. In these peripheral zones, radical worlds, such as those that convene around amphibious subjectivity, are always constituted and decomposed.

Moreover, the communities sasso reside in are also places of world-, self-, and freedom-making that are dense and tense scenes of queer self-fashioning. They are domains where queering queer Africa, to once again return to Stella Nyanzi's provocative remark, occurs. One might ask about some of the ways that organizations like PORSH and LGBT+ Rights Ghana, SOLACE Initiative, Rightify Ghana, Courageous Sisters Ghana, unlike BURJ or AIDSPAN, are engaging in projects that "queer" queer Africa. I am of the view that by their very existence in a state of uncertainty overseen by a heteronationalist government navigating the collusion between neoliberalism and neocolonialism, these organizations, despite their unique and familiar shortcomings, forge livable spaces where queer Ghanaians both converge and commiserate.

For example, they capitalize on social media platforms like Facebook, Instagram, Twitter, and especially WhatsApp to apprise themselves of the happenings occurring in and outside of the community, what affects members of the queer community, and what both PORSH and LGBT+ Rights Ghana can do to create and sustain a safer space for all involved, including nonqueer members. Some if not most members of the sasso community are now involved in these activities, making one wonder whether LGBT+ categories will subsume sasso in the future or not. Does queering queer Africa as a project, practice, experience, and epistemology also entail retaining these vernacular formations of queerness such as the ones sasso embody and live? Will sasso be here ten years from the publication of this book? Are sasso, by entering the categories LGBT+, changing how the desires, intimacies, and identities attached to those categories are imagined, felt, embodied, thought, and performed? In sum, how are they engaging either overtly or covertly in queering queer Africa?

NOTES

INTRODUCING AMPHIBIOUS SUBJECTS

1. Elsewhere in this book, I discuss how the increased visibility of LGBT+ human rights politics in Ghana undermined homosociality in Ghana, wherein homosocial actions are now interpreted as undergirded by homosexual acts.

2. On pondering the complexity of gender in the contemporary Ghanaian context, Takyiwaa Manuh suggests that "whatever its source, gender has become indigenized around Africa and Ghana and is being used to chart an agenda for social and political transformation, as African women and some men do for themselves, in light of realities on the ground in Africa" (2007, 126). Manuh's point also illuminates a genealogy of gender theory in sub-Saharan Africa that is clearly distinguishable from gender theorization in the context of Euro-America. In fact, gender in the former has been restricted to women, whereas in the latter it has involved linking gender together with sex, an approach that has enabled an environment in which to have conversations on gender. I try to highlight how neoliberalism's appearance in Ghana, for example, produced a narrative of gender that emphasized saving African women. Rather than deploy gender more expansively, the term's political utility was only accessible to women. Thus, the underside of gender politics, which I elaborate throughout this book, has been the resistance being shown to the emergent queer political movements in postcolonial Ghana.

3. Most of the sasso I encountered during fieldwork lived in Jamestown. Jamestown has designated locations like Club House, Akoto Lante, and Wato bar, which were domains or hangouts where sasso living within and outside of Jamestown mostly converged.

4. The Ga are mostly a coastal ethnic group indigenous to Greater Accra, and the hinterlands of the Greater Accra Region. They are situated on the south-central coastline. The Ga are contiguous with the Adangbe; thus the hyphenation Ga-Adangbe. The latter, too, are mostly coastal, but like the Ga, have hinterland connections with the Krobos.

5. The Chale Wote Festival was started by Accra[dot]Alt, a collectivity of creatives and artists invested in demonstrating the viability of African artistic products. http://accradotaltradio.com/chale-wote-street-art-festival/.

6. In section 104(1) of the Criminal Offences Act, 1960 (Act 29), the provision states that "a person who has unnatural carnal knowledge: (b) of another person of not less than sixteen years of age with the consent of that other person commits a misdemeanor." "Unnatural carnal knowledge," though presumed to be clearly about homosexuality or even anal sex (which is not exclusive to homosexual men), is extremely ambiguous and tied up in the biblical story of Sodom and Gomorrah. Also, nowhere in the Ghanaian constitution is homosexuality mentioned. That unnatural carnal knowledge is reducible to homosexuality neglects the range of actions, intimacies, and desires that constitute homosexuality.

7. In a milieu where, hegemonically, gender is interchangeable with woman, it comes as no surprise that gender is not invoked or imagined as a category that transcends women. The history of gender in Africa, consistent with the trajectory of gender politics, is particularly distinct from examinations and politics of "gender" in the West. Perhaps this is one of the key reasons why addressing LGBT+ human rights politics is not seen as an issue of gender but rather an issue that primarily has to do with, if not entirely reducible to, sex/sexuality.

8. A news item appearing in *Foreign Policy* titled "The Closeted Continent," by Suzanne Nossel, ominously evinces how thirty-eight out of fifty-five African nations have laws punishing sodomy. And things may get worse before they get better. http://foreignpolicy.com/2014/10/08/the-closeted-continent/.

9. I am using a pseudonym for this organization based on conversations with the then executive director, who requested that I not use the organization's actual name.

10. By paradox, I mean that sasso instrumentalize aspects of queer politics and iconography to their advantage, for example, in the realm of public health outreach and projects that focus on sexual and gender-based violence in Ghana.

11. It is worth noting here that homosexuality is not explicitly criminalized as demonstrated in Ghana's Fourth Republican Constitution, an observation also made by legal scholars.

12. For more information on the origins and changing meanings of the word *amphibian*, see https://www.lexico.com/en/definition/amphibian.

13. I am particularly aware of the freight that accompanies using *queer* to describe the subjectivities of sasso here. What interests me in this book, however, is in fact how sasso subjectivities compel us to think about "queerness" in the context of Ghana in particular and Africa in general. I consider, then, what it means to study queerness using sasso as a point of departure rather than studying sasso using queerness as point of departure. This is my objective in this book.

14. The emergence, a few years ago, of the National Coalition for Proper Human Sexual Rights and Family Values, run by the anti-gay activist Moses Foh-Amoaning, exemplifies the mainstreaming as well as the politicization of homophobic rhetoric in public discourse. The coalition, whose membership encompasses religious organizations and some civic institutions, has lobbied proactively against LGBT+ human rights interventions in Ghana.

15. Kwadwo is the name for a male born on Monday and *besia* is female; *ntow*, the prefix in Ntowbea, translates as "male" and the suffix *bea* is female.

16. Signorini distinguishes between two levels of friendship among the Nzema as follows: "In fact, there are two levels of friendship which are, in a certain sense, inferior to agɔnwole agyalɛ. There is the simple agɔnwole which resembles the normal relationship involving friendship and affection found in Western society; this involves no fixed norms of behavior between the partners other than those reflected by the ethical ideal of Nzema society (loyalty, honesty, mutual help). Then there is agɔnwole kpalɛ (kpalɛ—great) in which friendship with a certain person assumes a particular value which emphasizes, if not its 'exclusiveness' (it is possible to have this relationship with more than one person at the same time), at least its importance in the eyes of the community" (1973, 222).

17. For more on the raid launched by Ghana's National Security Forces at the request of the government, see "Ghana Security Forces Shut Down LGBTQ Office," *Aljazeera*, https://www.aljazeera.com/news/2021/2/24/ghana-shuts-down-lgbt-office-rights-group.

18. President Mills's statement was made at the National Convention of the Pentecost Church of Ghana, "Christ is President-Atta Mills," GhanaWeb, https://www.ghanaweb.com/GhanaHomePage/NewsArchive/Christ-Is-President-President-Mills-208162.

19. For more information on the National Coalition for Proper Human Sexual Rights and Family Values, visit their Facebook page at https://www.facebook.com/ncphsrfv/?ref=page_internal.

20. Section 104(1) of the Criminal Offences Act, 1960 (Act 29).

21. One only needs to Oyèrónkẹ́ Oyěwùmí's *The Invention of Women* (1997) and Ifi Amadiume's *Male Daughters, Female Husbands* (1987a) to identify how they jettison Western conventions of gender.

22. For more of the debates on African communalism see Leopold Senghor's *On African Socialism* (1964) and Ifeanyi Menkiti's *Person and Community in African Traditional Thought* (1984).

23. I quite appreciate how poetic and philosophical domains have been mobilized by Black thinkers and artists to imagine worlds unimaginable. Gyekye's ability to call the crocodile an amphibian here does not, I speculate, signify his disrespect of science but in fact represents a certain play with language marked by an attempt to indigenize the term. This reminds me of one of the famous quotes by the Martinican poet and thinker Aimé Césaire that "poetic knowledge is born in the great silence of scientific knowledge" (1990, 7).

24. This analysis is critical to the book because other queer theorists and critical development scholars have long established how development projects undertaken to enhance and better the lives of those regarded as the targets of development instead heighten their states of vulnerability and precarity. The queer literary theorist Lauren Berlant (2011) captures this paradox as "cruel optimism." Chandan Reddy (2011) notes that these irreconcilable projects rely on violence to be executed or serve as the breeding grounds for violence.

25. "Ghana Security Forces Shut Down LGBTQ Office."

1. SITUATING SASSO: MAPPING EFFEMINATE SUBJECTIVITIES AND HOMOEROTIC DESIRE IN POSTCOLONIAL GHANA

1. Chester's is a hangout known to be popularly queer friendly and located in Osu, a suburb in Accra known for attracting expats and having high-end shops and restaurants. It is also one of the gentrified areas in Ghana, appealing to tourists who often traverse the

popular Oxford Street. Adabraka, the location of Terry's (a pseudonym), unlike Osu, is much closer to the central business district of Accra. The cosmopolitan characteristics of these spaces and the fact they are construed as quite accepting to LGBT+s make them appealing to sasso.

2. The Ga, or Ga-Adangbe, are mostly a southern ethnolinguistic group, found in the Greater Accra Region and parts of the Eastern Region of Ghana. As the British social anthropologist Margaret Field observes: "The Ga are not one people. Each town is an independent republic, having its own unique constitution which has grown out of its own unique history. By intermarriage and proximity, the different peoples have come to have a language and many everyday customs in common" (1940, vii). The Akan are ethnolinguistically the largest group of people in Ghana, with several dialects of Twi and Fante. The proximity of the Ga and Akan peoples points to pronunciation similarities between *saso* and *sasso*, both of which have a wide array of meanings, as I have discussed.

3. According to the linguist Esther Kropp Dakubu, "Ga, the language of Accra, arose in a multilingual context and has existed in one ever since. The split between Ga and its only close relative, Dangme, was undoubtedly triggered mainly by the influence of other languages, some of them spoken by much larger and more powerful groups, and many of whose speakers were assimilated into the Ga-speaking society" (1997: 5).

4. "Homosexuality Is Unacceptable," BusinessGhana, https://www.businessghana.com/site/news/general/135455/Homosexuality-is-unacceptable-Moderator.

5. I am grateful to Professor Ato Quayson for confirming this cultural attribution among the seagoing fishermen in Jamestown. While it is mainly anecdotal, I hope to investigate further the historical basis informing this rather critical cultural observation. To this day, there are very few ethnographic monographs about the phenomenon of young boys cross-dressing in the community, despite the profanations exacted by colonialism and Christianity. Thus, I find it rather unexpected that there is no documentation on the act of dragging articulated in the community.

6. In several instances in the field, most sasso had very little to say regarding what they thought was the etymological source for the word. In fact, there was no unified explanation. This perhaps has to do with the nebulousness of the term, and how sasso individually interpret the term as they see fit.

7. I draw on my understanding of and familiarity with this typology and the degree to which its meaning is contingent on the context in which it is used.

8. It is still possible that effeminacy as a denominating feature among the men who participated in this project might also reinforce that because they are feminine they are the same as women, resulting in a sexist framework that views them as "lesser men."

9. Never did I come across the verb "to sasso" during my fieldwork. The sasso with whom I interacted often used "to do sasso" when describing engaging in effeminate performance/exhi biting effeminate tendencies, or engaging in homoerotic sex.

10. It is not my intention here to superimpose a Western categorical distinction on the men for whom sasso have sexual and intimate preferences. Rather, I use this term to help me clarify the modulations of sasso identity and how they trouble the neat and tidy placeholders articulated by LGBT+ human rights movements.

11. Despite the integral presence of logs and gentors in sasso lives, I was unable to interview any of them since they were secret partners to the sasso I engaged with. Because of their masculine self-presentations and the fear that any open association with sasso in the public sphere would mark them as homosexuals, most engaged with sasso furtively.

12. In Ghana, "kubolor boys" are synonymous with hustlers. However, it is a derogatory term used to describe school dropouts or young boys who are not serious in school but are engaged in nefarious or deviant activities.

13. It has been noted in several studies on sex work and sexually transmitted diseases such as HIV that transactional sex is rife in many parts of Africa (Oppong and Kalipeni, 2004). Operationally, I use it here to capture the reciprocation of sex for gifts, financial benefits, and other material products.

2. CONTESTING HOMOGENEITY: SASSO COMPLEXITY IN THE FACE OF NEOLIBERAL LGBT+ POLITICS

1. The constitutional review was held to review and debate portions of the 1992 constitution which require changes. It was composed of some members of the judiciary, the Ghana Bar Association, and members of parliament. It was held in 2011 in Akosombo.

2. For information on Oxford Street, Osu, please see Ato Quayson's rich spatial ethnographic analysis, *Oxford Street*, in which he traces the lines of flight articulated by modernity and coloniality in the neoliberal and postcolonial moment. This street is often touched upon by Jemima Pierre in her astute analysis of race-making in postcolonial Ghana (2013).

3. The disavowal of homosexuality and homoerotic intimacy as a possibility clearly resonates with Gayatri Gopinath's (2005) incisive analysis of how queer desire is rendered "impossible" in particular sociocultural landscapes.

4. Anthropologists such as Rudy Gaudio (2009), Jafari Allen (2011), and Gloria Wekker (2006) have faced similar questions regarding revealing their intention to study same-sex sexual formations or sexual orientation in the field.

5. I am inspired by Veronique Benei's book, entitled *Schooling Passions: Nation, History, and Language in Contemporary Western India* (2008), in which she discusses the ways in which educational institutions were fecund sites for planting nationalist seeds. Thus, nationalist sentiments were deeply ingrained in school curricula in ways that were meant to be embodied by elementary school students. As Hillary's narrative reveals, schools are sites of heterosexual preservation, and any breach of heterosexual mores invited severe penalties.

6. Okada is a form of local transportation. The word *okada* is of Nigerian origin and has been popularized in Ghana through Nollywood movies (Nigerian movies). It is very common in Jamestown and other low-income communities in Accra. As a profession, okada is barred, yet in this community it is a preferred source of transportation as a result of the ease it presents.

7. A detailed description of the range of sasso and sasso behavior is presented in chapter 1.

8. Jemima Pierre (2013) writes that widespread skin-bleaching practices articulate the existence of racial formations in postcolonial Ghana. Shelley's reliance on skin-bleaching products to look fairer reflects the colorist economy in Ghana and how it is entangled with anti-Blackness.

9. It should be made clear here that the art and the act of going to the market is a gendered responsibility in many parts of Ghana. Appearances made at the market for the purpose of buying foodstuff is a woman's duty. Boys, until they reach a certain age, can go to the market to engage in the act of buying foodstuffs. But once they become recognizably men, that responsibility is curtailed. Although some men continue to go the market, and that is seen as admirable, purchasing foodstuff is largely recognized as women's responsibility.

10. Like the nation's poor more generally, Shelley experiences the negative effects wrought by neoliberalism, as reflected in the high inflation and the escalating fuel prices, which in turn affect the price of foods and other utilities in Ghana. The deals the women offer him allow him to keep his head above water.

11. The queer theorist Judith Halberstam (1998) notes another variant of gender amorphousness, what she refers to as "masculinities without men."

12. See Miescher (2005).

13. Raewyn Connell (1993) distinguishes between hegemonic masculinity and subordinate masculinity. Such a distinction maybe useful insofar as the in-betweens, that is to say what happens between hegemonic and subordinate masculinities, are recognized as complex and dynamic. For example, the market women thought of Shelley as the perfect husband or father because he went to the market. However, that very fact also reduced his perceived masculinity. Such paradoxes raise questions about how categories fix and hide the incoherencies of social constructs. The oral historian Stephan Miescher (2005) in his study of masculinities among Kwahu men in Ghana critiques Connell's distinction.

14. Jamestown was a trading post and a harbor at the dawn of colonization. It had two big forts, which doubled as colonial posts and sites for the exchange of slaves for other commodities. In colonial iconography, Jamestown is thus central, named, perhaps, after King James of England. In contemporary times, however, it is one of the poorest suburbs of Accra. Although multiethnic, it is predominantly populated by the indigenous Ga population. The colonial and postcolonial intersections are crucial to the demarcation of this space as a habitation not only for sasso, but also for society's poor, those considered in the Ghanaian imagination as the urban detritus.

15. "Gays and Lesbians Invade Takoradi," GhanaWeb,http://www.ghanaweb.com/GhanaHomePage/NewsArchive/Gays-and-lesbians-invade-Takoradi-182531.

16. "Minister Orders Arrest of Homosexuals," GhanaWeb, http://www.ghanaweb.com/GhanaHomePage/NewsArchive/Minister-orders-arrest-of-all-homosexuals-214188.

17. In the Ghanaian context, a compound house is residential complex with a compound within it. The compound is a public area where a range of domestic activities and ritual festivities are held. Historically, they represent traditional Ghanaian architecture, intended to knit together families residing within the compound.

18. This is a common Adinkra symbol that is often printed on fabrics. "Gye Nyame" is Twi for "Except for God."

3. AMPHIBIOUS SUBJECTIVITY: QUEER SELF-MAKING AT THE INTERSECTION OF COLLIDING MODERNITIES IN NEOLIBERAL GHANA

1. For more information about Aidspan, see their website, http://www.aidspan.org/.

2. A recent Centers for Disease Control (CDC) study shows that African American men are at more risk at becoming infected with HIV. For more information, see http://www.cdc.gov/hiv/group/msm/brief.html.

3. This was a good friend. The terms of their friendship were not sexual at all. Yet, she was very accepting of Hillary's sexual disposition, aware that he engaged in homoerotic sex with men within and from outside Jamestown.

4. The president had consistently challenged people who supported homosexuality. In 2011, he castigated both David Cameron and Hillary Clinton for attempting to impose

gay rights on the Ghanaian government. See "Forcing Africa to Embrace Homosexuality," Modern Ghana, https://www.modernghana.com/news/479905/forcing-africa-to-embrace-homosexuality.html.

5. I often referred to him with that appellation because of the notable role he played among sasso and the fact that among his peers he was held in high regard because of just how vociferous and unapologetic he was.

6. For Michel Foucault (1978), there is not one but many silences, and they are an integral part of the strategies that underlie and permeate discourses.

7. There is substantial literature on herbalists in Ghana; see, for example, Amoah et al. (2014).

8. In public health discourse, the term "key populations" is used to describe populations believed to be most at risk of contracting HIV. It refers to men who have sex with men (MSM); female sex workers (FSW), and persons living with HIV/AIDS (PLHIV). The term is also deployed to minimize the stereotype and stigma that these populations are likely to face.

9. The moderator of the Presbyterian Church of Ghana has consistently decried homosexuality. In fact, he has on several occasions described homosexuals as being lower than animals.

10. King James Version (KJV).

4. THE PARADOX OF RITUALS: QUEER POSSIBILITIES IN HETERONORMATIVE SCENES

1. This is traditional wear for women in Ghana and in many parts of West Africa. It consists of a blouse and an accompanying long skirt made to fit. It is usually sewn out of African fabrics.

2. The sartorial play performed by Kissi here is not only intended to evoke his desire to distinguish himself from other sasso. In fact, it is reminiscent of his desire to also participate in a universe in which sartorial citizenship is essential to being and becoming sasso. Here, I am reminded of Monica Miller's (2009) erudite elucidation of Black dandyism. It is clear that Kissi's sartorial production integrates African and Afro-diasporic fashion statements.

3. It is possible that the acquisition of the different forms of capital herein described serves as an insurance for sasso, who perhaps seek to neutralize the repercussions that being effeminate present in their communities. To have wealth therefore presents one with an opportunity to trump effeminacy in a way that boosts masculinity. Here wealth and hegemonic masculinity are regarded as two sides of the same coin.

4. This phrase captures a certain tendency among Ghanaians to do everything ranging from social events like birthdays to funerals in excess. In chapter 4, I show how ritualized spaces enact these surpluses in ways that vernacularize Thorstein Veblen's (1899) notion of conspicuous consumption.

5. PALIMPSESTIC PROJECTS: HETEROCOLONIAL MISSIONS IN POST-INDEPENDENT GHANA (1965–1975)

1. The coalition's membership includes the Christian Council of Ghana, the Catholic Bishops' Conference, the Ghana Muslims Mission, the Ghana Pentecostal and Charismatic Council, the Ghana Baptist Convention, and the Ahmadiyya Muslims Mission. In February

2021, the coalition, together with the National Security Service in Ghana, closed down an LGBT+ human rights organization's office in Accra. The organization, LGBT+ Rights Ghana, not only retained the name LGBT+ but also widely publicized its inauguration, attracting the attention of some high-ranking foreign diplomats in the country. That the organization boldly opened an office in the capital, Accra, drew the ire of the coalition and some leading members of Ghana's Christian and Islamic community as well as politicians. "Anti-Gay Uproar after Ghana Opens Its First LGBT+ Community Centre," Reuters, https://www.reuters.com/article/us-ghana-LGBT+-rights-trfn/anti-gay-uproar-after-ghana-opens-its-first-LGBT+-community-centre-idUSKBN2AO04Q.

2. The introduction of the CES will generate a heated debate in the country, as demonstrated by the campaign pursued by the coalition to stop the government's efforts to introduce the program into the curriculum. The backlash will compel the government and some UN agencies to join in the efforts to rectify any misconceptions associated with the policy, especially those emphasizing that it was a ploy by the West to introduce LGBT+ issues and topics in schools. For more about the debates, see "Here's Why Ghana's Sex Education Program Is Controversial," AfricaNews.com, https://www.africanews.com/2019/10/03/here-s-why-ghana-s-sex-education-program-is-controversial//; "Understanding the Outcry against Comprehensive Sexuality Education in Ghana," https://medium.com/@Appiah/understanding-the-outcry-against-comprehensive-sexual-education-in-ghana-1dfd77b4baf2.

3. In 2018, the coalition was at the forefront of a campaign that lambasted Western governments for forcing African governments to embrace same-sex marriage. In particular, Mr. Foh-Amoaning was responding to then British prime minister Theresa May's demand that African governments legalize gay marriage. Members of the coalition represented the demand as a Western "ploy to deplete the African race" by reducing the continent's population. These concerns were made public at a consultative meeting on the rise of LGBT+ persons and organizations in Ghana organized by the coalition. Furthermore, the meeting was a strategic session at which efforts were made to caution Ghanaians against the so-called values of a civilized West. Mr. Foh-Amoaning described the assembly as an exposé that would "enable Ghanaians, Africans and the world at large to react appropriately . . . to the degenerated western moral behaviour which is in essence a veritable vestige of modern neo-colonialism, cultural imperialism and aggressive western cultural humanism." On June, 1 2018, the coalition launched a national prayer festival against Ghana's spiraling morality, which was aggressively publicized nationwide. In fact, the festival was to be held simultaneously in regional and district capitals across Ghana to combat what the coalition described as "the LGBT+ problem in Ghana."

4. Surprisingly, some Ghanaians took to Twitter to express umbrage, defending the possible implementation of the Comprehensive Sexuality Education policy, the very policy which had outraged the coalition and its conservative allies. See "Here's Why Ghana's Sex Education Program Is Controversial."

5. See "LGBT Group Opens Administrative Office in Accra," GhanaWeb, https://www.ghanaweb.com/GhanaHomePage/NewsArchive/LGBT-group-opens-administrative-office-in-Accra-1179199.

6. See "LGBTQ Community Cries for Help as National Security Raid Office," GhanaWeb, https://www.ghanaweb.com/GhanaHomePage/NewsArchive/LGBTQ-community-cries-for-help-as-National-security-raid-office-1188331.

7. Accessed from Evangelical Presbyterian Church Volta Region Committee on Christian Marriage and Family Life Secretary's Report to the Synod, September 1966, "Ghana: Volta Region Committee on Christian Marriage and Family Life," Ref no: CA/CA1/01/070, ordering reference number: Christian Aid (first deposit) Box CA/A/11, Missionary Collections, School of Oriental and African Studies, London. Hereafter, Volta Region Committee.

8. See the Christian Council of Ghana's website: http://www.christiancouncilofghana.org/Pages/History.php.

9. See "Homosexuality not on Ghana's Agenda—President Akufo-Addo, AfricaNews, https://www.africanews.com/2017/11/26/homosexuality-not-on-ghana-s-agenda-president-akufo-addo//.

10. The CCG's mission statement is available here: http://www.christiancouncilgh.org/Vision%20&%20mission.htm.

11. Evans-Pritchard writes that "boy marriage was owing, Azande say, to *zanga ade* 'lack of women'" (1970, 1429).

12. Here is what Evans-Pritchard says about the prevalence of homosexuality in precolonial Sudan: "It is beyond question that male homosexuality, or rather a sexual relationship between young warriors and boys, was common in pre-European days among the Azande, and as Czekanowski (1924:56), citing Junker (1892:3–4), has pointed out, there is no reason to suppose that it was introduced by Arabs as some have thought" (1970, 1429).

13. Here, the customary public designates the realm of the non-European. The African realm, if you will.

14. I, for one, am interested in the term *customary* since it subsumes those customs and cultural practices, and so forth, that were in competition with the colonial practices legitimized and enforced by the colonial state. *Primordial*, for me, reads as uncouth and atavistic, and somehow places the civic in a civilized timescape, as if to suggest that both publics did not exist in parallel worlds that then generated the collusions and collisions between them.

15. Several African and African American feminist writers have discussed the ways in which the Black female form became the prism for the exercise of imperial and colonial power. Some have even asserted that the domination of Africa was predicated on a logic of racial and gendered power. In order to be penetrated, Africa had to be imagined then as terra nullius, a land without people (McFadden 2011; McClintock 1995; Amadiume 1987a, 1987b).

16. As an institution of marriage, monogamy was distinguished from polygamy as being better suited to civilization from the viewpoint of missionary Christians and colonial administrators (Willey 2006; Miescher 2005; Stoler 1995). An aspect of the civilizing mission, the institutionalization of monogamy was regarded as the surest way out of atavistic polygamy. With polygamous practices, branded backward, monogamy emerged as the primary heterosexual union. In the postindependent nation, Christian organizations were established both to supervise and to sustain monogamy. While the case is made that this institution enabled marital stability, it was also seen as promoting healthier and happier children. The historical observations made by Stephan Miescher (2005) in *Making Men in Ghana* attest to these readings.

17. Conferences were held in many parts of Africa in the sixties and seventies, most of which emphasized the not only the social significance of Christian monogamy and family life for postcolonial Africans, but the also the economic significance—as catalysts for the

development of these postindependent nations. One such conference was the All-Africa Seminar on the Christian Home and Family Life, which was held in Kitwe, North Rhodesia, in April 1963. Accessed from Volta Region Committee.

18. The entrance into the top 40 of such performers as the Beatles in the United States triggered the British invasion, which also coincided with the emergence of the countercultural movement on the American side of the Atlantic. As chronicled by Miles (2009), these alternative cultural productions meteorically transformed sociopolitical and religio-moral structures of the time.

19. Frantz Fanon (1967) captured the waning, slow collapse of white supremacist behemoths in Africa in the phrase "a dying colonialism." Fanon's allusion hints eloquently at the possible destabilization of the colonial structure in Algeria, a country that consistently fought for its freedom, thus weakening French colonial rule.

20. In John Akomfra's recent documentary *The Stuart Hall Project*, we see the extent to which the demise of British imperialism in the early fifties ushered in a moment in which formerly colonized peoples migrated to the heart of what used to be an empire. Following the activities of Stuart Hall, and his role in the New Left and the racial politics of the Black Atlantic, the documentary foregrounds the destabilizing forces that enabled the cracks in postimperial England.

21. The moral desire to protect and preserve monogamous values saw Christian humanitarian organizations in Europe work closely with Christian organizations, in Africa historically established by missionaries in the colonial era. In Ghana, as I have indicated earlier, it was the Christian Council of Ghana.

22. For more information on the history of Christian Aid and its activities, see its website: http://www.christianaid.org.uk/aboutus/who/history/.

23. Ibid.

24. Accessed from Volta Region Committee.

25. Ibid.

26. Accessed from Volta Region Committee.

27. Ibid.

28. Ibid.

29. Letter exchanged between Mrs. C. F. Paton and Miss Janet Lacey on May 20, 1965, asking for funding to engage in a project on Christian families and the alleviation of gonorrhea and sterility, accessed from Volta Region Committee.

30. Letter from Mrs. C. F Paton to Miss Janet Lacey, October 9, 1965, accessed from Volta Region Committee.

31. Ibid.

32. Lecture Organized by the Christian Council of Ghana, "Why a Christian Marriage?" Accessed from Volta Region Committee.

33. Ibid.

34. Ibid.

35. Excerpts from Mrs. Vivian Hazel's letter to Miss Janet Lacey dated September 21, 1966, accessed from Volta Region Committee.

36. *Let Us Plan for Healthy Happy Children!*, accessed from Volta Region Committee.

37. Ibid.

38. Accessed Letter from Mrs. Vivian Hazel to Miss Janet Lacey dated September 21, 1966, accessed from Volta Region Committee.

39. Ibid.

40. Here, I use the term *postcustomary* not to suggest that it is after the customary but to suggest that it has been transformed by what we now refer to as the postcolonial. In other words, the impingement upon the customary by both the postcolonial moment and the nation-state has engendered the postcustomary.

6. QUEER LIBERAL EXPEDITIONS: THE BBC'S *THE WORLD'S WORST PLACE TO BE GAY?* AND THE PARADOXES OF HOMOCOLONIALISM

1. As noted in the introduction, Bring Us Rights and Justice (BURJ) is a pseudonym for the organization I temporarily worked at during my fieldwork in Ghana. Pseudonyms are also used for BURJ staff members, with the exception of those who authorized me to use their names.

2. In 2014, the event was described as International Day Against Homophobia (IDAHO). The celebration now includes transphobia and biphobia; thus the new name is International Day Against Homophobia, Transphobia and Biphobia (IDAHOTB).

3. "The Conference That Never Was!" GhanaWeb, https://www.ghanaweb.com/GhanaHomePage/NewsArchive/The-conference-that-never-was-110384.

4. These NGOs can be viewed as one of the first-generation organizations to engage directly with homosexual issues especially from the perspective of health.

5. A brilliant interview of the Ghanaian novelist and essayist Ama Ata Aidoo distills the important roles Ghanaian women played to advance the interests of women in a highly patriarchal culture. "We Were Feminists in Africa First," *Index on Censorship*, https://journals.sagepub.com/doi/pdf/10.1080/03064229008534948.

6. During my tenure there I worked with interns from Kenya and Nigeria, but few interns from other African nations; most were non-African.

7. The internship fee was one source of income for the organization. Interns could be there as long as they wanted as long as they paid the fee every month. Also, interns were required to take care of their living expenses for the duration of the internship. The only time they received money was when they were reimbursed for things like BURJ-related travel and accommodation.

8. Arguably, BURJ is one of few human rights organizations that has an intersectional framework at the core of its mission to fight against oppression in Ghana.

9. Here, I say amphibious because BURJ strategically engages in LGBT+ human rights politics, not overtly, but quite carefully just in the same way that most sasso navigate the homophobic contexts in which they reside.

10. It is understandable that Richard would disclose his gay identity to interns from Western countries because of the prevailing assumption held by the majority of Ghanaians that they are more tolerant of members of the LGBT+ community. The pervasiveness of this assumption is not only seen in BURJ, but also in expatriate spaces in Ghana which are likely to be populated by Westerners. I reckon that this is why Ghanaians are quick to claim that homosexuality is a Western imposition.

11. During my fieldwork at BURJ, there was hesitation among the queer Africans in the office to openly self-identify as gay. Meanwhile, some staff members relied on these queer Ghanaians to serve as gatekeepers into the community of men who have sex with men that BURJ was interacting with. I found this to be paradoxical for many reasons, but I also

understood that the staff of the organization, and especially its queer staff, operated in an environment that was largely uncertain. It was also known through rumors that some of the organization's staff had expressed homophobic sentiments in the past, making it quite difficult for some to talk openly about LGBT+ topics.

12. Strengthening Transparency, Accountability and Responsiveness (STAR-Ghana Foundation) is an NGO in Ghana that is constructed as belonging to and run by the people. For more on STAR-Ghana, visit their website, https://www.star-ghana.org/about-star-ghana.

13. It remains unclear how this unofficial policy came into being. What I know, however, is that LGBT+ workers at BURJ often hushed their identities. In a way, our identities were like a public secret: known but not expressed visibly.

14. For more on PORSH and LGBT+ Human Rights Ghana, visit http://afedghana.org/node/23#:~:text=In%20November%202013%2C%20PORSH%20was,populations%20in%20Ghana%20and%20beyond.

15. For more on the SOLACE Initiative, visit https://solaceinitiative.org/who-we-are/.

CONCLUSION

1. For more on this statement, see "Ghana's Speaker of Parliament Says the LGBT+ Pandemic Is Worse Than COVID-19," PinkNews, https://www.pinknews.co.uk/2021/07/01/ghana-alban-bagbin-lgbt-covid-19/.

2. For more information on PORSH and LGBT+ Human Rights Ghana, see http://afedghana.org/node/23#:~:text=In%20November%202013%2C%20PORSH%20was,populations%20in%20Ghana%20and%20beyond.

3. Courageous Sisters Ghana (CSG), https://www.facebook.com/Courageous-Sisters-Ghana-466635700579572; Alliance for Equality and Diversity (AfED), https://afedghana.org/; SOLACE Initiative, https://solaceinitiative.org/.

4. Some parliamentarians are working aggressively to enact a statute that criminalizes not only self-identifying as LGBT+ but also engaging in advocacy efforts to respect and acknowledge the rights of Ghanaians identified as LGBT+. "Parliament Will Provide Clear Legislation on LGBTQI+ in Ghana—Bagbin," https://www.modernghana.com/news/1069794/parliament-will-provide-clear-legislation-on-lgbtq.html.

BIBLIOGRAPHY

Acheampong, Emmanuel

1996 *Drink, Power, and Cultural Change: A Social History of Alcohol in Ghana.* Portsmouth: Heinemann.

Achebe, Chinua

1977 *An Image of Africa: Racism in Conrad's "Heart of Darkness."* London: Penguin Books.

Adomako Ampofo, A., M. P. K Okyerefo, and M. Pervarah

2009 "Phallic Competence: Fatherhood and the Making of Men in Ghana." In *Culture, Society and Masculinity.* Vol. 1. No. 1. Pp. 59–78.

Agathangelou, Anna M.

2013 "Neoliberal Geopolitical Order and Value: Queerness as Speculative Economy and Anti-Blackness as Terror." In *International Feminist Journal of Politics.* Vol. 15. No. 4. Pp. 453–476.

Agyekum, Kofi

2006 "The Sociolinguistic of Akan Personal Names." In *Nordic Journal of African Studies.* Vol. 15. No. 2. Pp. 206–235.

Ake, Claude

1996 *Democracy and Development in Africa.* Washington, DC: Brookings Institution.

Alexander, Bryant K.

2006 *Performing Black Masculinity: Race, Culture and Queer Identity.* New York: Alta Mira Press.

Alexander, M. Jacqui

2005 *Pedagogies of Crossing: Meditations on Feminism, Sexual Politics, Memory and the Sacred.* Durham, NC: Duke University Press.

Alcock, Chris, dir.

2011 *The World's Worst Place to Be Gay?* Film. BBC Three.

Allen, Jafari

2011 *¡Venceremos? The Erotics of Black Self-Making in Cuba*. Durham, NC: Duke University Press.

Altman, Dennis

1997 "Global Gaze/Gays." In *GLQ: A Journal of Lesbian and Gay Studies*. Vol 3. No. 4. Pp. 417–436.

Alvarez, Sonia

1999 "Advocating Feminism: The Latin American Feminist NGO Boom." In *International Feminist Journal of Politics*. Vol. 1. No. 2. Pp. 181–209.

Amadiume, Ifi

1987a *Male Daughters, Female Husbands: Gender and Sex in an African Society*. London: Zed Books.

1987b *Afrikan Matriarchal Foundations: The Igbo Case*. London: Karnak House.

Amartey, A. A.

1985 *Omanye Aba*. Accra: Presbyterian Press.

Amoah, S. K., L. P. Sandjo, M. L. Bazzo, S. N. Leite, and M. W. Biavatti

2014 "Herbalists, Traditional Healers and Pharmacists: A View of Tuberculosis in Ghana." In *Brazilian Journal of Pharmacology*. Vol. 24. No. 1. Pp. 89–95.

Appiah, Kwame Anthony

1992 *In my Father's House: Africa in the Philosophy of Culture*. Oxford: Oxford University Press.

Ashforth, Adam

2000 *Madumo: A Man Bewitched*. Chicago: University of Chicago Press.

Atuguba, Raymond

2019 "Homosexuality in Ghana: Morality, Law, Human Rights." In *Journal of Politics and Law*; Vol. 12. No. 4. Pp. 112–126.

Bailey, Marlon

2013 *Butch Queens Up in Pumps: Gender, Performance and Ballroom Culture in Detroit*. Ann Arbor: University of Michigan Press.

Bakhtin, Mikhail

1984 *Rabelais and His World*. Bloomington: Indiana University Press.

Bambara, Toni Cade

1970 "On the Issue of Roles." In *The Black Woman: An Anthology*. New York: Pocket Books. Pp. 123–136.

Banks, William

2011 "'This Thing Is Sweet': Ntetɛɛ and the Reconfiguration of Sexual Subjectivity in Post-Colonial Ghana." In *Ghana Studies*. Vol. 14. Pp. 265–290.

2013 *Queering Ghana: Sexuality, Community, and the Struggle for Cultural Belonging in an African Nation*. Unpublished dissertation. Wayne State University.

Benei, Veronique

2008 *Schooling Passions: Nation, History, and Language in Contemporary Western India*. Palo Alto, CA: Stanford University Press.

Berlant, Lauren

2011 *Cruel Optimism*. Durham, NC: Duke University Press.

Biruk, Cal

2020 "'Fake Gays' in Queer Africa: NGOs, Metrics, and Modes of (Queer) Theory." In *GLQ: A Journal of Lesbian and Gay Studies*. Vol. 26. No. 3. Pp. 477–502.

Bleys, Rudi

1995 *The Geography of Perversion: Male-to-Male Sexual Behavior outside the West and the Ethnographic Imagination, 1750–1918*. New York: New York University Press.

Bocahut, Laurent, dir.

1998 *Woubi Chéri*. Film.

Boddy, Janice

2007 *Civilizing Women: British Crusades in Colonial Sudan*. Princeton, NJ: Princeton University Press.

Bourdieu, Pierre

1986 "The Forms of Capital." In *Handbook of Theory and Research for the Sociology of Education*. J. Richardson (Ed.). New York: Greenwood. Pp. 241–258.

Brodwin, Paul

1996 *Medicine and Morality in Haiti: The Contest for Healing Power*. Cambridge, UK: Cambridge University Press.

Brown, Vincent

2010 *The Reaper's Garden: Death and Power in the World of Atlantic Slavery*. Cambridge, MA: Harvard University Press.

Buc, Phillipe

2001 *The Dangers of Ritual: Between Early Medieval Texts and Social Scientific Theory*. Princeton, NJ: Princeton University Press.

Burton, Richard

1885 *The Book of the Thousand Nights and a Night*. Burton Club for Private Subscribers Only.

Burke, Timothy

1996 *Lifebuoy Men, Lux Women: Commodification, Consumption, and Cleanliness in Modern Zimbabwe*. Durham, NC: Duke University Press.

Butler, Judith

1990 *Gender Trouble: Feminism and the Subversion of Identity*. New York: Routledge.

Camara, Mohamed, dir.

1997 *Dakan*. Film.

Camp, Stephanie

2002 "The Pleasures of Resistance: Enslaved Women and Body Politics in the Plantation South, 1830-1861." In *Journal of Southern History*. Vol. 68. No. 3. Pp. 533–572.

Césaire, Aimé

1990 *Lyric and Dramatic Poetry, 1946–82* (Trans. Clayton Eshleman and Annette Smith). Charlottesville: University of Virginia Press.

Cohen, Cathy

1997 "Punks, Bulldaggers, and Welfare Queens: The Radical Potential of Queer Politics?" In *GLQ: A Journal of Lesbian and Gay Studies* Vol. 3. No. 4. Pp. 437–465.

1999 *The Boundaries of Blackness: AIDS and the Breakdown of Black Politics*. Chicago: University of Chicago Press.

Collins, Patricia Hill

1991 *Black Feminist Thought: Knowledge, Consciousness, and the Politics of Empowerment*. London, UK: Routledge.

Connell, Raewyn

1993 *Masculinities*. Berkeley: University of California Press.

Cooper, Frederick
2014 *Africa in the World: Capitalism, Empire, Nation-State*. Cambridge, MA: Harvard University Press.
Currier, Ashley
2012 *Out in Africa: LGBT Organizing in Namibia and South Africa*. Minneapolis: University of Minnesota Press.
Dangaremba, Tsitsi
2004 *Nervous Conditions*. Accra: Ayebia Clark Publishing.
Dankwa, Serena
2009 "It's a Silent Trade: "Female Same-Sex Intimacies in Postcolonial Ghana." In *NORA-Nordic Journal of Feminist and Gender Research*. Vol. 17. No. 3. Pp. 192–205.
2021 *Knowing Women: Same-Sex Intimacy, Gender, and Identity in Postcolonial Ghana*. Cambridge: Cambridge University Press.
Decena, Carlos U.
2011 *Tacit Subjects: Belonging and Same-Sex Desire among Dominican Immigrant Men*. Durham, NC: Duke University Press.
Deflem, Mathieu
1991 "Ritual, Anti-Structure, and Religion: A Discussion of Victor Turner's Processual Symbolic Analysis." In *Journal for the Scientific Study of Religion*. Vol. 30. No. 1. Pp. 1–25.
D'Emilio, John
1983 "Capitalism and Gay Identity." In *Powers of Desire: The Politics of Sexuality*. A. Snitow, C. Stansell, and Sharon Thompson (Eds.). New Feminist Library Series. New York: Monthly Review Press. Pp. 101–113.
Diawara, Manthia
2010 *African Film: New Forms of Aesthetics and Politics*. Munich: Prestel Publishing.
Du Bois, W. E. B.
1903 *The Souls of Black Folk*. Chicago: A. C. McClurg and Co.
Duggan, Lisa
2003 *The Twilight of Equality? Neoliberalism, Cultural Politics, and the Attack on Democracy*. Boston: Beacon Press.
Dzobo, N. K.
1992 "African Symbols and Proverbs as Sources of Knowledge and Truth." In *Person and Community: Ghanaian Philosophical Studies*. Vol. 1. K. Wiredu and K. Gyekye (Eds.). Washington, DC: Council for Research in Values and Philosophy. Pp. 85–100.
Edmondson, Scott
2009 *Striking Prayers and Mediating Powers: An Ethnographic and Hypertextual Interpretation of Pentecostal and Charismagic Cultural Production in Ghana*. Unpublished dissertation. University of California, Los Angeles.
Ekeh, P. P.
1975 "Colonialism and the Two Publics in Africa: A Theoretical Statement." In *Contemporary Studies in Society and History*." Vol. 17. No. 1. Pp. 91–112.
El-Saadawi, Nawal
1997 *The Nawal El-Saadawi Reader*. New York: Zed Books.

Eng, David
2010 *The Feeling of Kinship: Queer Liberalism and the Racialization of Intimacy.* Durham, NC: Duke University Press.
Epprecht, Marc.
2004 *Hungochani: The History of a Dissident Sexuality in Southern Africa.* Montreal: McGill-Queen's University Press.
2008 *Heterosexual Africa?: The History of an Idea from an Age of Exploration to an Age of AIDS.* Athens: Ohio University Press.
Evans-Pritchard, E. E.
1970 "Sexual Inversion among the Azande." In *American Anthropologist.* Vol. 72. No. 6. Pp. 1428–1434.
Eze, Emmanuel, ed.
1998 *African Philosophy: An Anthology.* Malden, MA: Blackwell.
Fabian, Johannes
1983 *Time and the Other: How Anthropology Makes Its Object.* New York: Columbia University Press.
Fanon, Frantz
1967 *A Dying Colonialism.* New York: Grove Press.
Farmer, Paul
2006 *Aids and Accusation: Haiti and the Geography of Blame.* Berkeley: University of California Press.
Fayorsey, Clare
1992 "Commoditization of Childbirth: Female Strategies towards Autonomy among the Ga of Southern Ghana." In *Cambridge Journal of Anthropology.* Vol 16. No. 3. Pp. 19–45.
Ferguson, James
2006 *Global Shadows: Africa in the Neoliberal World Order.* Durham, NC: Duke University Press.
Ferguson, Roderick
2003 *Aberrations in Black: Toward a Queer of Color Critique.* Minneapolis: University of Minnesota Press.
Field, Margaret
1940 *Social Organization of the Ga People.* London: Crown Agents of the Colonies.
Foucault, Michel
1978 *History of Sexuality: An Introduction.* Vol. 1. New York: Pantheon Books.
Fowler, Lorenzo
1847 *Marriage: Its History and Ceremonies; with a Phrenological Exposition of the Functions and Qualifications for Happy Marriages.* New York: Fowler and Wells.
Gaudio, Rudolph Pell
2009 *Allah Made Us: Sexual Outlaws in an Islamic African City.* Malden, MA: Wiley-Blackwell.
Gifford, Paul
2004 *Ghana's New Christianity: Pentecostalism in a Globalizing African Economy.* Bloomington: Indiana University Press.

Gill, Lyndon
2018 *Erotic Islands: Art and Activism in the Queer Caribbean*. Durham, NC: Duke University Press.
Goffman, Erving
1959 *The Presentation of Self in Everyday Life*. New York: Random House.
Goldberg, David. T.
2008 *The Threat of Race: Reflections on Racialized Neoliberalism*. Malden, MA: Wiley-Blackwell.
Gopinath, Gayatri
2005 *Impossible Desires: Queer Diasporas and South Asian Public Cultures*. Durham, NC: Duke University Press.
Gyekye, Kwame
1987 *An Essay on African Philosophical Thought: The Akan Conceptual Scheme*. Philadelphia: Temple University Press.
1992 "Person and Community in Akan Thought." In *Person and Community: Ghanaian Philosophical Studies*. Vol. 1. K. Wiredu and K. Gyekye (Eds.). Washington, DC: Council for Research in Values and Philosophy. Pp. 101–122.
1995 *An Essay on African Philosophical Thought: The Akan Conceptual Scheme*. (Rev. Ed.). Philadelphia: Temple University Press.
1997 *Tradition and Modernity: Philosophical Reflections on the African Experience*. Oxford: Oxford University Press.
Halberstam, Judith
1998 *Female Masculinity*. Durham, NC: Duke University Press.
Hall, Stuart
1987 "Minimal Selves." In *Identity: The Real Me*. H. Bhabha (Ed.). London: Institute of Contemporary Arts. Document No. 6.
Harper, Phillip B.
1997 "Introduction: Queer Transexions of Race, Nation, and Gender." In *Social Text*. Vol. 53/54. Phillip Brian Harper, Ann McClintock, José Esteban Muñoz, and Trish Rosen (Eds.). Durham, NC: Duke University Press. Pp. 1–4.
Herzfeld, Michael
2004 *Cultural Intimacy: Social Poetics in the Nation-State*. New York: Routledge.
Hoad, Neville
2007 *African Intimacies: Race, Homosexuality, and Globalization*. Minneapolis: University of Minnesota Press.
Human Rights Watch.
2017 "No Choice but to Deny Who I Am: Violence and Discrimination against LGBT People in Ghana." https://www.hrw.org/report/2019/02/04/no-choice-deny-who-i-am/violence-and-discrimination-against-lgbtpeople-ghana.
Igoe, Jim, and Tim Kelsall
2005 *Between the Rock and a Hard Place: African NGOs, Donors, and the State*. Durham, NC: Carolina Academic Press.
Johnson, E. P.
2005 "'Quare' Studies, or (Almost) Everything I Know about Queer Studies I Learned from my Grandmother." In *Black Queer Studies: A Critical Anthology*. E. P. Johnson and Mae Henderson (Eds.). Durham, NC: Duke University Press. Pp. 124–159.

Jones, Andrew
2014 *British Humanitarian NGOs and the Disaster Relief Industry, 1942–1985*. Unpublished dissertation. University of Birmingham.

Kandiyoti, Deniz
1988 "Bargaining with Patriarchy." In *Gender and Society*. Vol. 2. No. 3. Pp. 274–290. Kanneh, Kadiatu
1998 *African Identities: Race, Nation and Culture in Ethnography, Pan-Africanism and Black Literatures*. London: Routledge.

Kaoma, Kapya
2009 *Globalizing the Culture Wars: US Conservatives, African Churches, and Homophobia*. Somerville, MA: Political Research Associates.

Keane, Webb
2007 *Christian Moderns: Freedom and Fetish in the Mission Encounter*. Berkeley: University of California Press.

Korten, David
1990 *Getting to the 21st Century: Voluntary Action and the Global Agenda*. Hartford, CT: Kumarian Press.

Krafft-Ebing, Richard Von
1924 (1886). *Psychopathia Sexualis: With Especial Reference to Antipathic Sexual Instinct: A Medico Forensic Study* (Trans. F. J. Rebman). New York: Physicians and Surgeons Book Company.

Kropp Dakubu, Mary E.
1997 *Korle Meets the Sea. A Sociolinguistic History of Accra*. New York: Oxford University Press.

Livermon, Xavier
2012 "Queer(y)ing Freedom: Black Queer Visibilities in Postapartheid South Africa." In *GLQ: A Journal of Lesbian and Gay Studies*. Vol. 18. No. 2–3. Pp. 297–323.

Lorde, Audre
1984 "Poetry Is not a Luxury." In *Sister Outsider: Essays and Speeches by Audre Lorde*. New York: Ten Speed Press.

Lorway, Robert
2015 *Namibia's Rainbow Project: Gay Rights in an African Nation*. Bloomington: Indiana University Press.

Lowe, Lisa
2015 *The Intimacies of Four Continents*. Durham, NC: Duke University Press.

Macharia, Keguro
2016 "On Being Area-Studied: A Litany of Complaint." *In GLQ: A Journal of Lesbian and Gay Studies*. Vol. 22. No. 2. Pp. 183–189.
2019 *Frottage: Frictions of Intimacy Across the Black Diaspora*. Durham, NC: Duke University Press.

Madison, D. Soyini
2005 *Critical Ethnography: Method, Ethics, and Performance*. New York: Sage.

Manuh, Takyiwaa
2007 "Doing Gender Work in Ghana." In *Africa after Gender?* C. Cole, T. Manu, and S. Miescher (Eds.). Bloomington: Indiana University Press. Pp. 125–149.

Marshall, Ruth
2009 *Political Spiritualities: The Pentecostal Revolution in Nigeria*. Chicago: University of Chicago Press.
Massad, Joseph
2007 *Desiring Arabs*. Chicago: University of Chicago Press.
Matebeni, Zethu, ed.
2014 *Reclaiming Afrikan Queer Perspectives on Sexual and Gender Identities*. Athlone, South Africa: Modjaji Books.
Matera, Marc
2015 *Black London: The Imperial Metropolis and Decolonization in the Twentieth Century*. Berkeley: University of California Press.
Mbiti, John
1995 "African Religions and Philosophy." In *African Philosophy: Selected Readings*. Albert Mosley (Ed.). Englewood Cliffs, NJ: Prentice Hall. P. 101.
McCune, Jeffrey Jr.
2014 *Sexual Discretion and the Politics of Passing*. Chicago: University of Chicago Press.
McClintock, Ann
1995 *Imperial Leather: Race, Gender, and Sexuality in the Colonial Contest*. New York: Routledge.
McDowell, Deborah E.
1995 *The Changing Same: Black Women's Literature, Criticism, and Theory*. Bloomington: Indiana University Press.
2006 "Recovery Missions: Imaging the Body Ideal." In *Recovering the Black Female Body: Self-Representation by African American Women*. M. Bennett and V. Dickerson (Eds.). New Brunswick, NJ: Rutgers University Press. Pp. 296–317.
McFadden, Patricia
2011 *Resisting Neocolonial/Neoliberal Collusion: Reclaiming Our Lives, Our Futures*. Lecture delivered at the Africa Gender Institute. University of Western Cape.
Melamed, Jodi
2011 *Represent and Destroy: Rationalizing Violence in the New Racial Capitalism*. Minneapolis: University of Minnesota Press.
Menkiti, Ifeanyi
1984 "Person and Community in African Traditional Thought." In *African Philosophy: An Introduction*. R. Wright (Ed.). New York: University Press of America. Pp. 171–181.
Mercer, Kobena, and Isaac Julien
1988 "Race, Sexual Politics, and Black Masculinity: A Dossier." In *Male Order: Unwrapping Masculinity*. Rowena Chapman and Jonathan Rutherford (Eds.). London: Lawrence and Wishart. Pp. 68–96.
Meyer, Birgit
1999 *Translating the Devil: Religion and Modernity among the Ewe in Ghana*. London: International African Institute, Edinburgh University Press.
Miescher, Stephan
2005 *Making Men in Ghana*. Bloomington: Indiana University Press.
Miles, Barry
2009 *The British Invasion: The Music, the Times, the Era*. New York: Sterling Press.

Miller, Monica
2009 *Slaves to Fashion: Black Dandyism and the Styling of Black Diasporic Identity.* Durham, NC: Duke University Press.
Muñoz, José E.
1999 *Disidentifications: Queers of Color and the Performance of Politics.* Minneapolis: University of Minnesota Press.
Mustakeem, Sowande'
2016 *Slavery at Sea: Terror, Sex, and Sickness in the Middle Passage.* Urbana-Champaign: University of Illinois Press.
Narayan, Uma
1997 *Dislocating Cultures: Identities, Traditions, and Third World Feminism.* New York: Routledge.
Newman, Michele
1999 *White Women's Rights: The Racial Origins of Feminism in the United States.* New York: Oxford University Press.
Nkrumah, Kwame
1965 *Neocolonialism: The Last Stage of Imperialism.* London: Thomas Nelson and Sons Ltd.
Nyanzi, Stella
2014 "Queering Queer Africa." In *Reclaiming Afrikan Queer Perspectives on Sexual and Gender Identities.* Zethu Matebeni and Jabu Pereira (Eds.). Athlone, South Africa: Modjaji Books. Pp. 65–68.
Nyerere, Julius
1968 *Freedom and Unity.* New York: Oxford University Press.
Nzegwu, Nkiru
2006 *Family Matters: Feminist Concepts in African Philosophy of Culture.* Albany: SUNY Press.
Odotei, Irene
1996 "Precolonial Economic Activities of the Ga." In *Research Review.* Vol. 2. Nos. 1 and 2.
Oglesby, Carl
1969 *The New Left Reader.* New York: Grove Press.
O'Mara, Kathleen
2013 "Making Community and Claiming Sexual Citizenship in Contemporary Ghana." In *Sexual Diversity in Africa: Politics, Theory, and Citizenship.* S. N. Nyeck and Marc Epprecht (Eds.). Montreal: McGill-Queens University Press. Pp. 188–207.
Opoku, Kofi Asare
1978 *West African Traditional Religion.* FEP International Private Limited.
Oppong, Joseph R., and Ezekiel Kalipeni
2004 "Perceptions and Mis-perceptions of AIDS in Africa." In *HIV and AIDS in Africa: Beyond Epidemiology.* E. Kalipeni, S. Craddock, and J. R. Oppong (Eds.). Malden, MA: Blackwell. Pp. 47–69.
Otu, Kwame Edwin
2014 "Reluctantly Queer: Sasso and the Shifting Paradigms of Masculinity and Sexual Citizenship in Postcolonial Ghana." In *Democratic Renewal versus Neoliberalism: Towards Empowerment and Inclusion.* CLACSO (Ed.). Buenos Aires: Claudio Lara Cortés and Consuelo Silva Flores.

2016 "Saints and Sinners: African Holocaust, 'Clandestine Countermemories,' and LGBT+ Visibility Politics in Postcolonial Africa." In *Being and Becoming: Gender, Culture and Shifting Identity in Sub-Saharan Africa.* Chinyere Ukpokolo (Ed.). Denver: Spears Media Press. Pp. 195–216.

2017 "LGBT Human Rights Expeditions in Homophobic Safaris: Racialized Neoliberalism and Post-Traumatic White Disorder in the BBC's *The World's Worst Place to Be Gay?*" In *Critical Ethnic Studies.* Vol. 3. No. 2. Pp. 126–150.

Oyěwùmí, Oyèrónkẹ́

1997 *The Invention of Women: Making an African Sense of Western Gender Discourses.* Minneapolis: University of Minnesota Press.

p'Bitek, Okot

1998 "The Sociality of Self." *In African Philosophy: An Anthology.* E. Eze (Ed.). Malden, MA: Blackwell. Pp. 73–78.

Pierre, Jemima

2013 *The Predicament of Blackness: Postcolonial Ghana and the Politics of Race.* Chicago: University of Chicago Press.

Povinelli, Elizabeth

2001 "Radical Worlds: The Anthropology of Incommensurability and Inconceivability." In *Annual Review of Anthropology.* Vol. 30. Pp. 319–334.

Puar, Jasbir

2007 *Terrorist Assemblages: Homonationalism in Queer Times.* Durham, NC: Duke University Press.

Quayson, Ato

2014 *Oxford Street, Accra: City Life and the Itineraries of Transnationalism.* Durham, NC: Duke University Press.

Ray, Carina

2015 *Crossing the Color Line: Race, Sex, and the Contested Politics of Colonialism in Ghana.* Athens: Ohio University Press.

Reddy, Chandan

2011 *Freedom with Violence: Race, Sexuality, and the US State.* Durham, NC: Duke University Press.

Reid, Graeme

2013 *How to Be a Real Gay: Gay Identities in Small-Town South Africa.* Natal: University of KwaZulu-Natal Press.

Rich, Adrienne

1980 "Compulsory Heterosexuality and Lesbian Existence." In *Signs.* Vol. 5. No. 4. Pp. 631–660.

Rodney, Walter

1972 *How Europe Underdeveloped Africa.* London: Bogle-L'Ouverture Publications.

Said, Edward

1978 *Orientalism.* New York: Pantheon Books.

Senghor, Léopold

1964 *On African Socialism.* New York: Praeger.

1995 "Negritude: A Humanism of the Twentieth Century." In *I Am Because We Are: Readings in Black Philosophy.* F. Hord and J. Lee (Eds.). Amherst: University of Massachusetts Press. P. 52.

Shohat, Ella, ed.
1998 *Talking Visions: Multicultural Feminism in a Transnational Age*. Cambridge, MA: MIT Press.
Signorini, Italo.
1973 "Agonwole Agyale: The Marriage between Two Persons of the Same Sex among the Nzema of Southwestern Ghana." In *Journal de la Société des Africanistes*. Vol. 43. No. 2. Pp. 221–234.
Smallwood, Stephanie
2007 *Saltwater Slavery: A Middle Passage from Africa to the American Diaspora*. Cambridge, MA: Harvard University Press.
Snorton, C. Riley
2014 *Nobody Is Supposed to Know: Black Sexuality on the Down Low*. Minneapolis: University of Minnesota Press.
Stoler, Ann
1995 *Race and the Education of Desire: Foucault's History of Sexuality and the Colonial Order of Things*. Durham, NC: Duke University Press.
2008 "Imperial Debris: Reflections on Ruins and Ruinations." In *Cultural Anthropology*. Vol. 23. No. 2. Pp. 191–219.
Szreter, Simon
2003 "The Population Health Approach in Historical Perspective." In *American Journal of Public Health*. Vol. 93. No. 3. 421–431.
Tallie, T. J.
2019 *Queering Colonial Natal: Indigeneity and the Violence of Belonging in Southern Africa*. Minneapolis: University of Minnesota.
Taussig, Michael
1999 *Defacement: Public Secrecy and the Labor of the Negative*. Palo Alto, CA: Stanford University Press.
Thiong'o, Ngugi Wa
1992 *Moving the Centre: The Struggle for Cultural Freedoms*. London: James Currey.
Thomas, Greg
2007 *The Sexual Demon of Colonial Power: Pan-African Embodiment and Erotic Schemes of Empire*. Bloomington: Indiana University Press.
Tinsley, Omise'eke Natasha
2010 *Thiefing Sugar: Eroticism between Women in Caribbean Literature*. Durham, NC: Duke University Press.
Turner, Victor
1969 *The Ritual Process: Structure and Anti-Structure*. New Brunswick, NJ: Transaction.
1974 "Liminal to Liminoid, in Play, Flow, and Ritual: An Essay in Comparative Symbology." In *Rice Institute Pamphlet*—Rice University Studies. Vol. 60. No. 3.
Uchendu, Victor
1965 *The Igbo of Southeast Nigeria*. New York: Harcourt Brace.
Valentine, David
2007 *Imagining Transgender: An Ethnography of a Category*. Durham, NC: Duke University Press.
Van Gennep, Arnold
1960 *The Rites of Passage*. Chicago: University of Chicago Press (Reprint Ed.).

Van Klinken, Adriaan

2019 *Kenyan, Christian, Queer: Religion, LGBT Activism, and Arts of Resistance in Africa*. University Park: Penn State University Press.

Veblen, Thorstein

1899 "Conspicuous Consumption." In *The Theory of the Leisure Class: An Economic Study of Institutions*. New York: Macmillan. Pp. 68–101.

Wahab, Amar

2012 "Homophobia as the State of Reason: The Case of Postcolonial Trinidad and Tobago." In *GLQ: A Journal of Lesbian and Gay Studies*. Vol. 18. No. 4. Pp. 481–505.

Wekker, Gloria

2006 *The Politics of Passion: Women's Sexual Culture in the Afro-Surinamese Diaspora*. New York: Columbia University Press.

Willey, Angela

2006 "'Christian Nations,' Polygamic Races' and Women's Rights: Toward a Genealogy of Non-Monogamy and Whiteness." In *Sexualities*. Vol. 9. No. 5. Pp. 530–546.

Wiredu, Kwasi, and Kwame Gyekye, eds.

1992 *Person and Community: Ghanaian Philosophical Studies*. Vol. 1. Washington, DC: Council for Research in Values and Philosophy.

Zouhali-Worrall, M., and Fairfax Wright, K., dirs.

2012 *Call Me Kuchu*. Film.

INDEX

Founded in 1893,
UNIVERSITY OF CALIFORNIA PRESS
publishes bold, progressive books and journals on topics in the arts, humanities, social sciences, and natural sciences—with a focus on social justice issues—that inspire thought and action among readers worldwide.

The UC PRESS FOUNDATION
raises funds to uphold the press's vital role as an independent, nonprofit publisher, and receives philanthropic support from a wide range of individuals and institutions—and from committed readers like you. To learn more, visit ucpress.edu/supportus.